Studies in Anglo-French Cultural Relations

Imagining France

Edited by

Ceri Crossley
Senior Lecturer in French
University of Birmingham

and

Ian Small
Lecturer in English
University of Birmingham

M
MACMILLAN
PRESS

First published 1988

Published by
THE MACMILLAN PRESS LTD
Houndmills, Basingstoke, Hampshire RG21 2XS
and London
Companies and representatives
throughout the world

Printed in Hongkong

British Library Cataloguing in Publication Data
Studies in Anglo-French cultural relations: imagining
France.
1. Great Britain – Civilisation – French
influence   2. Great Britain – Civilisation –
19th century   3. Great Britain – Civilisation –
20th century
I. Crossley, Ceri   II. Small, Ian
941.08   DA533
ISBN 0–333–38971–9

Contents

Acknowledgements

The editors would like to thank Professors James Boulton and David Lodge for their help and advice in the planning of this volume.

Notes on the Contributors

J. B. Bullen is Lecturer in English at the University of Reading. He has written widely on English nineteenth- and twentieth-century literary and artistic culture. His previous publications include an edition of Roger Fry's *Vision and Design*.

John J. Conlon is Associate Professor of English at the University of Massachusetts at Boston. He has written widely on English, European and Latin American literatures. He is the author of *Walter Pater and the French Tradition*.

Ceri Crossley is Senior Lecturer in French at the University of Birmingham. He is the author of *Edgar Quinet (1803–1875): A Study in Romantic Thought, Alfred de Musset: 'Lorenzaccio'*, and articles on intellectual history and comparative literature.

Vanessa Davies is a research fellow at King's College, London. She is writing a study of the literary review *Adam* and is currently engaged in a descriptive cataloguing of the library and archive of *Adam* in the possession of King's College.

Richard Ellmann was Professor of English at Emory University and formerly held the Goldsmiths' Chair of English at the University of Oxford. His publications include *The Identity of Yeats, Yeats: The Man and the Masks, Eminent Domain* and a biography of James Joyce. He was the editor of Joyce's *Letters* and of *The New Oxford Book of American Verse*. He died in 1987.

Jill Forbes has taught at the Ecole Normale Supérieure and been a Lecturer at the Université de Paris III and the University of Loughborough. She is currently head of Modern Languages at the South Bank Polytechnic. She has been a governor of the British Film Institute and a member of its production board. She is the editor of *INA French for Innovation* and the author of the forthcoming *French Cinema since 1968*.

John Fowles was born in 1926 and read French at New College, Oxford. His main novels are *The Collector*, *The Magus*, *The French Lieutenant's Woman*, *Daniel Martin* and *A Maggot*; two of the stories in *The Ebony Tower* are set in France.

Susan James is Assistant Lecturer in the Faculty of Philosophy, at the University of Cambridge, and Fellow of Girton College. She is the author of *The Content of Social Explanation*.

Christopher Norris is Reader in English at the University of Wales in Cardiff. He has written extensively on various aspects of philosophy and literary theory. His publications include *William Empson*, *Deconstruction: Theory and Practice*, *The Deconstructive Turn* and *The Contest of Faculties*. At present he is completing a book on Jacques Derrida.

Norma Rinsler is Professor of French Language and Literature at King's College, London. She has published books on Nerval and articles on nineteenth- and twentieth-century literature, especially poetry, and on comparative literature.

Ian Small is Lecturer in English at the University of Birmingham. His previous publications include *The Aesthetes*, editions of Walter Pater's *Marius the Epicurean* and, with Russell Jackson, of Oscar Wilde's four society dramas.

Colin Wilson was born in Leicester in 1931. He left school at the age of sixteen and began to write a novel when he was seventeen. An offshoot of this novel, a study in 'existential sociology' called *The Outsider*, appeared when he was twenty-four and brought him overnight notoriety as an 'Angry Young Man'. The novel *Ritual in the Dark* appeared in 1960. Wilson has written sixteen novels and forty works of non-fiction, including biographies of Shaw, Rasputin and Wilhelm Reich and the psychologist Abraham Maslow.

Introduction

CERI CROSSLEY AND IAN SMALL

> *It is absurd to generalize – all we can say is that Anglo-French culture exists, that Byron and Constable have intoxicated Paris, as Voltaire and Rousseau have shaken London, but that, if we are to understand what Anglo-French cultural relations are going to mean, we must try to isolate the particular element with which French culture has enriched us, which we cannot do without, and which we pine for when deprived of; and this I would identify as the sense of intellectual reality.*
>
> Cyril Connolly[1]

By all the usual yardsticks by which relations between countries are measured – mutual trade, travel, cultural exchange and so forth – the British and the French enjoy a familiarity never known before. Since 1945 Channel crossings have become swifter, safer and more popular. Paris and Provence are home for numbers of British expatriates, be they artists, writers or pop stars or just the merely rich. Despite this recent familiarity, it would be unwise to conclude that the age-old British sense of both unease and anticipation at the prospect of crossing the Channel has been dispelled. Certainly the English Channel remains a hostile and unpredictable natural environment; but in addition it still possesses the attributes of a symbolic as well as a physical barrier, which historically has been instrumental in forming in the minds of us British those famous perceptions of ourselves as a nation of islanders. On embarkation at one of the Channel ports we feel securely enclosed within a system of language and so within a system of recognisable cultural values. The very ships designed to transport us seem to make statements about us: ferries are all car ferries now and all one-class ships. Closer inspection, however, suggests the limitations of such a unitary way of interpreting the signs. Perhaps the ships and their companies embody national obsessions. Certainly French and British vessels encode different sets of values, of food, style and so forth. How disconcerting for us it is to board a Sealink

1

boat at Dover only to discover that the reassuring external appearances conceal a totally French vessel! But this is the first manifestation, and a fairly trivial example at that, of the changes that are involved in a Channel crossing, which, simply put, is leaving behind the *English* Channel. To cross that stretch of water that the English (not the British) have arrogated to themselves is to question our identity, to ask ourselves who we really are. Where does Britain stop and France begin? Crossing sea frontiers involves a different kind of transition from crossing land frontiers. In the Channel fixed boundaries are replaced by a shifting, fluid one; indeed this ambiguity about boundaries has a more focused counterpart in mainland British attitudes to the Channel Islands, which historically have enjoyed or endured an ambiguous status with regard to mainland British law, tax systems and sovereignty (they, after all, were the only part of Britain to be occupied during the Second World War).

To arrive in France, moreover, is to have questions of national and self-identity posed very sharply. Until the late 1950s British national prejudices could allow France to be viewed with a degree of condescension, an attitude reinforced by a combination of its cheapness for British middle-class holiday-makers between the wars and its apparent 'failure' during the war itself. Since then, however, the image of France as a predominantly rural country inhabited by untranslatable *paysans* has largely given way to a perception of France as a modern, efficient, industrially advanced and culturally progressive nation whose apparent success contrasts sharply with commonly expressed British perceptions of British industrial and political decline. The comparisons which strike the modern British visitor completely dispel that former condescension and have something to do with the widely held sentiment that the French have managed to 'do things better'. Crossing the Channel points this up in a particularly painful way. Why, for example, are France's motorways only rarely bedevilled with contraflow systems? The traveller who exchanges dilapidated British Rail rolling-stock for the comfort of a SNCF *train corail* is overcome with a mixture of anger and hurt national pride.

In contrast to this general view of France, however, the role that has been ascribed to it by British intellectuals, writers and artists has always been secure from condescension. The qualities in French life that Cyril Connolly identifies in the quotation used as epigraph to this introduction are those that have been central to

British intellectual and artistic life for the past hundred years or more. A decade later Wallace Stevens made a substantially similar point about the influence of Paris on the American imagination:

> I am one of the many people around the world who live from time to time in a Paris that has never existed and that is composed of the things that other people, primarily Parisians themselves, have said about Paris. That particular Paris communicates an interest in life that may be wholly fiction, but, if so, it is precious fiction.[2]

France has been a necessary 'otherness', whether, as Stevens notes, fictional or not: aspects of this intellectual 'otherness' of France, the ways in which French influence, or aspects of it, have operated upon British high culture in the last century, are explored in the present volume of essays. But the view of France produced by British high culture, although widespread and constant, has not been one universally held. There have been other, equally powerful, 'images' of France that have been constructed by the British; these different views of France and what they correspond to in British society are central to the general thesis of the present volume.

The ways in which the culture of one nation assimilates or imagines the cultures of other nations is always a complex and profoundly subtle process. Initially, of course, the experience of those other cultures is realised in terms of how they are different, how they are foreign, alien or unknown. Against the certainties of the native culture they are represented as the 'other'. European nations, for example, historically have defined Muslim and Hindu religions in terms of their values being other-than-Christian, Africa and India in terms of their geography being other-than-European. But 'foreignness' is itself a concept which is constantly undergoing discrimination. So, to give a very obvious example, for the nineteenth-century traveller, France may have been perceived as alien in a wide variety of ways, but it was not as alien as, say, India. The 'otherness' of foreign cultures is in itself subject to a variety of distinctions which are always encoded for the native culture in subtle ways, and subject themselves to a whole variety of other determinants, particularly political and economic, and therefore constantly undergoing historical change. This is true of any cultural interaction, but it is particularly true of the history of cultural relations between France and Britain, because from all the foreign cultures that have to a greater or lesser extent been formative influences upon British culture, historically by far the most complex and pervasive has been that exercised by France. The 'otherness' of France has been a constant presence in the British imagination for almost a thousand years. Despite all this – perhaps even because of it – the precise forms of this elusive 'otherness' are not easy concepts to formulate and depend in the first instance upon what is meant by a set of related terms, particularly 'influence', 'culture' and the name 'France' itself.

To put matters at their simplest, to the British imagination the term 'France' cannot connote what it connotes to the French; in the same way, 'France' cannot be a defined political, social or geographical entity for the Briton in the way it manifestly has to be for the French man or woman. For the British tourist in the last hundred years, for example, the geography of France has tended to bring to mind specific but narrow regions or towns – Normandy, Provence, Britanny, the Dordogne and so on; the last forcing itself into the general consciousness of the British as recently as the past twenty years or so. The consequence of all this is that for the British imagination – an admittedly shorthand term that also will require much subtler definitions – the term 'France' is always subject to an intervening and hence defining context. In the case of some aspects of French culture, these contexts have remained consistent and constant; so for a Briton to admire French *haute couture* or French *cordon bleu* cuisine has always announced something specific about his or her values and priorities in the native culture – among other Britons, that is. But other aspects of French life (in, for example, the case of the reception of French politics in Britain) have evoked much less predictable reactions. Hence the sign ⟨France⟩ (as it will henceforward be designated) has always to be understood by referring it to the code in which it is placed, for in fact it is that code alone which can give significance and interpretative value to the plurality of its occurrences. In these senses our description and interpretation of some aspects of recent French culture and its significance for British culture will inevitably be a semiotic one.

For British culture, knowledge of France is produced by a process of encoding. Within these encodings France is both a concrete reality which impinges upon consciousness and an 'elsewhere' or 'other' in which problems are posed, alternative values explored, different intellectual strategies practised. Moreover while France is acknowledged as different, its difference is one which the British can always endorse or reject or, more often, use to redefine concepts of 'Englishness' or 'Britishness'. While the precise meanings of ⟨France⟩ can undergo surprising modifications, some of the most significant of which are explored here, its prime function for the British literary or artistic consciousness has been that of providing an external point of reference, an element of comparison which offers the writer or artist a way of thinking about his or her own social world and hence of confronting it. Of course, such a process is a much larger undertaking than simply endorsing or resisting those received opinions and entrenched prejudices which constitute national myths. Rather, to represent France or Frenchness for British culture is to acknowledge that, from among its many meanings, the sign ⟨France⟩ has for the moment become fixed and hence has been registered as intelligible.

It would be as well to admit at the outset, though, that we are aware that we and our contributors face an insurmountable methodological difficulty, for it is impossible to describe objectively a phenomenon in which we are all so deeply involved. Ethnographers and anthropologists as varied as Clifford Geertz and Pierre Bourdieu have alerted contemporary students of culture to the fact that there is no privileged location from which cultures can be surveyed and described. Because, in Geertz's striking phrase, 'culture is located in the minds and hearts of men',[3] there cannot be a neutral or objective vantage point for such a survey, for every such point is in itself subject to cultural determinants. The aspiring commentator inevitably brings to his description of foreign culture a mental portmanteau of values and assumptions that predispose him to observe in particular ways; hence observations become interpretations. Most of the contributors to this volume are British; some are American; and it is simply not possible for us, individually or collectively, not to have been affected by the intellectual and cultural processes that we are attempting to describe and account for. Indeed this volume in its own small way becomes a part of those processes that it tries to analyse, in the sense that we too are caught up in those webs or codes of signification that give to any part of the cultural transactions between the British and the French their precise meanings. So we openly acknowledge that our attempts to describe the relationships between the cultures of Britain and France are, and necessarily have to be, an interpretation

of them. Such a self-consciousness of the limitations of our abilities
to describe the significance of ⟨France⟩ is not an attempt to claim
a counterfeit objectivity or to brush aside some fundamental problems of methodology; rather the opposite, it is intended to confess
the provisionality and the relativity of our conclusions.

Like the name 'France', the terms 'influence' and 'culture' also
are problematic. In the course of this volume, the term 'culture'
will generally stand for high culture: artistic, intellectual and literary culture, that is. Now we are aware of, but not in the first place
concerned with, the ideological implications of the concepts 'high'
and 'mass' culture, and we are aware as well that we are to some
extent marginalising 'mass' reactions to ⟨France⟩, a tendency that
is regrettable but inevitable. The term 'influence' is also a vexed
one; generally it will denote the assimilation of a set of values
generated by French high or intellectual culture into British high
culture. Whether it is defined as a fundamentally mechanical
process, as in the case of, say, Oscar Wilde's reactions to J.-K.
Huysmans's *A Rebours*, or as an intricate set of interrelated processes, as with recent British responses to French structuralism,
one thing is certain: that the concept of 'influence' is a complex
one, in both high and mass culture. One aspect of this complexity
is that influence, whatever its nature or source, is never simple nor
straightforward in the way that it operates. It is not just the case
that French intellectual culture has been appropriated by British
intellectual culture and rejected by British mass culture (in a manner, for example, totally dissimilar to the operation and influence
of American culture in Britain). Clearly attitudes to France do not
just simply coincide with British class differences. Quite often they
actually allow them to be exhibited. It is as if opposed attitudes to
France are being enlisted as a way of defining those very differences between British mass and high culture. One or two examples
make the point in an obvious way. France, from Matthew Arnold
onwards, has been used to bring to mind a standard of intellectual
seriousness that in its turn has been used to define and to con-
demn British mass philistinism. Or, in the case of the British tourist
industry, France as a holiday centre has always required a Spain or
a Blackpool to define it. The *Sun*, in appropriately unsubtle headlines, can direct its readers to specific forms of francophobia over
some perceived injustice in the operations of the EEC trade rules.
In this respect, the adopting of French terms and names by the
British has a specific cultural and class significance; so, beyond the

domain of the restaurateur, French *pommes frites* can become simple Saxon chips once more. Attitudes to France, that is, and receptivity to French values, are not only related to the British class system but are actually often used to define the operations of that system; it is significant that no other country has been so consistently used to help define British class differences. We shall return to comment on some of the ways in which popular or mass images or readings of France have become specifically political for the British, but for the moment it is enough to note that such considerations are at the margins of the subjects of the essays that follow, as the silent domain of French 'otherness'.

The contributors to this volume are most concerned with the ways the sign ⟨France⟩ has come to be understood as anti-Britain or as non-Britain. In these senses France has been primarily understood in terms of escape. It would be fruitless to attempt to draw up an exhaustive list of those writers and artists who, since the time of Oscar Wilde's self-imposed exile in the last years of the nineteenth century, have sought to escape from British insularity or moral hypocrisy, from a social and a cultural reality which imposed restrictions on the pursuit of intellectual inquiry and which limited the freedom of artistic expression. The reasons adduced for this flight from the British Isles are well-known: the need to escape from British philistinism, complacency, mercantilism, cultural and intellectual isolation. In each case France always presented itself in terms of a set of *possibilities*. For example, in 1929, in 'England Not My England', the young Cyril Connolly surveyed the difference between intellectual life in France and its counterpart in Britain at a period when, to many, Britain seemed to have retreated into cultural isolationism; he forcefully articulated this sense of France encompassing and accommodating the possibility of a fundamental intellectual seriousness in a manner which was wholly alien to Britain:

> London was created for rich young men to shop in, dine in, ride in, get married in, go to theatres in, and die in as respected householders. . . . Every writer and artist must feel a sense of inferiority in London unless he is (like Browning or Henry James) a romantic snob. . . . Of course, there are Bohemians, but they have to be smart ones, otherwise they are afraid to show themselves; without a quarter, without cafés, their only chance is to get rich and fashionable and give cocktail parties. In

Paris they have a quarter assigned to them, and are lords of it.
They aren't much better as artists, but they are freer, happier,
and harder-working, and live in an atmosphere where great art
is more likely to arise.[4]

Connolly's choice of James as a 'romantic snob' is perhaps mis-
placed in the light of the substantially similar comparisons between London and Paris made in novels such as *The Tragic Muse*,
where France stands for essential seriousness in matters of art;
moreover Connolly's complaint is conditioned by that special
sense of provincialism produced in Britain in the 1920s (the subject
of some of the essays in this volume). But Connolly does indeed
capture a familiar and consistent complaint made by British intellectuals and artists: that uniquely in France the life of the mind is
easier to sustain. The essays in this volume make the overall point
that at the times when British academics and intellectuals were still
attempting to stem the tide of contemporary French ideas –
whether Impressionist or Post-Impressionist, at the turn of the
century, or existentialist or structuralist, after the Second World
War – those ideas were already becoming outmoded in Europe.
France thus has always presented itself as the natural ally of the
British *avant-garde*. In this respect the writers of the inter-war years
reinforced the attitudes developed in late Victorian and Edwardian
England. In *Abroad: British Literary Travelling between the Wars*, Paul
Fussell has described how the necessity to flee the drab awfulness
– intellectual, cultural, climatic – of Britain was proclaimed by
Lawrence, Norman Douglas, Huxley, Graves, Orwell, Isherwood
and others. Here France is obviously only one among a number of
locations – Italy or Spain or India also spring to mind – in which the
British literary exile imagined that a different self might be realised:
none the less it has been the principal one.

However, while the idea of escape is attractive and useful, it
needs to be manipulated with care. Escape from the perceived
cultural or social actualities of Britain is clear, even if that actuality
and the perception of it differ from writer to writer or from artist to
artist. But escape *to* what? As far as France is concerned, some
qualifications are necessary. In the first instance it must be emphasised that, for the British, France is both culture and nature. France
also presents a perplexing diversity of distinctive locations and
sites, urban and rural: Dieppe, Paris, Versailles, Provence, Brit-
tany, the Côte d'Azur, and so on. And a complex process of

selection, evaluation, classificaton and grading is at work even when its operations are not made explicit. Indeed, within Paris itself the various districts (Montmartre, Quartier Latin, Montparnasse, and so on) carry quite different meanings and associations. Such discriminations often parallel those produced internally within French culture itself, but they are not rigorously identical with them. Moreover, the British consciousness encounters these associations and discriminations in terms of what seem to be conflicting traditions. So France can stand at the head of a revolutionary inheritance and at the same time be the eldest daughter of the Church.

As we have already indicated, the analysis of the cultural transactions between nations is a hazardous undertaking. The writer tries to fix something which is inherently fluid, constantly capable of taking on new meanings and of discarding former associations. Despite these reservations, however, it is possible, as we have suggested, to advance the thesis that for the British literary and artistic consciousness, ⟨France⟩ can become a physical and a metaphorical location which can accommodate unacknowledged and hitherto unvalued aspects of selfhood and restore to the artistic conscience a sense of belonging, purpose and order. It would, however, be wrong to interpret the reference to France made by writers, intellectuals and artists as signalling an unqualified appeal to an external source of authority. The presence of France and the example of French writers and artists has doubtless often served to guide both the choice of a subject matter and of the mode of its representation. But their appropriation by the British artist or writer does not in its turn betoken a denial of his consciousness of a specifically British or English literary tradition. Indeed, some of the essays in this volume – particularly John Fowles' account of the influence of France upon him as a writer (Ch. 12) – make this point explicitly. It is rather that British cultural isolation has encouraged the estrangement of the writer from the forms considered appropriate for the rendering of the reality of the modern age. In other words, since the 1880s the writer's or artist's encounter with ⟨France⟩ has brought with it sharpened awareness of history, and consequently of the individual's responsibility for representing the conditions of collective or social life. In 1932 Edgell Rickword remarked that the recent influence of French poetry in England was quite understandable, since such writing revealed 'a keener sense of the requirements of the modern

sensibility'.[5] There is a sense in which Britain both participates in
and stands outside movements in intellectual history, especially
those of Europe. Contact with France has always promised the
possibility of a relocation in that history. A different example of
this phenomenon is given by Rayner Heppenstall, who in the
years after the Second World War sought to alert his readers to the
deep bonds which unite French and British culture over the centuries despite national rivalries and the barriers of language. 'We
cannot live without France', declared Heppenstall in *The Fourfold
Tradition* (1961).[6] At a time when significant elements of British
culture were inward-looking and even arrogantly insular, Heppenstall asserted that the British and French traditions formed a
continuum, vital and productive.

It is clear, then, that France may be necessary to British literary
and artistic consciousness. But which France? Certainly we need to
distinguish between France the reality, or realities, and the manifold forms of its representation in art and in literature. It would be
tempting to inquire whether the reality often, or indeed, ever,
fulfilled the pattern of expectations generated by the discourses
about France. Did the crossing of the English Channel produce the
joys of recognition or the pangs of disappointment brought about
by the discrepancy between image and reality? Such questions,
although enticing, are unfortunately elusive because, as we have
already suggested, the simply antimony between image and reality
fails to take account of the complexity of the relationship between
France the country and ⟨France⟩ the unstable sequence of signs
by which the country is known; and the Channel passage (considered both literally and figuratively as a *rite de passage*) is therefore
merely the exchanging of one set of unstable meanings of ⟨France⟩
for another. One thing, however, is certain. For the creative British
artist or writer, the role of the French environment seems designed
to liberate energies, to offer the promise of a personal contact with
great Continentals, and to transform the aspirations of the individuals concerned. Related to this idea of the role of France is the
problem of language and the temptation of a bilingualism which is
also a biculturalism. Since the exhortations of Matthew Arnold in
the 1860s, countless Britons have adopted France as the source of a
new or alternative identity. Richard Cobb has remarked, 'Balliol
did *not* make me. But France did; at least it gave me a new identity,
into which I slip almost unconsciously as soon as I cross to the
other side.'[7]

Specific perceptions of France have of course altered quite significantly over the course of the past century. What has remained constant, though, is that image of France as 'escape' which we have described above. The contemporary traveller's image of France and the contemporary British intellectual's image of France coincide at this point. France as alterity is a constant British preoccupation. However this modern tradition of France as a mental, physical, intellectual or artistic escape, which this volume attempts to document, has a set of very specifically literal antecedents.

Historically one of the most persistent reasons for the association of France and exile or escape has involved what appeared to the British as quite different French sexual ethics. 'Naughty' Paris and France have a long history. For example, at the beginning of the period with which we are concerned, the comfortable complacencies by which the upper-middle-class British conducted their lives proclaimed the self-evident superiority of marriage as a national and racial institution, a sacred ideal distinguishing the British from their less fortunate, immoral neighbours, and in particular from the French, their allegedly most immoral neighbours. France, therefore, in a way already well established historically in the language itself (the etymology of terms such as 'French leave', 'French kisses', 'French diseases', and so on, is a very long one) came to figure in the careers and works of writers such as Charles Dickens and Wilkie Collins quite literally as an escape from the claustrophobia of British social and domestic life. Escape to the Continent came to signify simply escape to less regimented forms of social and sexual life. Certainly it is an exotic Paris in which the mysterious and predatory Svengali operates in *Trilby* (1894), George Du Maurier's novel of French artistic life. This tradition of France as a version of Bohemia was one associated with those works of French drama which crossed the Channel in the 1880s and 1890s. Indeed, as our essays show, the unease of British audiences at the different and so dissident sexual mores depicted in French drama at the end of the century was one of the most significant features of its reception. It is precisely the force of these commonplaces that Oscar Wilde captured in his social dramas of the 1890s. His 'fallen' men and women escape to a France that sanctions or regularises what in Britain had been irregular sexual morals and manners. So, in *Lady Windermere's Fan*, the 'fallen' Mrs Erlynne can announce her intention of escaping London by the 'Club Train', an express that made the journey between London and Paris in under eight hours. Indeed, during the course of the nineteenth century, faster and larger trains and boats brought the possibility of a passage to France within the reach of far greater numbers of the British population than in the early decades of the century. In its turn, this increased proximity of France became part of popular fictional and dramatic devices. ⟨France⟩ became not merely that world of cosmopolitanism and sexual liberty, the possession of a Mrs Erlynne, or, in Thomas Hardy's *The Return of the Native*, a Clym Yeobright: it became part of the furniture of popular genres such as the detective story. Criminals, bigamists, murderers are, in popular late-nineteenth-century detective stories – including the tales of Sherlock Holmes – apprehended on the boat or on the boat train on the very point of making good their departure from Britain. Indeed, the reality of escape is so close to the boat train that the train itself comes to stand as a 'part' of France in England; escape to the ferry or ferry train, in popular fiction, is as effective as escape to the Continent itself.

Perhaps the main point to notice about these popular traditions of exiles and refugees from British law and British morals is simply the fact that they *are* illicit. Historically, France, as we have argued, has consistently been presented as the natural ally of the British *avant-garde*. In other contexts, and in particular in some products of English mass culture, France has been presented as the natural ally of the illicit or the exile. Within both *avant-garde* high culture and some forms of popular culture, then, ⟨France⟩ resumes one of the most persistent roles that we have claimed has been ascribed to it: ⟨France⟩ on both occasions is simply anti-Britain.

Indeed, the role of France as the automatic and natural ally of the British *avant-garde* forms the underlying and unifying theme of the first few essays in this volume. Richard Ellmann (Ch. 1) demonstrates how French programmes for decadence, particularly those found in the work of Théophile Gautier, Paul Verlaine and J.-K. Huysmans, were accommodated into the work of British and Irish writers a generation later, particularly into that of Oscar Wilde, W. B. Yeats and James Joyce. But, as Ellmann goes on to demonstrate, that appropriation of French notions of decadence was also a revaluation or redefinition of them; so much so that decadence comes to stand not for the abnegation or inversion of moral values – as in the Britain of the late nineteenth century French decadence was commonly understood to involve – but a means of relocating moral questions, or of redefining them in terms of the individual.

The topic is pursued by John J. Conlon (Ch. 2) in his survey of the reception of French literature in England in the final decades of the nineteenth and the first decades of the twentieth centuries. Although, as Conlon suggests, French literature was advertised widely and loudly by a group of literary francophiles (amongst whom, Conlon points out, Walter Pater was the most consistent and the most catholic) it remained very much a minority and *avant-garde* interest. French culture, particularly French literature, was establishing itself as a key influence on early British modernism. The extravagant espousal of things French that is now associated with the modernism of the early years of this century, especially in the work of propagandists such as Ezra Pound and T. S. Eliot, was already present in the preceding decades. Yet, as we have stressed, this alliance of ⟨France⟩ with the British *avant-garde* was not achieved without cost. The nature of that cost is outlined by Conlon. It occurred locally too in British reactions to contemporary French drama: French theatrical and dramatic craftsmanship could be admired, but the social and ethical values that the plays themselves seemed to be proposing squared uncomfortably with the safe and accepted British ways of ordering things. The same general pattern of *avant-garde* adulation but widespread popular condemnation was repeated in British reactions to French pictorial art. As J. B. Bullen shows (Ch. 3), French Impressionist and Post-Impressionist works found their admirers, but they also encountered miscomprehension, distrust and simple abuse. As Bullen notes, contemporary psychopathology could happily identify foreignness and so modernity with the pathological and the deranged. The role or general image of France and things French as being simply and axiomatically anti-English is at work here and explains precisely the virulence and persistence of British reactions to French Impressionist and Post-Impressionist painting.

The next few essays describe some of the changed reactions to France during the inter-war years. Norma Rinsler (Ch. 5) discusses the view of France and French culture that was proposed by Arnold Bennett, and how he endorsed the (by then) familiar image of French 'otherness'. Already in Bennett's transactions with France, though, there is a hint of the émigré or exile, of the writer not entirely at ease in either culture. Vanessa Davies (Ch. 7) documents how in the inter-war years, marked generally by a renewed British provincialism, the main means by which knowledge of French culture and literature was transmitted to Britain was through the little literary magazines. A further aspect of this rediscovered sense of the 'otherness' or 'foreignness' of France is the theme that connects the pieces by Ceri Crossley (Ch. 6) and Ian Small (Ch. 4), who attempt to explore how the well-established conjunction between France and the British *avant-garde* underwent a series of redefinitions in the years following the First World War, and how knowledge of France became the ground upon which a renewed sense of national identity could be located.

Most of the essays in this volume concern cultural relations between Britain and France in the years after the Second World War. There are good reasons for this. Some of our contributors have themselves been significant voices in constructing our post-war image of France. Colin Wilson (Ch. 8) was one of the most significant propagandists for existentialist novels in the late 1950s and 1960s – a time when, with the aggressive provincialism of the 'Movement' and the wholesale rejection of the experimentalism of the *nouveau roman*, British culture was threatening another phase of parochialism, of which perhaps a novel such as Kingsley Amis's *I Like It Here* is fairly representative. Jill Forbes (Ch. 9) picks up this idea of a continued British resistance to French influence in her essay on the relationship between French film culture and British cinema, and how, even after the comparative success of such publications as *Screen*, British film criticism is only slowly absorbing the concepts and language familiar for decades among French critics. Still, it was perhaps impossible to avoid the actuality of the events of May 1968; and in British reactions to French political life it is difficult to underestimate the significance of Louis Althusser. Although, as Susan James notes in the first paragraph of her essay on Althusserian materialism (Ch. 10), the French philosopher's star has waned in recent years, his name can still evoke strong reactions. Indeed, this waxing and waning of the influence of ideas and things French has a predictable element to it. So E. P. Thompson in *The Poverty of Theory* drew attention to the way that certain elements in British political life produced a view of French political theory totally dissimilar to the one that obtained in France itself:

> it is necessary to note the consistent misinformation as to French political realities, and mystification as to French intellectual affairs, which has been passed upon the English-speaking Left by the British francophiles. . . . I make no objection to franco-philia. There is very much in French intellectual and political life

to learn from and to admire. But our own agencies, who have taken out their franchises to import Althusser, Balibar, Poulantzas, Lacan, & c., have consistently presented images of French life and politics which are little more than fairy-tales derived from Parisian café gossip.[8]

If this is indeed the case, then, as we have pointed out, things have always been much the same. Certainly there have been occasions since the Second World War when some hybrids of contemporary French intellectual life have not thrived in Britain. The *nouveau roman*, as indicated above, has been one such case. Another seems to be those theories generated by French psychoanalysis. These are examples, that is, of the occasions when France has provided Britain with a practically unusable *avant-garde*. But these cases are the exception, not the rule. A fascinating study in this respect is that by Christopher Norris (Ch. 11), who points out that Oxford, long held to be the centre of Anglo-Saxon philosophical traditions, is in fact considered by some contemporary French thinkers to have much in common with those Continental schools of philosophy that it has traditionally been held to oppose.

Certainly, since the last years of the 1960s and the early years of the 1970s the tide of French intellectual influence has proved difficult to resist. It is increasingly difficult to imagine the heyday of F. R. Leavis, when literary criticism enjoyed what now seems like a complete immunity from having to make clear the assumptions that underwrote its practices. Indeed literary criticism is the area in which French ideas have found their most receptive contemporary audience, where the 'new' is welcomed virtually for its own sake. But it is one of the ironies of intellectual history that those whose gaze is firmly set towards France as the fountain of newness strike a very old pose indeed. It is one shared by many contemporary creative writers and artists. One of the most distinguished of recent British novelists, John Fowles, concludes this volume (Ch. 12) by describing how for him France has been, as it has been for countless other writers, an external point of reference which allows concepts like nationality and creativity and artistic responsibility to be addressed.

16 *Introduction*

NOTES

1. Cyril Connolly, 'French and English Cultural Relations' (1943), *The Condemned Playground* (London: Hogarth Press, 1985) p. 80.
2. *The Letters of Wallace Stevens*, ed. Holly Stevens (London: Faber, 1967) p. 773.
3. Clifford Geertz, *The Interpretation of Cultures* (London: Hutchinson, 1975) p. 11. Geertz is in fact quoting Ward Goodenough. See also Pierre Bourdieu, *Esquisse d'une théorie de la pratique* (Geneva: Droz, 1972), translated as *Outline of a Theory of Practice* (Cambridge University Press, 1977).
4. Connolly, *The Condemned Playground*, pp. 203–4.
5. Edgell Rickword, *Literature in Society*, ed. A. Young (Manchester: Carcanet, 1978) p. 1.
6. Rayner Heppenstall, *The Fourfold Tradition* (London: Barrie and Rockcliff, 1961) p. 247. Heppenstall is of course not alone in this view. Cf., for example, Theodore Zeldin, *The French* (London: Collins, 1983).
7. Richard Cobb, *A Second Identity* (London: Oxford University Press, 1969) p. 50.
8. E. P. Thompson, *The Poverty of Theory* (London: Merlin Press, 1978) p. 404.

1

The Uses of Decadence: Wilde, Yeats, Joyce

RICHARD ELLMANN

Victorian melancholy disclosed its uneasiness in the concept of decadence. The word began to be used in England about 1850, as if the distentions of empire necessarily entailed spiritual decline and fall. 'Decadent' was not a word that Ruskin or Arnold found congenial: Ruskin preferred 'corruption' and Arnold 'philistinism' and 'barbarism'. But decadence, with implications of the fading day, season and century, had an unfamiliar ring and gradually came to seem the right word. As if to confirm its rightness, the principal guardians of the Victorian age in statecraft and in literature ailed and then died symbolically as well as literally. Most were gone by the time the nineties started. 'The woods decay, the woods decay and fall.'

What distinguished decadence from corruption or philistinism was that it could be discussed with relish as well as with concern. Gautier, whose writings were in vogue in England as well as in France, declared in his preface to Baudelaire's *Les Fleurs du mal* in 1868 that the decadent spirit was in harmony with the contemporary crisis. He interpreted decadence as the extreme point of maturity of a civilisation. Paul Verlaine could accordingly announce in 1883 with *Schadenfreude* rather than discomfiture, 'Je suis l'Empire à la fin de la Décadence.' Dying cultures make the best cultures. A few months after Verlaine's poem came Huysmans's novel *A Rebours*, to give decadence the force of a programme. His decadent nobleman (decadents are always male and preferably noble; female decadents are called by other names) has no normal tastes. A determined quester for unheard-of pleasures, he collapses at last in neurasthenia, but of the most glamorous kind. This powerful work outlasted all other decadent prose because it established a new type – the sampler, who keeps changing his drink, who moves from one inordinate and esoteric fancy to another. *A Rebours*

17

became at once a favourite book of Whistler, Wilde, George Moore, Arthur Symons. Wilde and Moore wrote books that in part derived from it, and something of the book's effect rubbed off on Wilde's life as well. The cult of the green carnation, for instance, probably stemmed from Des Esseintes's peculiar notion that, while artificial flowers were to be preferred to natural ones, best of all would be natural flowers that looked like artificial ones. (A florist in the Burlington Arcade painted white carnations green every day.) What was also valuable about *A Rebours* was that it criticised decadence even while touting it. The intricate schemes of Des Esseintes to amuse himself with new sensations are checked as much by Huysmans's sardonic irony as by their inherent futility, and Huysmans, while never indifferent to his hero, avoids identification with him.

A Rebours was read with more solemnity than it was written with, and remained for a time the bible of decadence. Devotees of that movement were as determined in their advocacy as its bourgeois adversaries in their rejection. They flourished, however, for only a few years in Paris, during the eighties. By the time English writers took an interest in decadence it had already lost its lustre, or what they labelled (in a mistranslation of Baudelaire) 'its phosphorescence of putrescence'. In England nobody called himself a decadent, though it was a fine epithet to ascribe to someone else. Ten years after Verlaine's poem Arthur Symons published in *Harper's* his article 'The Decadent Movement in Literature'. Symons expressed a wry fondness for decadence as 'a new and interesting and beautiful disease', but within a few years he acknowledged that the decadent movement had been 'an interlude, a half-mock interlude'. He was persuaded later to call the movement 'symbolist' rather than decadent, a change of title which had already taken place in Paris ten years earlier. The element of mockery was overt in Oscar Wilde's references to decadence in the late 1880s. He spoke of a new club called 'The Tired Hedonists' who, he said, 'wore faded roses in their buttonholes' and 'had a sort of cult for Domitian'. The essay in which he evoked this fantasy movement was 'The Decay of Lying', the title itself a mockery of decadence.

The fact that in England decadence never gained the status of a literary movement did not keep people from taking sides about it. It was a subject of debate, it affected the course of literature, it did everything but exist. What opponents of decadence meant by the word was principally its parent movement, aestheticism. The battle lines had been drawn early in the century in two books. One was Gautier's *Mademoiselle de Maupin* (1837), the other Kierkegaard's *Either/Or* (1843). Gautier provided a heroine with bisexual tastes; in his preface he scorned morality, social utility, and nature as points of reference for art. Art was amoral, useless, and unnatural. Kierkegaard took up aesthetic man, as opposed to ethical man, and anatomised the way in which aesthetic man sought to be absorbed in a mood, a mood which must necessarily be only a fragment of himself. For fear of losing the mood, he cannot afford to reflect, nor can he attempt to be more than what he for that mood-moment is. He moves from sensation to sensation, much in the manner that Pater was later to extol; Kierkegaard seems to be refuting Pater before Pater wrote.

During the century both aestheticism and anti-aestheticism gathered force. In Joyce's *Stephen Hero* the president of the college warns Stephen, 'Estheticism often begins well but ends in the vilest abominations . . . .' The term could still be used without reproach, however. In 1868 Pater described the Pre-Raphaelites under the honorific title of the 'aesthetic movement'. But the counter-movement had its weapons of ridicule. In 1881 Gilbert's *Patience* presented an aesthete – Bunthorne – as effeminate and narcissistic. Up to now no memorable type of decadent aestheticism had been evolved in English literature to match Huysmans's character Des Esseintes, but Pater tried to establish one with his *Marius the Epicurean*, published two years after *A Rebours*. Marius is also a sampler, attracted to a series of cults like a series of sensations; one of them is a new Cyrenaicism, which, as Pater explains, 'from time to time breaks beyond the limits of the actual moral order, perhaps not without some pleasurable excitement in so bold a venture'. As his double negative indicates, Pater was a cautious man. His Marius is cautious too, and cannot be said to succumb to Cyrenaicism or to Christianity either; he seeks the impassioned realisation of experience, but in so sober-sided a way as to deprive aestheticism of its unwholesomeness. (For true decadent aestheticism a gamy whiff of the Borgias is required.) Pater situated his story in imperial Rome during the reign of Marcus Aurelius, and so left it open for someone else to provide a more modern and English instance. This was exactly what Wilde tried to furnish in *The Picture of Dorian Gray*, first published four years after *Marius* and part of the same cycle of novels.

The familiar ways of attacking decadent aestheticism were to quarrel with its supposed morbidity and pretentiousness, its narcissism, its excesses in technique and language, its concern with mere sensation, its artificiality and abnormality. Most of these criticisms could easily be turned against those who made them. Wilde said that, if one looked for examples of decay, one would find them among the sincere, the honest, the earnest. In *Ecce Homo* Nietzsche declares, 'Agreed that I am a decadent, I am also the reverse.' By his lights 'morality itself' was 'a symptom of decadence'. It was a revenge upon life, an attempt to 'unself man' (*Ecce Homo*). In *Stephen Hero* Joyce acknowledged that at moments Stephen showed signs of decadence, then added, 'But we cannot but see a process to life through corruption'. One man's decadence was another man's renaissance. Mallarmé saw in the dying century 'the fluttering of the veil of the temple', as if some infinite revelation were in store ('Crise des vers'). So Yeats wrote an essay under the title 'The Autumn of the Flesh' in 1896, and said, in ninetyish rhythm, 'I see, indeed, in the arts of every country those faint lights and faint colours and faint outlines and faint energies which many call "the decadence" and which I, because I believe that the arts lie dreaming of things to come, prefer to call the autumn of the flesh.' The best season is autumn, and the best time of day is of course the Celtic twilight, which also heralded a victory of moonlit spirit over sunlit matter. Wilde, less mystically, offered the heraldic figure of the new man, the *do-nothing*, a creature who emerges only after five in the afternoon, what used to be called 'the lounge lizard'. In a period when Victorians were infernally busy in misdoing everything, what really needed to be recognised was what he called 'the importance of doing absolutely nothing'. Under cover of indolence, which others were free to call decadence if they liked, Wilde proposed to transform society.

The debate about decadence achieved such resonance that any account of the nineties must take notice of it. C. E. M. Bowra reports in his *Memoirs* that Yeats wrote to him, 'The 'nineties was in reality a period of very great vigour, thought and passion were breaking free from tradition.' The allegation that they were decaying prompted writers to disprove the charge. In so doing, they had to rethink problems of art, language, nature, life, religion, myth. Wilde is the supreme example. He had adopted aestheticism while still at Trinity College, Dublin, and in the early 1880s he went to America to present the doctrine under the title of the English

renaissance. At the time he was between two versions of aestheticism. One, deriving from Gautier, and supported by Whistler,
extolled art for its absolute uselessness and its elitism, and denied
that it had any but a perfunctory connection with life and nature.
The other held that art could remake the world. In America Wilde
spent most of his time extolling beauty, but he also urged that
artistic principles might beautify houses and dress as well as life
generally. This meant that it was not useless, nor necessarily
elitist.

Wilde preached renaissance for a whole year to the Americans,
then returned and went to Paris. He found himself there *en pleine
décadence*. Parisian decadence made his inveterate proselytising for
undefined beauty seem somewhat out of date. Soon after returning to England, Wilde made clear in a review that he did not at all
accept that art was for art's sake. That slogan referred only to what
the artist feels when he is composing, and had nothing to do with
the general motive of art. Towards the end of the eighties Wilde
propounded such a general motive of art in 'The Decay of Lying'.
In this he turned Aristotle on his head by saying that art does not
imitate nature, nature imitates art. It was a paradox that no one
had been able to state so succinctly before, though it had certainly
been implied by the Romantics. The effect was not to divorce art
from life, as Whistler and Gautier would do, but to bring the two
together again, though with the priorities changed. The difference
between Wilde and the Romantics was not in estimating the value
of art, but in putting so much emphasis as Wilde did on artifice.
When he said, 'A sunset is no doubt a beautiful thing, but perhaps
its chief use is to illustrate quotations from the poets', he was
suggesting that artists were not only the Shelleyan unacknowledged legislators, but the quickeners of perception. Nature as we
know it is built up out of imaginative fictions. Strip as we will, we
will never be naked. People fall in love because poets have talked
up that sentiment. They limp because Byron limped, they dress up
because Beau Brummel did, Wilde's point here being that people
are affected not only by the works of art that are written down, but
by the works of art that are lived. This view of art was not at all
elitist; it was democratic and inescapable. Wilde set himself against
the contempt that Whistler expressed for art critics, which derived
from Gautier's comment, 'There was no art criticism under Julius
II.' Wilde's contrary view was, 'The Greeks were a nation of art
critics', and he would have said the same of the Italians of the

Renaissance. For criticism was one way in which expression could recognise its cultural antecedents. In his other great essay, 'The Critic as Artist', he explained that if it were not for criticism art would merely repeat itself. But, since all fine imaginative work is self-conscious and deliberate, the role of criticism is to subvert what has just been done, by confronting it with what was done before and elsewhere. The critical faculty brings to bear 'the concentrated experience of the race' as opposed to momentary consolidations arrived at by individual artists. Art is a great subverter, but always in danger of forgetting to subvert. Criticism prevents art from forgetting, prevents it from sinking into conformity. The image of subversion leads Wilde to see the artist and the critic within the artist as in some sense criminal. He disrupts, he destroys as he creates. In pursuing ever ampler and as yet unaccepted versions of the world, the artist is always breaking bonds.

The effect is to challenge all effigies, all that is established, such as the established virtues. Chastity is a virtue for which, as Renan says, nature cares little, and art, according to Wilde, correspondingly little. Charity creates a false sense of obligation, since the rich have no right to their wealth any more than the poor to their poverty. As for self-sacrifice, Wilde says that only a thoroughly secular age such as our own deifies it, for self-sacrifice is a survival of the self-mutilation of the savage and part of the old worship of pain. (This was not his final word on the subject.) It involves exactly that contraction of impulse, that narrowing in, which art sets itself to overcome. Wilde examines, or rather cross-examines, all the accepted virtues. So he takes up the virtue of presence of mind. He had a story to illustrate this. Once, in a crowded theatre, the audience saw smoke rising from the wings. They panicked and ran for the exits. But a leading actor, a man with presence of mind, went to the proscenium and called out, 'Ladies and Gentlemen, there is nothing to worry about. This tiny disturbance is of no consequence. The real danger to you is your own panic. The best thing for you to do is to go back to your seats.' They all turned and went back to their seats, and . . . were burned to a crisp.

The virtues are all to be tested afresh, then, and in fact all things require testing. The artist, equipped with a critical eye that constantly enforces a larger context – as, for example, of Greece and Rome as well as Christianity, has this task to perform. We speak of the artistic imagination, but what we mean is this eye for 'the concentrated experience of the race' which keeps the new from solidifying. Writ large, this shift in perception brings a new dispensation – Wilde speaks of it as the 'new Hellenism' as in youth he had spoken of it as the Renaissance. Does it matter whether we call it decadent or resurgent? He thinks not, and simply says, 'When that day dawns, or sunset reddens', as if either phrase would do so long as we recognise that the world will be changed.

Without having read Nietzsche, Wilde had arrived at something of the same view of things. In their different ways, both were constructing a new man, what Wallace Stevens called a 'major man'. Wilde did not share Nietzsche's elaborate view of the genealogy of morals, by which Christianity overturned the pagan virtues and put a morality of slavery in their places; but he did see hypocrisy all about him, masquerading as seriousness. His conception of the major man was of the artist who dared to 'harrow the house of the dead'. Nietzsche would have agreed.

In making the artist an advance man rather than a camp-follower of his society, Wilde implied that the artist is by necessity as well as choice a deviant. His sense of his own sexual deviation helped him to find justification for this view. (Later writers such as D. H. Lawrence also made an alliance between their sexual and their artistic needs.) In Wilde's time the word 'homosexual' was not in use, but there was no less need to find warrant for what it signified. Wilde became the first writer in English since Christopher Marlowe to make a case for it in public. One of his ways of doing so is to attack homosexuality's enemies the puritans. He does so in his plays in the nineties as he demonstrates, in one play after another, that moral questions are too complex to be solved by puritan mottoes. He never defended homosexuality overtly, except once at his trial, and the present generation, happily uncloseted, are sometimes indignant with him for not having made himself more convincingly and openly the victim of society, the first 'Homintern martyr' (in Auden's phrase). I think Wilde felt he could be more effective by opening a window here and there than by seeking martyrdom through taking off the roof, and, given the age in which he lived, that monstrous age, who can say that he was wrong? He saw himself as a rebel, not as a missionary. Homosexuality was not a cause; it was a way of affronting complacency. In three works, between 1889 and 1892, Wilde therefore outraged heterosexual smugness.

The first was *The Portrait of Mr W. H.*, which played with the idea that Shakespeare was a homosexual, and that he wrote the sonnets to his 'dearmylove', Mr W. H. He does not actually endorse the view, but he disseminates it. Wilde had begun his perilous campaign to bring this forbidden theme into literature by reconstructing the image of Shakespeare himself. He continued this campaign in *The Picture of Dorian Gray*. Dorian not only espouses decadence; he decays in every way except physically, the physical decay being consigned till the book's end to his portrait. He is driven to ruin men and women alike, as if his love in either mode were genuine only to the extent that it is tainted. As in *A Rebours* or, for that matter, in *The Waste Land*, a later decadence, both forms of love are introduced as equally corrupt. Wilde did not celebrate homosexuality, but, then, neither did Proust. In both writers, this deviation is described in terms of unhappiness. But to mention it at all in a society which pretended it did not exist was courageous, and for Wilde, as events proved, foolhardy. The book is also a criticism of the aesthete type, who samples sins and regrets it. Dorian lacks the motive of art, has only its artificialising mechanism. He enslaves instead of emancipating himself. We almost forgive him because he is so beautiful. In *Salomé* the pageboy loves the Syrian soldier, but this in only one of the erotic relationships suggested. For the Syrian, like Herod, loves Salomé; Salomé loves John the Baptist; John the Baptist loves Jesus. All love appears as deviation, and no deviation is superior to any other. All bring their tragic consequences. Wilde improves upon the Bible also by making Iokanaan as hysterical in hatred as Salomé is hysterical in love, so that the reader feels about the same concern for his being decapitated and for her being smothered. Originally Wilde intended to have both of them decapitated as if to confirm their parity. Wilde said elsewhere that renunciation, like excess, brings its own punishment, chastity being just as tendentious as debauchery. Mario Praz finds that the play exhibits the *femme fatale* in all her cruelty, but it seems to exhibit rather the uncontrollability of passion. Though Praz claims it is all plagiarised, and is baffled by its surviving better than other versions, the reason is simple – only Wilde's *Salomé* reconstitutes the entire legend, St John as well as Salomé, and in terms of a strong and original attitude.

With these writings Wilde stretched the domain of literature: he suggested that art might deal critically with moral taboos as part of an effort to remake the world. As Herbert Marcuse says, art shatters everyday experiences and anticipates a different reality principle. Wilde did for English literature almost singlehandedly what a score of writers in France had been attempting for a dozen years. The result was soon apparent. A. E. Housman was empowered to write, in the year of Wilde's trial, *A Shrosphire Lad*, with its thinly veiled interest in boys; he sent it to Wilde as he was being released from prison. The next year Rhoda Broughton, who did not like Wilde but was quick to sense the way the wind was blowing, wrote her novel *Faustina*, which is the first lesbian novel in English. Even Henry James wrote a series of works which took advantage of the freedom that Wilde had won for art even while losing his own freedom. Among them perhaps the most important for my purpose is *The Turn of the Screw* (1897), in which James indicates that boy and valet, and girl and governess, pair off for long hours together, and that the boy is expelled from school for some unnamable act of corruption of his schoolmates, which is described as being 'against nature'. Of course his offence is never specified. By presenting, even if with deliberate vagueness, homosexuality in terms of the corruption of children by adults, James follows Wilde's lead in broaching the subject, and he too associates it with bad conduct, though he too was inclined that way. It is in large part thanks to Wilde, then, both to his books and to his trial testimony, that the taboo against writing about homosexual behaviour or other forms of sexuality begins to be lifted in England. Opening our eyes has been the principal labour of modern literature.

In only one of his works did Wilde attempt to say what the renaissance would be like. That is *The Soul of Man under Socialism*. It would be a time when art would be triumphant, when people would develop freely, when there would be a new Hellenism devoid of the slavery that marked the old Hellenism, when nobody would have to be concerned about the poor, because there would be no poor, nobody would fight for property, because there would be none, nobody would marry, because marriage, being merely an extension of property, would also be abolished. In his letter to Douglas *De Profundis*, Wilde imagined in muted terms that Christ, whom he now accepted at last, but as the supreme aesthete, would bring about a renaissance by being recognised as a model – for Christ created himself, out of his own imagination, and asserted the imagination as the basis of all spiritual and material life. There are no laws, only exceptions. Sin and suffering were for him modes of perfection. So Wilde found place for suffering, at last, as leading to reconstitution of the terms of existence.

Yeats was in many ways a disciple of Wilde. When he was

eighteen he heard Wilde give a lecture in Dublin, and when he was twenty-two he met Wilde at the home of William Ernest Henley. This was the famous occasion when Wilde praised Pater's book on the Renaissance – 'It is my golden book. I never travel anywhere without it, but it is the very flower of decadence; the last trumpet should have sounded the moment it was written.' 'But,' someone interjected, 'would you not have given us time to read it?' 'Oh, no,' said Wilde, 'there would have been plenty of time afterwards, in either world.' Wilde was praising Pater for his decadence, and also suggesting that Pater's readers might as likely go to hell as to heaven. He recognised the ambiguity of Pater's morality. But the decisive moment in the early relationship of Wilde and Yeats came after the Christmas dinner at Wilde's to which Yeats was invited in 1888, when he was twenty-three. At 16 Tite Street he saw the extraordinary decor – drawing-room and dining-room done in white, not only walls but furniture and rugs too, the only exception being the red lampshade suspended from the ceiling. This cowled a terracotta statue which stood on a diamond-shaped cloth in the middle of a white table. After dinner Wilde brought out the proofs of his essay 'The Decay of Lying', and read it to Yeats. It had a profound effect. Yeats was quite prepared to believe that lies were better than truth, for he had already written in 'The Song of the Happy Shepherd',

> The woods of Arcady are dead,
> And over is their antique joy;
> Of old the world on dreaming fed;
> Grey Truth is now her painted toy.

He would say this more vigorously in his verse dialogue 'Ego Dominus Tuus', where the first of the two speakers, Hic, pleads for sincerity and veracity so that one can be what one really is, and the second, Ille, pleads for masks and images to enable one to be more than one really is. Ille of course wins. In his edition of Blake, Yeats redefined truth in the light of aestheticism: it is 'the dramatic expression of the most complete man'. Pater and Wilde would have approved.

Much of 'The Decay of Lying' deals with the value of images in shaping our awareness of the world. Wilde insists, for example, that 'the whole of Japan is a pure invention. There is no such country, there are no such people.' It is a concoction of the artists, to which they have given the name 'Japan'. Yeats would do something similar with Byzantium, which in his poems must be taken as a pure invention also. It bears no resemblance to the historical Constantinople, but is a city of imagination made by its artists, a magnificent 'instead' conjured up by an aging Irishman seeking an antidote for his own time. In his first poem on the subject, Yeats made the city somewhat static, and he wrote a second poem to give it the dynamism that he, like Wilde, regarded as essential to avoid art's repeating itself.

Although Yeats in the nineties scouted the idea of literary decadence, he wrote many poems about the decadence of the modern world. When he says in 'The Second Coming,' 'Things fall apart, the centre cannot hold, / Mere anarchy is loosed upon the world', he has at least the satisfaction of finding in the rough beast that 'slouches towards Bethlehem to be born' an image of the mock-renaissance that decadence will bring. His poetry is full of anguish over the world's decadence in poem after poem:

> Though the great song return no more
> There's keen delight in what we have:
> The rattle of pebbles on the shore
> Under the receding wave.
> ('The Nineteenth Century and After')

When Edward VII is crowned he writes,

> I have forgot awhile
> Tara uprooted, and new commonness
> Upon the throne and crying about the streets
> And hanging its paper flowers from post to post.
> ('In the Seven Woods')

But it was not only English decadence he resented; it was Irish decadence too, as in 'Romantic Ireland's dead and gone, / It's with O'Leary in the grave', or, more largely, 'Many ingenious lovely things are gone'. Yet he never loses hope, and a renaissance is almost always in the offing. 'Easter 1916', which declares that 'A terrible beauty is born', makes the claim that in tragic failure Ireland has achieved heroic rebirth. The great sacrifice is a true Easter, as the poet is the first to recognise.

Yeats identified decadence, much as Wilde did, as all the things that the Victorians celebrated as evidences of health. He spoke derisively of 'that decadence we call progress'. The Victorian poets had allowed morality and religion to fill their art with impurities, such as the 'doctrine of sincerity'. Victorian morality was particularly blameworthy. So he says in *A Vision* (1925), 'A decadence will descend, by perpetual moral improvement, upon a community which may seem like some woman of New York or Paris who has renounced her rouge pot to lose her figure.' He insisted even in his early work that fantasy and caprice would lose their necessary freedom if united either with good or with evil. Wilde sometimes referred distantly to a *higher ethics*, which would completely revise moral standards, and Yeats was prompted to try to redefine good and evil, in terms of an aesthetic point of view. In *A Vision* (1925) he said that, for men of the coming age, good would be that 'which a man can contemplate himself as doing always and no other doing at all'. This definition underlies poems such as the ones in which Yeats sanctions 'the wild old wicked man', or praises Crazy Jane against the Bishop, or pleads for vital personality instead of dead character, for laughter instead of solemnity. For he too, like Wilde, knew the terrible unimportance – or even danger – of being earnest. Artists are in league with lovers because they too are in search of an amplified consciousness. Appropriately, however, when Yeats in 'Under Ben Bulben' denounces the present –

> Scorn the sort now growing up
> All out of shape from toe to top,
> Their unremembering hearts and heads
> Base-born products of base beds

(as if it were not the case that all beds could be called base, – or no beds at all) – he asks the Irish *poets* to overcome this decadence. It is they who must engender renaissance of the imagination, to rescue 'this foul world in its decline and fall,'

> gangling stocks grown great, great stocks run dry,
> Ancestral pearls all pitched into a sty,
> Heroic reverie mocked by clown and knave.
>
> ('A Bronze Head')

Like Wilde, Yeats insists on the ulterior motive of art to reshape the world in which we live. This renaissance is always in the making.

Sometimes it is present in the deeds of great men, in intense love, in images of poets or in the way the language, often clogged and impeded, suddenly begins to dance.

And here we come to recognise that each Yeats poem is likely to begin in decadence, and to end in renaissance. The decay may be physical, as in 'The Tower', or 'Sailing to Byzantium', or cultural, as in 'Nineteen Hundred and Nineteen'. There are of course many variations – sometimes the point is to show that apparent decadence is not true decadence, as in 'No Second Troy', and sometimes, as in 'The Cold Heaven', the decadence continues into the afterworld, where heaven proves to be hell. But in general the poems present decadence in order to overcome it. The mind contends with some decadent fact or thought or image, then puts it aside in favour of some radiant recovery, a renaissance in little. Yeats does the same thing when he takes up whole civilisations, as if they too at recurrent intervals were artistically rescued from decadence. He expresses this idea most powerfully in 'The Gyres':

> Conduct and work grow coarse, and coarse the soul,
> What matter? Those that Rocky Face holds dear,
> Lovers of horses and of women, shall,
> From marble of a broken sepulchre,
> Or dark betwixt the polecat and the owl,
> Or any rich, dark nothing disinter
> The workman, noble and saint, and all things run
> On that unfashionable gyre again.

Lovers of horses and of women – Yeats could have said 'artists' directly, but he avoids the term, not wishing to be totally aesthetic. The term 'artist' had become much less honorific than it was in Wilde's time, yet the artist's role in conjuring up the best of life out of marble or air is implicit.

In Wilde and Yeats 'decadence' becomes the term to turn upon their antagonists. The decadents are those who accept the acquisitive, insensitive, unimaginative world, with all its morality, sincerity and seriousness. This world exists only as a distortion of reality, as Blake would also have said. Wilde could celebrate art more directly in his time than was possible in Yeats's more ironical age, and, while Yeats believed as fully as Wilde did that the mind of man can be rescued by art, he had to be wary in praising a faculty that others were quick to belittle. If Yeats is occasionally circumspect, Joyce is even more so. By his time silence, exile and cunning are required. Yet, though she would not have said so, Joyce was in the same tradition.

He rarely discusses decadence or renaissance in general terms as Wilde and Yeats had. The word 'aesthetic' was used by him to describe a philosophical theory, not adjectivally to pat art on the back. He even called Yeats an aesthete in a derogatory way, meaning that Yeats had been too ethereal and so had drifted about. Joyce wanted his renaissance closer to earth. He began by particularising the waste-land qualities of life in Ireland. He has Mr Dedalus say at the Christmas dinner in *A Portrait of the Artist as a Young Man*, 'A priestridden godforsaken race.' In 'The Day of the Rabblement', Joyce's first published work, he called the Irish the 'most belated race in Europe'. Later Stephen Dedalus in *A Portrait* says that Ireland is 'the old sow that eats her farrow'. Joyce, as a writer of fiction based on close observation, makes a more detailed attack upon hypocrisy than either Wilde or Yeats – he shows his countrymen pretending to piety and goodness but actually using religion and morality to curb individual lives with cruelty and repressiveness. In *Dubliners* he presented his initial indictment of Ireland in terms of its inertness, repression and corruption. Yet *Dubliners* does not rest in the portrayal of decadence. It establishes by tacit antithesis what it is the country lacks. Even while he portrays the fallen state of his countrymen, Joyce introduces three elements of possible relief. The first is a sympathy, usually latent and unstated, for thwarted lives. The second is the evident pleasure taken by the author in Dublin humour. If Joyce were merely excoriating, the humour would be a continual irrelevance. But it is not irrelevant; it keeps suggesting that even squalor can be funny, as if to enable us to withdraw a little from mere disgust or horror, and yet by prodding the muscles with which we laugh to keep us from detachment. Through humour we tumble to our likeness with others. The third is the reserved, fastidious diction and occasional bursts of lyricism. It is as if Joyce were proclaiming that all is chaos, but doing so in heroic couplets. When even the most mentally impoverished situations are described so deftly, so reservedly, so lyrically, the style itself offers the lost rhythms, the missing emotional possibilities, the absent structure. The age weeps, the rhythm smiles. So, as hopes are dashed, enterprises doomed, love unrequited or warped, sympathy, humour and lyricism keep reminding us that life need not necessarily be so incomplete. Joyce is not being inconsistent then, in the last story of

Dubliners, 'The Dead', where his hero is forced to acknowledge that there can be passion in parochialism and primitivism. The country may be decadent, yet still worth saving.

If the description of decadence is by example rather than generalisation, so is the description of renaissance. Yet that Joyce hoped for a renaissance was something he did say explicitly, though in less grandiloquent language, on a few rare occasions. The first was in his semi-autobiographical narrative essay entitled 'A Portrait of the Artist', not the book that came later. He ends that essay with a promise of what, thanks to the artist, is to come:

> To those multitudes, not as yet in the wombs of humanity but surely engenderable there, he would give the word: Man and woman, out of you comes the nation that is to come, the lightening of your masses in travail; the competitive order is employed against itself, the aristocracies are supplanted, and amid the general paralysis of an insane society, the confederate will issues in action.

The later novel *A Portrait of the Artist as a Young Man* uses a different method from *Dubliners* in that decadence is described not from various points of view, but entirely through the growing consciousness of it in mind of the inchoate artist. The criticism of decadence is much the same but looks different because of this focus. Stephen's future depends upon his becoming an artist, but the future of Ireland depends upon it too. So he asks himself, as he thinks of his decadent countrymen, 'How could he hit their conscience or how cast his shadow over the imaginations of their daughters, before their squires begat upon them, that they might breed a race less ignoble than their own.'

At the book's end, Stephen announces that he is going forth for the millionth time to 'encounter the reality of experience and to forge in the smithy of my soul the uncreated conscience of my race'. Joyce has stolen conscience away from the Church and given it to art. He wishes to emphasise that his art will work with reality, not Zolaesque reality, which is distortion in the name of the body, and not mystical distortion, which is the name of the soul – but it is through art that he hopes to bring about his great change. As he wrote in a letter to his wife on 22 August 1912, 'I am one of the writers of the generation who are perhaps creating at last a conscience in the soul of this wretched race.'

Joyce had read Wilde, regarded him as a hero of literature, a victim of society; he had Buck Mulligan mock Wilde's idea of a new hellenism, but what Mulligan mocks is what Joyce doesn't mock. Even if Joyce would not have used that slogan, *Ulysses* with its Greek title was intended to bring something like a new hellenism about. Because *Ulysses* does so many things – Joyce worried at one point whether he was trying to do too much – this basic impulse has been lost. Yet Joyce, like Stephen in *Stephen Hero*, considered art to be the vital centre of life. When he speaks of a conscience he means something different from the conscience then prevalent – something in tune with Wilde's higher ethics, more hellenic than Christian. It is a conscience which is always in search of more freedom for itself, and hence for both artist and his audience. Readers of *Ulysses* have pondered endlessly whether the principal characters are reborn. They do not need to be. Their consciences have gradually defined themselves as exemplary in action and thought against the powers of the world. In 'Circe' they resist final attempts to subdue them. They are the race less ignoble than their fellows for which the artist has forged a conscience. Stephen poses the negative aspect of the new era and the new conscience when he points to his head and quotes Blake against subjugation of his spirit or body, 'But in here it is I must kill the priest and the king.' Bloom poses the affirmative aspect when he advocates 'the opposite of force, hatred, history, all that' as truly life – and when pressed says, 'Love, I mean the opposite of hatred.' Molly Bloom is needed to complete the picture to raise their fragmentariness to lyricism, and to show by her general approval of Bloom and Stephen that nature, to which she may be a little closer than they, responds to the values of art – sensitivity, discrimination, sympathy, understanding, and intensity of feeling. Although she is described as fleshy, she is not fleshlier than Hamlet. For her too the mind affects everything. The tenor of her thoughts is to acknowledge grudgingly that her husband, who recognises her wit and musical talent and inner nature, is a better man than Blazes Boylan. 'I saw he understood or felt what a woman is', she says. Penelope recognises Ulysses not by his scar but by his imagination. All three characters achieve a freedom from hypocritical spirituality or empty materiality. In reading about them, the reader takes on the new conscience too. Joyce, like Wilde and Yeats, had a fifth gospel, a vision, a new bible. So reading *Ulysses*, if that book is properly understood, is a means of emancipation. One is freed by it to read about freedom.

Decadence, then, had its uses for Wilde, Yeats and Joyce, as a pivot around which they could organise their work. All in their different ways summon up an opposite to decadence, the promise of an 'unfashionable' age for which as artists they constitute themselves heralds. They are not decadents but counter-decadents. Or we could say that they went through decadence to come out on the other side.

Reprinted by permission of Bennington College, Vermont, this essay was originally delivered at Bennington College as Lecture 6 in the Ben Bellitt Lectureship Series, 28 September 1983, and subsequently published in 1984 as one of the *Bennington Chapbooks in Literature* with an introduction by Stephen Sandy.

2

The Reception of French Literature in England, 1885–1914

JOHN J. CONLON

In their discussion of the aesthetic movement, the implications of 'art for art's sake', and the phenomenon of the 1890s, Walter E. Houghton and G. Robert Stange focus on a curious occurrence: 'Out-of-the-way and queer writers were sought out; the elaborate metres of medieval French and Italian poetry were revived. But most important was the sudden addiction to, and liberal borrowing from, the works of nineteenth-century Frenchmen.'[1] To explain how this addiction came to exist and indeed to endure through the first decade of the twentieth century one must look first to the writers who preceded the writers of the 1890s and influenced the course of their literary lives. Beginning in the 1860s, several writers and critics contributed to a newly developing sense of the importance of French literature and began to exercise a profound influence upon the course of English attitudes towards the literature, culture and intellectual history of France; chief among them were Matthew Arnold, Algernon Charles Swinburne and, above all, Walter Pater, although such writers as John Morley and Andrew Lang also set the stage for a growing appreciation of French literature.

In Swinburne, especially in his work of the early 1860s, a considerable body of new and, in part, startling French literature found an English apostle. His essays on the poetry of François Villon and reviews of the work of Victor Hugo and Charles Baudelaire were truly partisan efforts but were not generally well received. Despite Edmund Gosse's assertion that his essays 'became a very remarkable element in current literature' Swinburne's advocacy of Baudelaire's work and his endorsement and practice of the motto of Les Jeunes France, *épater le bourgeois* ('to shock the

34

middle class') put the vast majority of English readers out of sympathy with him.[2] Further, his own poetry and the cause of art for art's sake, which it both springs from and illustrates, did not foster a wide appreciation of his French masters, Baudelaire and Théophile Gautier.[3] Swinburne's pioneer work in evangelising England for nineteenth-century French writers did help prepare for much more widespread work later in the century, but, having begun a thirty-year reformation in 1879, he ceased to be a force in the British literary world in the 1880s.

Matthew Arnold was the first literary figure of generally acknowledged respectability to lay open in an extensive way the literature of France to his countrymen. In his celebrated essay 'The Function of Criticism at the Present Time' (1864), he asserts that his chief object is to examine 'the best that is known and thought in the world' and that his critical perspective 'regards Europe, as being, for intellectual and spiritual purposes, one great confederation, bound to a joint action and working to a common result; and whose members have, for their proper outfit, a knowledge of Greek, Roman, and eastern antiquity, and of each other'.[4] Arnold follows these statements with the claim that more French and German literature ranks among the best of what is known and thought than does English literature. Commenting on Arnold's special diligence in exploring French literature, F. J. W. Harding writes, 'Yet within the span of the nineteenth century at least, Arnold probably made more references to and drew more parallels with French literature in his diverse publications than predecessors such as Carlyle, Coleridge, De Quincey, Lamb and Hazlitt, or near contemporaries like G. H. Lewes and Thackeray.'[5] If one excepts Pater's more important and far-reaching use of French literature and more lasting influence in that regard, Harding's point has extraordinary merit. He does, indeed, point out Arnold's change of mind about George Sand and his limitations as a disinterested critic, and continues, 'In his moral and religious objections to the modern French drama and novel he was perhaps as guilty as those very countrymen of his, Philistines and Puritans, whom he criticised for putting obstacles to the free play of the mind. But at least he kept his eyes turned towards France and the Continent throughout his life.'[6] Although Arnold's eyes remained turned towards the French coast he had, by the 1880s, undergone a change about advocating French literature and had, like Swinburne but for different reasons, ceased to do so.

Before turning to the case of Walter Pater it is helpful to recall that other writers assisted at the birth of a francophile movement that would flourish later in the century. John Morley did much to advance the cause of French literature in England in the late 1860s and early 1870s as editor of the *Fortnightly Review* by encouraging such writers as Swinburne, Frederick Harrison, Leslie Stephen and Pater to write on topics related to France and by setting them an example in his own 'Life of Turgot' (1870); his major works on Voltaire, Rousseau and Diderot were still ahead of him, but he had already done much to introduce French literature to a wide readership early in his editorial career. Similarly, the polymath Andrew Lang helped prepare for a more general and open reception of French literature in late-nineteenth-century England through his translation of early French literature, *Ballads and Lyrics of Old France* (1872) and *Aucassin and Nicolette* (1886). In fact, Pater had recourse to Lang's translations of the poets of the Pléiade for his essay on Joachim du Bellay (1873); he anticipated Lang's interest in *Aucassin and Nicolette* in *The Renaissance* (1873), and also helped Lang publish a review of a new edition of *La Chanson de Roland* in the *Westminster Review* (1873).[7]

By far the most influential writer and critic who opened the multifaceted world of French culture to his countrymen and whose works and disciples altered the course of English literature in that regard was Walter Pater. In large measure the story of French literature in England from the 1870s onward is the story of Pater and his circle. Encouraged by Morley, partially abetted by Lang and directly influenced by the work of Arnold and Swinburne, Pater, more than any of these, made a major contribution to the Victorian consciousness of French literature, a consciousness that would grow in the 1890s and continue to grow in the course of the present century. From his earliest essays and reviews, in the 1860s, to his last works, including an unfinished essay on Pascal that occupied his last days in 1894, Pater consistently infused his writings with references to French literature of the Middle Ages, the Renaissance, and especially to the varied manifestations of French Romanticism in 'the works of nineteenth-century Frenchmen'. Pater's best known and most popular work, *The Renaissance* (1873), exerted an extraordinary, and sometimes surprising, influence upon such self-styled disciples as Ernest Dowson, Lionel Johnson, George Moore, Arthur Symons and Oscar Wilde.[8] Other writers, such as Edmund Gosse, William Sharp and Humphrey

Ward, shared Pater's appreciation of French writers; and writers of quite diverse artistic power and temperament, such as William Butler Yeats, Virginia Woolf, James Joyce, Ezra Pound and T. S. Eliot, came directly under Pater's influence.[9]

Pater's *The Renaissance* sounded a new note in criticism and in critical theory by presenting an eclectic 'aesthetic' criticism drawn from principles enunciated by the critic Charles Augustin Sainte-Beuve and the historian Jules Michelet. The work also has as its premises an appreciation of the art and literature of the ancient world, the Middle Ages, the Renaissance and Pater's own era that is founded upon the principles of French Romanticism. In the several *portraits littérairies* (literary portraits) in his work Pater incorporated notions from Sainte-Beuve and Michelet; he also uses the work of Renan, Chateaubriand, Rousseau, Madame de Staël, Victor Hugo, Théophile Gautier, Blaise Pascal and Joseph Joubert to explain and amplify his theories of a proto-Renaissance in the Middle Ages, of a cultural continuity from that time to the present, and of France as the principal locus and fount of cultural activity.

In his Preface, Pater explains his inclusion of the stories *Aucassin and Nicolette* and *Amis and Amile*, by writing that they not only illustrate Renaissance qualities he finds in the 'middle age itself' but also 'help the unity of my series, inasmuch as the Renaissance ends also in France, in French poetry, in a phase of which the writings of Joachim du Bellay are in many ways the most perfect illustration'.[10] 'The Renaissance,' Pater continues, 'in truth, put forth in France an aftermath, a wonderful later growth, the products of which have to the full that subtle and delicate sweetness which belongs to a refined and comely decadence . . .'(*Renaissance*, p. xxiii). Pater begins the first essay in his volume by reinforcing his sense of France's primary role in the Renaissance and writes, 'The history of the Renaissance ends in France and carries us away from Italy to the beautiful cities of the country of the Loire. But it was in France also, in a very important sense, that the Renaissance had begun' (p. 1). One additional element of French theory Pater incorporated into *The Renaissance* is in its Conclusion, where, following his famous phrase 'to burn always with this hard, gem-like flame, to maintain this ecstasy, is success in life', he counsels his readers that the wisest of 'the children of this world' will spend their time in art and song and that, 'of such wisdom, the poetic passion, the desire of beauty, the love of art for its own sake, has most' (p. 190).[11] The importance of Pater's use of 'art for art's sake' cannot be overstated; and this use has been the subject of numerous studies, including, in part, Richard Ellmann's essay reprinted above (Ch. 1). Without diminishing in any way the importance of the phrase and its impact upon Victorian readers, I suggest that several other aspects of French thought and literature Pater included in *The Renaissance* and in other of his writings between 1873 and 1894 also influenced those who adhered to the aesthetic creed of burning with a hard, gem-like flame and seeking poetic passion, the desire of beauty, and art for art's sake.

Unlike Arnold and Swinburne, Pater is the only major precursor of the generation of the 1890s who remained an active advocate of French literature and continued to explore it. In exploring Wordsworth's thought and poetry (1874) he traced the growth of a singular chapter in the history of the human mind from Rousseau to Chateaubriand, to Victor Hugo and included an appreciative statement about George Sand's novels. In a review of J. A. Symonds' *The Renaissance in Italy* (1874) he presented Stendhal to English readers; in so doing he was well ahead of his time not only in England but also in France, where Stendhal had, except in the writings of Hippolyte Taine and Prosper Mérimée, suffered general neglect. And in the first of what would become his *Greek Studies*, 'Demeter and Persephone' (1875), he tentatively explored what he saw as a connection between the paintings of Camille Corot and François Millet and the poetry of Wordsworth and began a limited discussion of symbolism. Symbolism, in this essay, does not carry the meaning of French symbolist poetry, as it would later be introduced by Arthur Symons, but it does provide a starting-point for further artistic and critical speculation.

Of even greater significance in the pre-1885 era of Pater's work are two highly important essays, 'Romanticism' (1876) and 'The School of Giorgione' (1877), which he included in the third edition of *The Renaissance* (1888). 'Romanticism' did for French literature of the eighteenth and nineteenth centuries what 'Two Early French Stories' and 'Joachim du Bellay' in *The Renaissance* had done for earlier periods of French literature. In that essay Pater examines the perennial question of what constitutes a classic, and breaks with Sainte-Beuve and Goethe to claim for the poetry of Henry Murger, Théophile Gautier and Charles Baudelaire the qualities of 'energy, freshness, comely order' which Sainte-Bauve and Goethe had posited as hallmarks of classic work. Baudelaire's place in this essay is as an accomplished writer of later Romanticism; and, although when Pater republished this essay as the Postscript to *Appreciations with an Essay on Style* (1889) he excised all reference to Baudelaire and replaced that name with Victor Hugo's, still the approval of Baudelaire's work, and the naming of such works as Murger's *Scènes de la vie de jeunesse*, Aloysius Bertrand's *Gaspard de la nuit*, Gautier's *La Morte amoureuse*, and Victor Hugo's *Les Travailleurs de la mer* make this one of the truly remarkable groundbreaking essays of Pater's career. 'The School of Giorgione' breaks new ground in quite a different way: in that essay Pater incorporates notions about synaesthesia and several other elements of the visual and musical arts which Baudelaire had written about in *L'Art romantique*, at times translating Baudelaire's statement directly into English, but without ever naming Baudelaire as his source.[12]

Pater's influence upon a younger generation relative to the reading and appreciation of French literature had, by the mid eighties, begun to grow. The unfortunate Oscar Browning was caught up in a minor scandal at Eton for allegedly lending a boy a copy of Gautier's *Mademoiselle de Maupin*, ostensibly upon Pater's recommendation, a scandal that widened later in the same year (1875), resulting in Browning's dismissal from Eton.[13] Emilia Francis Strong, Lady Dilke, a friend of Pater's and historian of French art, who had written an unfavourable review of *The Renaissance*, faulting Pater's sense of history, had herself produced a two-volume history, *The Renaissance of Art in France* (1879), which Pater referred to in the third (1888) edition of *The Renaissance*. While an undergraduate at Magdalen College, Oxford, Oscar Wilde met the renowned Fellow of Brasenose at Pater's invitation in 1877, a meeting that had a profound effect on Wilde's literary life and resulted, in the same year, in Pater's sending him a copy of Gustave Flaubert's *Trois contes* (1877); this included 'Hérodias', which Wilde would later refashion into *Salomé*.[14] The full effects of Pater's influence would not, however, be felt until he emerged from years of writing *Marius the Epicurean* (1885), and gave himself over to an active life in literary London when he was not otherwise engaged at Oxford.

The year 1885 represents a milestone for Pater in the publication of his only complete novel, and for the reception of contemporary French literature in England as Pater finally began to enjoy a salon life in which he counted among his intimates Violet Paget (Vernon Lee), George Moore, Arthur Symons, Oscar Wilde, Edmund

Gosse, William Sharp, Lionel Johnson, Ernest Dowson, Richard Le Gallienne, William Rothenstein, Herbert Horne, and Humphrey and Mary Ward (Arnold's niece). Many of these, soon to include William Butler Yeats, formed the Rhymers' Club, *les chevaliers de l'avenir* (the knights of the future) and frequently out-Patered Pater: they produced, on the one hand, studies of the French Symbolists, the *Yellow Book* and the *Savoy* and, on the other, the Celtic Renaissance. They were never slow to acknowledge their debts to Pater, even when they exaggerated debts paid back in false currency. Of some of these Germain d'Hangest writes, 'One must underscore the cosmopolitanism of this new school. . . . All were generally open to contemporary French influences, to the messages that came to them from Baudelaire and, more recently, from Verlaine, Huysmans or Mallarmé.'[15] Curiously, only some elements of Pater's cosmopolitanism surfaced in his essays and reviews from 1885 to his death in 1894: he chose to write about notable writers, Gustave Flaubert, Emile Zola, Prosper Mérimée and Pascal, and those whose work is less well-known today, Ferdinand Fabre, Henri-Frédéric Amiel, Octave Feuillet, Jules Lemaitre and Pierre Filon; he did not write about Paul Verlaine, Joris-Karl Huysmans, Stephane Mallarmé or Arthur Rimbaud, and touched upon such current topics in French literature as impersonality in art, realism and naturalism only in things he said 'by the way'. Although Pater withdrew from direct involvement with and advocacy of some of the newer movements in French and English literature in the last decade of his life, his earlier work on the French Romantics had begun a movement his reticence in the 1880s and 1890s would not alter.

A cursory examination of Pater's literary activity from about 1885 onward reveals a writer still propagandising England on behalf of the French, and whose efforts on behalf of French literature, though varied and uneven, helped fix English attention on a host of nineteenth-century Frenchmen and on three prose masters especially. His essay on Romanticism received a wider audience as the Postscript to *Appreciations* in 1889, the year after he published his borrowings from Baudelaire in 'The School of Giorgione' in the third edition of *The Renaissance*. His novel *Marius the Epicurean* is itself a highly Romantic work in which Pater quite consciously draws parallels between second-century Rome and nineteenth-century Paris and London and likens Apuleius to Gautier and Mérimée.[16] In that novel, however, Pater departs from both French and English models and conceptions of the novel by negating the ruling passion as a principle of novelistic action and anticipating writers such as Marcel Proust and James Joyce and the writers of the mid twentieth century by focusing on 'the sensations and ideas' of his protagonist. His other fiction of the period, ranging from *Imaginary Portraits* (1887) to his unfinished romance *Gaston de Latour*, to his last stories, 'Emerald Uthwart' (1892) and 'Apollo in Picardy' (1893), evidence the influence of Mérimée, Gautier and Flaubert.

'Of Flaubert', Arthur Symons wrote in his brief, appreciative biographical sketch of Pater, 'we rarely met without speaking. He thought "Julien l'hospitalier" as perfect as anything he had done. *L'Education sentimentale* was one of the books he advised me to read. . . .'[17] Pater's major discussions of Flaubert, in two reviews of editions of Flaubert's letters and in 'Style' (*Appreciations*, 1889), served to introduce Flaubert to a wide English readership as 'the martyr of literary style' who searched for *le mot juste* to express 'a relative, somewhere in the world of thought, and its correlative, somewhere in the world of language'.[18] This particular element of Flaubert's thought and Pater's presentation of it in 'Style' had considerable influence upon T. S. Eliot.[19] Pater's lecture on Mérimée at the Taylorian Institution (1890) likewise contains a discussion of art that fixes upon the state of nineteenth-century literature and provides a starting-point for critical discussions and artistic practice in the twentieth century. In assessing the state of art in his times he writes of contemporary man,

> The science he turns to will be a science of crudest fact; the passion extravagant, a passionate love of passion, varied through all the exotic phases of French fiction as inaugurated by Balzac; the art exaggerated, in matter or form, or both, as in Hugo and Baudelaire. The development of these conditions is the mental story of the nineteenth century, especially as exemplified in France.[20]

In focusing upon Mérimée's 'central literary aim' of impersonality, which would, before long, become a primary aesthetic tenet of Yeats, Joyce and Eliot, Pater appears as puzzled by it as he had in discussing the concept in Flaubert's work; while he does concede that Mérimée achieved some measure of impersonality, he is quick to state that this quality 'is itself but an effective personal trait and, transferred to art, becomes a markedly peculiar quality of literary beauty'.[21]

Pater's work on Zola, far less significant than his efforts on behalf of Flaubert and Mérimée, is none the less important both in itself and in the effects it had upon his fairly new circle of literary acquaintances who took up the new standard of francophilia and whose activity forms the second part of the history of the reception of French literature in England during this era. At this point in examining the English reception of French literature, it is also important to sound a cautionary note: those who by the mid-1880s were open to France were still in a decided minority. By the late 1880s Emile Zola's literary reputation in England, like the reputation of most French writers, was at a markedly low point. Henry Vizetelly, who published relatively sanitised translations of Zola's novels, had been tried twice on charges of obscenity and was sentenced to jail in 1888 on that account. A virtual crusade against the intrusion of French literary lubricity and vulgarity upon the English reading public was in full swing in the 1880s in the form of the National Vigilance Association.[22] Pater's published references to Zola in the late 1880s gather significance given the anti-French temper of the times and the unfortunate fate of Vizetelly. In April 1889 Pater reviewed Ferdinand Fabre's *Toussaint Galabru* for the *Nineteenth Century* and took the occasion to refer to 'realism' and to recommend Fabre's *Les Courbezon* as 'worthy of M. Zola at his best. And then, there is nothing in Fabre to shock the most scrupulous conscience, the daintiest taste.'[23] In June of the same year Pater again invoked Zola as a writer of 'undoubted power' whose work serves as a touchstone for Fabre's *Noirine*.[24] And in December 1889 Pater did a surprising thing: he reviewed a book he did not care for, a book that largely took issue with his old editor, John Morley, and used the review as an occasion for defending Zola's work. Specifically, he discounts the argument W. S. Lilly set forth in *A Century of Revolution* (1889) against Zola, *Nana* and 'naturalism' by claiming for naturalism a place in all living art and by claiming that *Nana* is not as representative of Zola's work as Lilly would have one think.[25]

Pater's defence of Morley and, more importantly, of Zola against Lilly and his acknowledgements of Zola in his reviews truly went against the currents of the time and helped encourage some members of his circle to read and write of Zola's novels. George Moore, one of the outspoken new generation of writers interested in

France, was an early disciple of Zola's and of Pater's, met Pater in 1885, sent him a copy of his naturalistic novel *A Mere Accident* (1887) and *Confessions of a Young Man* (1888), in which he praised Pater's *Marius* in the course of chronicling his life in the art-for-art's-sake movement. Moore had known Zola in Paris, served as an intermediary for the Vizetelly translations, especially for the translation of *La Terre* in 1888, and had written introductions to the Vizetelly translations of *La Curée* and *Pot-bouille*. Others of Pater's circle likewise took up the work of translating and writing of Zola. Edmund Gosse introduced Heinemann's edition of *The Attack on the Mill* (1892); Arthur Symons, whom Pater led to a study of French literature that would change English poetry in the twentieth century, translated *L'Assommoir* for the Lutetian Society's publication of the Rougon-Macquart series in 1894–5; Ernest Dowson translated *La Terre* for the same series. The change in English attitudes about Zola in the 1890s had varied implications: the publishing-firm of Chatto and Windus published Zola's works in translation; Macmillan published the translations in the United States; and, although he knew no English, Zola visited London in 1890, addressed the Institute of Journalists in 1893, and chose England as his place of exile in the furious period of the Dreyfus affair (1898–99).[26]

The involvement of Pater and his circle in the literary fortunes of Emile Zola in England is emblematic of the extent to which the Paterians helped alter British literary taste and activity in the 1890s and subsequently. Moore's *Confessions of a Young Man* is generally taken as the first work of the 'Beardsley Period', an out-and-out era of art for art's sake. Another manifestation of the era is the Rhymers' Club, a confederation of poets who claimed Pater as their master and who sought to capture the subtleties of French Symbolist poetry in English language and verse. The Rhymers' Club included such writers as Arthur Symons, Ernest Dowson, Lionel Johnson, George Moore, and William Butler Yeats, all of whom sought to integrate the poetic theory and practice of Verlaine, Rimbaud and Mallarmé into their own poetic practice. Characterised by a distinct but sometimes undistinguished poetry, their literary productions (Yeats's excepted) have not worn well and may appear to contemporary readers as yet more late-Victorian verse to be eschewed.

Lionel Johnson, a poet of the 1890s who wrote of Pater in 1894, had much to say of Pater's many endeavours and characterised his work by using Gautier's famous phrase 'Verse, marble, onyx, enamel' to describe the jeweller's work of Pater's prose.[27] Johnson himself wrote poetry that caught and held Ezra Pound's attention to the extent that he edited Johnson's collected verse in 1915, thereby forging another link between the late Victorians and modern poetry. Ernest Dowson spent much of his youth in France and, upon drifting to London from Oxford in 1887, became a stalwart Rhymer, a translator of French poetry, and a poet whose own practice incorporated elaborate French stanzaic forms. Yeats and Oscar Wilde participated fully in the importation of French literary theory and practice, frequented Bohemian Paris, and patterned much of their work in the 1890s on the new literature of France. In Yeats's case the influence of Pater led to a discovery of French poetry in his formative years; in Wilde's it led to an appreciation of Flaubert, Huysmans, Gautier and Baudelaire.

One of the most striking results of Pater's work on behalf of the French is the effect it had on Arthur Symons. Symons' poetry shares with that of his fellow Rhymers French leanings; his editorship of the *Savoy* and the *Yellow Book* was carried out in the spirit and letter of art for art's sake. Symons is, despite those achievements, best remembered for his own famous volume, one that reflects Pater's concerns in *The Renaissance*, mirrors its Conclusion and echoes Pater's phrases and ideas in most of its pages: *The Symbolist Movement in Literature* (1899). In that volume he introduced to a broad readership those works of French writers which he and his circle most admired and followed. At least one important aspect of that readership is that it bridged the period between the nineties and the thought and poetry of Ezra Pound and T. S. Eliot.

Symons had come under Pater's sway early in his own career; Pater reviewed his first volume, *An Introduction to the Study of Browning* (1886), quite favourably, and thereafter Symons and Pater struck up a literary friendship until an estrangement in 1891, possibly caused, as Lawrence Evans speculates, by Pater's disapproval of Symons' decadent eroticism in life as well as in literature.[28] One result of Pater's influence is Symons' studies of the French, many of which he collected and published in *Studies in Two Literatures* (1897) under the title 'Impressions and Notes: French Writers', to which he added some and from which he deleted others for the first edition of *The Symbolist Movement in Literature*, and added yet more in the second edition (1908). The authors about whom he wrote remain, for the most part, the acknowledged masters of the nineteenth century: Balzac, Mérimée, Nerval, Gautier, Flaubert, Baudelaire, the Goncourt brothers, Zola, Verlaine, Huysmans, Rimbaud, Laforgue and Maeterlinck. To these essays he added a superb bibliography, some notes, and translations from Mallarmé and Verlaine. Symons' work on these Symbolists, decadents, realists and naturalists marks a critical turning-point in the English reception of French literature; the reception may indeed have been mixed in the last decades of the nineteenth century and in the early years of the present century, but the work Symons produced had both immediate and long-term effects on the appreciation and study of French literature of the period in England and in the English-speaking world. The growing receptivity to French literature throughout the early part of this century has, then, its origins in the work of the writers of the 1890s; and their literary leanings and origins are in large measure traceable to the consistent advocacy for French literature of Walter Pater.

NOTES

1. W. Houghton and G. R. Stange, *Victorian Poetry and Poetics* (Boston, Mass.: Houghton Mifflin, 1968) p. 755.
2. Edmund Gosse, *Life of Swinburne* (London: Macmillan, 1917) p. 168.
3. Swinburne was the first in England to write of Baudelaire and is generally credited with introducing Gautier's formulation of 'art for art's sake' to English readers in his *William Blake* (London: Hotten, 1868) p. 101. For a more extensive discussion of Swinburne's place in introducing French literature to English readers, see John J. Conlon, *Walter Pater and the French Tradition* (Lewisburg Pa: Bucknell University Press; London: Associated University Presses, 1982) ch. 1.
4. See Matthew Arnold, *Lectures and Essays in Criticism*, ed. R. H. Super (Ann Arbor: University of Michigan Press, 1962) p. 230.
5. F. J. W. Harding, *Matthew Arnold: The Critic and France* (Geneva: Droz, 1964) p. 133. For an extended discussion or Arnold's uses of French literature and his interest in France, see Iris Sells, *Matthew Arnold and France* (1935; New York: Octagon, 1970) and Patricia Thompson, *George Sand and the Victorians* (New York: Columbia University Press, 1977) ch. 6.
6. Harding, *Arnold*, p. 133.
7. See *Letters of Walter Pater*, ed. Lawrence Evans (Oxford: Clarendon Press, 1970) p. 11.
8. For an examination of Pater's disciples and influence see John Pick, 'Divergent Disciples of Walter Pater', *Thought*, 23 (Mar 1948) 114–28.

9. See Richard Ellmann's essay above (ch. 1), and also John J. Conlon, 'Eliot and Pater: Criticism in Transition', *English Literature in Transition*, 25.3 (1982) 169–77.

10. Walter Pater, *The Renaissance: Studies in Art and Poetry*, ed. Donald L. Hill (Berkeley, Calif.: University of California Press, 1980) p. xii. Subsequent page references appear in the text, where possible.

11. See ibid., p. 457. All previous editions of *The Renaissance*, including the epoch-making first edition of 1873 and the *Ur*-Conclusion as it appeared in 'Poems by William Morris', *Westminster Review*, 90 (Oct 1868) 149, read 'art for art's sake.'

12. For a more extensive discussion of the Pater–Baudelaire connection see Conlon, *Walter Pater and the French Tradition*, ch. 3.

13. See *Letters of Walter Pater*, p. 16.

14. See ibid., p. 26.

15. Germain d'Hangest, *Walter Pater, l'homme et l'œuvre* (Paris: Didier, 1961), II, 16–17 (my translation).

16. See Pater, *Marius the Epicurean* (London: Macmillan, 1885) II, 14.

17. Arthur Symons, Introduction to *The Renaissance* (New York: Modern Library, n.d.) p. xxiii.

18. Pater, *Appreciations* (London: Macmillan 1889) p. 30. Pater's source for this and several other of his statements about Flaubert is Guy de Maupassant, Préface to *Lettres de Gustave Flaubert à George Sand* (Paris: Charpentier, 1880), repr. as 'Gustave Flaubert', in *Œuvres complètes de Guy de Maupassant*, ed. René Dumesnil (Paris: Librairie de France, 1938) XIV, 104–39.

19. See Conlon, 'Eliot and Pater', *English Literature in Transition*, 25.3.

20. Pater, *Miscellaneous Studies* (London: Macmillan, 1895) p. 13.

21. Ibid., p. 37.

22. See Clarence Decker, 'Zola's Literary Reputation in England', *PMLA* 59 (Dec 1934) 1140–53; and John J. Conlon, 'Walter Pater and Zola's Literary Reputation in England', *English Literature in Transition*, 19.4 (1976) 306–12.

23. Pater, 'Toussaint Galabru', *Nineteenth Century*, 25 (Apr 1889) 622.

24. Pater, *Essays from 'The Guardian'* (London: Macmillan, 1896) p. 121.

25. Pater, 'A Century of Revolution', *Nineteenth Century*, 26 (Dec 1889) 993.

26. For a more detailed listing of translations of Zola's work, a general sense of his reception in contemporary England, and a brief examination of his life and work see John J. Conlon, 'Emile Zola', *Critical Survey of Long Fiction: Foreign Language Series*, ed. F. Magill (Englewood Cliffs, N.J: Salem Press, 1984) pp. 1982–95.

27. Lionel Johnson, 'The Works of Mr Pater', (1894) in *Post Liminium* (London: Elkin Matthews, 1911) p. 20.

28. See *Letters of Walter Pater*, p. xl.

3

English Criticism and French Post-Impressionist Painting

J. B. BULLEN

*'Their debt to the French is enormous' – even
Mr Clive Bell, with all his enthusiastic admiration of the English Post-Impressionists at the Grafton
Galleries, is forced to make this admission. Every
word of their artistic language is traceable to some
French root. There is no eccentricity, no affectation, no mannerism in French that does not find
a ready echo in English Post-Impressionist art.*[1]

P. G. Konody's castigation of English francomania at the second
Post-Impressionist exhibition in 1912 is a symptom of the powerful
influence of France in the early years of this century. According to
Cyrena Pondrom in her book *The Road from Paris*, French intellectual currents were far more extensive and important than those of
any other foreign origin,[2] and her view is supported by Eric
Homberger in his essay 'Modernists and Edwardians'.[3] But the
continuity of the French tradition is probably more a feature of
literary life than of the world of art. In the middle decades of the
nineteenth century the English had observed with interest developments in French art. Towards the end of the period an indiffer-
ence had set in, and the English, priding themselves on their
national tradition in painting, became actively hostile to French
work of an experimental kind. When compared with the elaborate
medievalism of Burne-Jones, the monumental symbolism of G. F.
Watts or the statuesque classicism of Lord Leighton, French Impressionism appeared frothy and insubstantial and it took the full
critical effort of R. A. M. Stevenson and D. S. MacColl to convince
the English of the seriousness of the French enterprise. When

MacColl's *Nineteenth Century Art* was published in 1902 and the French dealer Durand-Ruel organised an extensive exhibition of late-nineteenth-century French art at the Grafton Galleries in 1905, the status of French Impressionism seemed secure. Both press and public responded favourably to the paintings of Monet, Manet, Renoir, Boudin, Morissot, Sisley and Pissarro. But between 1905 and 1910 not only did the reputation of Impressionist art fail to gain ground in Britain,[4] but those painters whom we now associate with Post-Impressionism were either unknown or overlooked. The Durand-Ruel exhibition, for example, contained ten pictures by Cézanne, but their muted tonal range was eclipsed by the startling brilliance of Monet's haystacks and the voluptuous richness of Renoir's bathers. 'What are these funny brown-and-olive land-scapes doing in a impressionist exhibition?'[5] the critic Frank Rutter remembered asking himself about the pictures by Cézanne as he passed through the galleries. But Rutter, who, together with Roger Fry, was later to become one of the most forceful exponents of Post-Impressionism in England, also 'walked through' the Cézanne exhibition at the Paris Salon d'Automne in 1904,[6] for he, like Fry, was 'sceptical about Cézanne's genius'[7] at this time.

Traditionally the 'Art-Quake of 1910'[8] is identified as an import-ant turning-point in the history of art in England. It is the year in which, in Quentin Bell's words, 'England met modern art'[9] and the year in which Virginia Woolf detected a change in English sensibility.[10] These exaggerations contain an important element of truth. Roger Fry's first Post-Impressionist exhibition in 1910 sub-verted not only established values about the nature of painting, but also the relations between art and the culture which produces it. But the exaggerations put too much stress on the instantaneous and dramatic quality of the impact of modern art in England and they overlook the important build-up to the first Post-Impressionist exhibition. In the years before 1910 there was extensive interest in new artistic forms in England and there was considerable aware-ness that there was a ferment of new techniques and new ideas on the Continent. But what the English lacked was not only the first-hand experience of the works of art themselves but also a perspective and an intelligible language by means of which they could respond to the new art. Roger Fry provided both, and it could be argued that the controversy over French art between the first and second Post-Impressionist exhibitions was as much an affair of language as one of images. In the months immediately following the first Post-Impressionist exhibition this controversy was focused on the term 'Post-Impressionism' itself. What was in the first place no more than a casual form of words immediately became a shibboleth, but one of such power that it polarised English attitudes to recent French culture.

It is significant that Desmond MacCarthy's introduction to the catalogue of the first Post-Impressionist exhibition opens with a discussion of terminology. MacCarthy, who wrote the piece under Fry's supervision, asserts in his first sentence that 'the pictures . . . are the work of a group of artists who cannot be defined by any single term', but by the end of the first paragraph of this same introduction he has adopted the term which was to become permanently attached to this 'group of artists'. 'This indeed', he says, 'is the first source of their quarrel with the Impressionists: the Post-Impressionists consider the Impressionists too naturalistic.'[11] The full title of the exhibition was 'Manet and the Post-Impressionists', and by its appropriation of the name of Manet it gave the term Post-Impressionism a sense of historical authenticity. Manet's work was known and admired by many connoisseurs in Britain; his pictures had been seen in significant numbers at the 1905 Durand-Ruel and subsequent exhibitions.[12] But in his history of Impressionism (translated in 1910 by J. E. Crawford Flitch under the title *Manet and the French Impressionists*), Théodore Duret assigned Manet a central role in nineteenth-century French art. The echo of Duret's study in the title of the exhibition at the Grafton Galleries is no coincidence, since it further supported the authenticity of what was an exceedingly new critical term.[13]

In its early days Post-Impressionism served to describe the miscellany of paintings which Fry could rapidly beg or borrow from French dealers already committed to serving the needs of established customers on the Continent and in Russia. As Benedict Nicolson has pointed out,[14] though the catalogue is unreliable and inaccurate, it is still possible to see that the sample of paintings which Fry brought from Paris tended to stress the romantic and expressionist aspects of Post-Impressionism rather than a preoccupation with form. Cézanne was represented by twenty-one works which were 'violent and dramatic in mood';[15] Gauguin by thirty-seven works and Van Gogh by twenty. No living artist was represented by more than nine pictures, so the emphasis was placed firmly on the old masters. There were nine pictures by Vlaminck, six by Rouault, five by Maurice Denis, three by Derain and three by

Friesz. There were three unrepresentative paintings by Matisse, of which *La Femme aux yeux vertes* created a disturbance as great as any in the show, and three by Picasso – *Young Girl with a Basket of Flowers* (1905), a portrait of Clovis Sagot and a landscape – but none in his latest, Cubist, style.

Nevertheless, many of the images in these paintings were frankly incomprehensible to English eyes and much journalistic copy was derived from the hysterical reaction of the first visitors to the Grafton Galleries, but the power of the term 'Post-Impressionism' was not derived exclusively from its connection with the pictures in Bond Street. It caught the public imagination because it served to concentrate ideas and feelings about modernism in a peculiar way. Strongly held attitudes to modern art were already latent within contemporary English criticism; they ranged from uncertain excitement about experimentalism to barely suppressed rage about the erosion of longstanding values. The paintings served to focus these extremes and the controversy which surrounded Post-Impressionism was considerably greater even than Fry had anticipated.

British attitudes to modern French painting in the period before 1910 are often misinterpreted as blank ignorance. However, this is not entirely true. Many British artists were familiar with the developments which had taken place in French art since the 1880s, and many of them had experimented with the techniques of Van Gogh, the pointillism of Seurat and the primitivism of Gauguin. The Scottish painter J. D. Fergusson, for example, had sent a number of decorative, Fauve-inspired pictures to the Salon d'Automne,[16] and, when Frank Rutter invited him to review this exhibition in 1909, Fergusson made it clear in his article that, for him, Matisse was the most important artist then working in France.[17] Walter Sickert, too, exhibited regularly in the modern salons and was no stranger to French art. When, in 1905, he returned from his self-imposed exile on the Continent, he wished to bring something of the French attitude to art to Britain, so he set up the Fitzroy Street Group – what he called his 'Salon d'Automne milieu in London'.[18] Spencer Gore, one of the original members of that group, was impressed by the works of Cézanne at the Durand-Ruel exhibition in 1905,[19] and was deeply moved by the Gauguins at the Salon d'Automne of the following year when he visited it in Sickert's company. This was the second year in which the Fauves showed their pictures, and Gore, unlike Sickert, was drawn to the works of Matisse. Charles Ginner, too, joined the Fitzroy Group, with a broad knowledge of French art. Born in France and educated at the Académie Vitti, he developed a strong admiration for the work of Van Gogh, with whose techniques he had already experimented.[20] Early in 1910 Rutter persuaded him, too, to write for *Art News*, and in his account of the International Society's exhibition he used the opportunity to express his admiration for Vallotton, Vuillard and Matisse.[21] The familiarity with modern French art amongst other English-speaking artists was considerable, and many of them were to rise to prominence in England on the high-tide of Post-Impressionism. Robert Bevan, for example, had met Gauguin as early as 1894 at Pont Aven; in 1905 Clive Bell and Vanessa Stephen visited Roderic O'Conor in his Paris studio and both expressed admiration for his collection of works by Cézanne and Gauguin;[22] Duncan Grant met Matisse several times on his visits to Paris, and C. R. W. Nevinson said that he had heard of 'the "mad" paintings of Van Gogh some five years before their "discovery" by Roger Fry and the dealers'.[23] The list of artists who were familiar with the painting at the independent salons in the first decade of the century could be extended to include J. B. Manson, Wyndham Lewis, Augustus John,[24] Henry Lamb, the Americans Nan Hudson, Ethel Sands and Anne Estelle Rice, and many others.

The public were, of course, much less well informed, and, though *The Times*, the *Burlington Magazine* and the *Nation* published reviews of the exhibitions at the Salon d'Automne and the Salon des Indépendants, these were frequently confused and misleading. The Salon d'Automne of 1905, which contained the famous *cages des Fauves*, was notable, said *The Times*, for its 'quiet harmony of effort to record frankly and honestly sensations', but the same paper led an attack on the 'unnatural and obtrusive colours' of paintings by Gauguin at the same salon in the following year.[25] Confusion about developments in Continental art reached their height in England in 1910, when, almost simultaneously, abstract paintings by Kandinsky were shown at the Royal Albert Hall, an article on Italian Futurism appeared in the journal the *Tramp*,[26] and paintings by Cézanne, Gauguin, the Nabis, the Fauves, Derain and Vlaminck were shown at an exhibition in Brighton. The divergence in critical attitude is admirably demonstrated by reviews of this last show. In a long piece in *The Times* the critic stressed the historical continuity between modernism and

early Italian art. He praised the 'primitive method' and the 'clear
and harmonious design' of Gauguin, Maurice Denis's attempt to
replicate the 'grandeur of Piero della Francesca', and Matisse's
work, which he described as 'more primitive than the early Sienese
in [its] reaction against photographic realism'.[27] Frank Rutter, on
the other hand, writing in *The Sunday Times*, applauded the effort
of André Derain for taking 'his courage in his hands . . . throwing
overboard the whole cargo of art history ancient and modern', and
attempting 'to forget that a picture was ever painted'.[28] The prevailing perplexity about modern art was summed up by the critic
Lewis Hind, writing in the *Art Journal*. He had recently seen
pictures by Matisse in the Stein collection and asked his readers (in
the full knowledge of the likely reply), 'Do you know his works?'

> Ninety-five out of a hundred laugh when they see them. Five
> think. Do you know the 'cube' pictures of Pecasso [*sic*], and the
> improvisations of Wassily Kandinsky, or the chaotic interpreta-
> tions of London by André Derain? Pause before you embark on
> that voyage. You will find yourself without a chart, without a
> compass.[29]

Inevitably the response to Post-Impressionist art in 1910 and
1911 was violent, widespread and highly emotional. The terms of
reference were often divergent, and, though some were determined by aesthetic considerations, most were shaped by ideological commitments. The ideological controversy was extremely
vociferous, and in the first weeks of the exhibition it effectively
drowned out Fry's patient, lucid and reasoned attempts to explain
what he saw to be the central principles of Post-Impressionism and
his attempt to address the works in their own terms.

Fry was a self-confessed newcomer to the generation of French
painters of the 1880s. Schooled in the criticism of early Renaissance
art and dissatisfied with the narrowness of Impressionist painting,
his 'discovery' of Cézanne began in 1906, when he was sponta-
neously moved by two paintings at an exhibition of the
International Society. His advocacy of French painting was part
formal, part psychological and part historical. In the first decade of
the twentieth century he developed a theory of art which involved
the relations between what he called the practical life and the
aesthetic life. In Fry's view the realist tendencies of Western art
since the Renaissance had appealed progressively to our practical

impulses; art had come more and more to imitate the forms of the physical world, degenerating into illusionism, on the one hand, and anecdotalism or sentimentalism, on the other. As a consequence it had lost its appeal to the imaginative life. Trecento art, in contrast, made no attempt mechanically to reproduce natural forms, and the correspondences between the painted image and the material world were simply those which were able to stimulate most economically an imaginative response in the beholder. Until 1908 Fry felt that modern art had lost this power, but a small exhibition of paintings by Cézanne, Gauguin, Maurice Denis and Matisse caused him to revise this opinion. An anonymous review entitled 'The Last Phase of Impressionism' in the *Burlington Magazine* described this group as the decadent remnant of a healthy Impressionist movement, and likened them to 'the now forgotten Flemish and Italian eclectics' that followed in the wake of the vigorous 'naturalistic movement in fifteenth century Florence'.[30] Fry found this interpretation historically unacceptable and in his reply he began to develop a theory of historical continuity which was to become central to his account of Post-Impressionism. Far from being the last phase of Impressionism, he said, this group were the beginning of something new. They were, he said, 'proto-Byzantines rather than neo-Impressionists' and grew out of a fundamental revision of the 'anarchic licence of Impressionism'.[31] This neo-traditionalist strain in Fry's argument was a persistent one and was his most powerful weapon against those critics who denounced Post-Impressionism for its anarchism and its flouting of the values inherited from previous generations.

Fry found the confirmation of his views in the work of two contemporary writers – Maurice Denis and Julius Meier-Graefe. Denis, in a long article published in the French journal *L'Occident* and translated by Fry for the *Burlington Magazine* early in 1910, argued for the 'classic' status of Cézanne's work. According to Denis, Cézanne, reacting against Impressionism, created an art which 'imitates objects without any exactitude and without any accessory interest of sentiment or thought'. 'He assembles colours and forms without any literary preoccupation; his aim is nearer to that of a Persian carpet weaver than of a Delacroix'.[32] Fry was later to extend this idea to the other painters whom he included in the Post-Impressionist movement, and in 1912 explained that when he called these painters 'Classic' he meant 'that they do not rely for their effect upon associated ideas, as I believe Romantic and

Realistic artists invariably do';[33] instead they rely on 'images which by the clearness of their logical structure, and by their closely-knit unity of texture appeal to our disinterested and contemplative imagination'.[34]

Fry's other mentor was Julius Meier-Graefe – the 'volcanic German', as Lewis Hind called him.[35] Meier-Graefe's *Modern Art* (written in 1904, and translated in 1908) was widely read by those in England as the only comprehensive history of modern painting which took account of the work of Cézanne, Gauguin, Van Gogh and the Neo-Impressionist painters led by Seurat. It was highly romantic, highly Teutonic, but must have appealed to Fry for the way, as Judith Falkenheim suggests, it 'upheld the notion that art is a recreation of the permanent structure that underlies appearances'.[36] What distinguishes Meier-Graefe from so many of his contemporaries is that he addressed himself directly to the formal quality of painting – the arrangement of light and colour in terms of brushwork and pigment. So in a painting by Cézanne 'where trees are growing, we see a light road, in which the tone of the canvas is merely enriched by pale yellow, grey, and faint touches of blue; then again we have a green field, flecked with touches of stronger green, but on the whole of exactly the same tone as the foreground'.[37] But there are two further ideas in Fry's writing at this time traceable to Meier-Graefe's influence. The first was connected with the expressive element in Post-Impressionist art. Meier-Graefe's account of late-nineteenth-century French painting lays great stress on the romantic and the passionate aspects of the artistic temperament. In one sense his book is a series of heroic biographies in which each of his characters finds personal expression in works of art. The only way in which Van Gogh could escape despair, says Meier-Graefe, was 'to loosen more and more the slender threads that bound his individuality to a failing body, and penetrate ever more deeply into the mystery that dazzles the eyes, to give bodily substance to the artistic soul, even when it was parting soul and body'.[38] Echoes of Meier-Graefe's account of Van Gogh can be heard in Fry's writing. 'To Van Gogh's tortured and morbid sensibility', said Fry in December 1910, 'there came revelations . . . of realities behind the veil of things seen'; he 'became a portrayer of souls; souls of broken, rugged, ungainly old women like the "Berceuse", [and] souls of girls brutalised by the associations of utter poverty'.[39] It was a tone which Fry was soon to abandon, and after 1910 he no longer stressed the expressive and romantic elements in Post-Impressionism; instead he concentrated on the abstract, formal constituents of French painting and their appeal to the imaginative life. By 1911 he was insisting that 'rhythm is the fundamental and vital quality of painting, as of all the arts – representation is secondary to that, and must never encroach on the more ultimate and fundamental demands of rhythm'.[40]

But the second idea which Fry may have found in Meier-Graefe's work had much further-reaching consequences. Meier-Graefe was a great systematiser. Throughout *Modern Art* painters are grouped and regrouped around a central structure made up of what he called 'The Pillars of Modern Art' – Courbet, Manet, Cézanne, Degas and Renoir – and 'Schools' and 'Circles' are integral to his interpretation of art history. This universal, encyclopaedic approach has its roots in eighteenth-century universal history. It is characteristically Germanic and makes a strong contrast with the way in which the same subject was treated in France; contemporary French criticism, tending to focus on the special and individual characteristics of individual painters, was much less preoccupied with bold historical sweeps. Fry was temperamentally more sympathetic to the French strategy, and certainly to the French use of critical language, but Meier-Graefe's structure, imposing as it did a logical development upon the history of art, must have attracted Fry. Consequently, while following the broad outlines, he modified and simplified the German's system. Fry's 'Post-Impressionism', like Meier-Graefe's 'Pillars of Modern Art,' fosters the idea of a tradition which started with Manet and extended onwards to the Fauves.[41] Fry's conception of Post-Impressionism was, of course, oversimplified and in many ways it presented a misleading view of the history of art. But, with the merit of comprehensibility and straightforwardness, cutting through a tangled and complicated web of painters and styles, it carried great weight with Fry's contemporaries. It was also a highly explosive theory. Fry's cavalier disregard of history and geography imparted to Post-Impressionism a much greater sense of unity than it actually possessed; he opened the way for many people, nervous about German militarism and foreign anarchism, to interpret it as yet another dangerous revolutionary 'movement'. Many of its critics saw it as an artistic conspiracy whose aim was to erode the traditions of high craftsmanship, artistic integrity and truth to nature for which late-nineteenth-century academic art had come to stand.

It is not difficult to see why, in 1910, critics were up in arms about Post-Impressionism, why academic painters closed ranks against it and why journalists were quick to report the extreme reactions. But the consequence for art criticism was considerable. Reviews, letters, articles and comments on Post-Impressionism appeared in every journal and newspaper in the first week of Fry's exhibition, and what was an unknown term on 8 November had passed into the language by 15 November.

The ideological objections to Post-Impressionist painting were concerned principally with the indirect threat to stable social and political order. A similar controversy had grown up around Degas's picture *L'Absinthe* in 1893, but then much of the objection had been levelled at the subject of the picture rather than its treatment.[42] Now, in 1910, the issues were more broadly cultural, and in the extremely heated exchanges which took place in the late months of that year the spectre of France with its malign influence on English traditions loomed large. Holbrook Jackson, for example, detected a sinister 'deep-rooted revolt against the past', which he connected with the 'dark and forbidding names' of the Continental anarchists Bakunin and Max Stirner,[43] and the critic of the *Spectator* (probably Harry Strachey) made the point that in France 'a reform movement always has its section who are for barricades, the guillotine, and the Anarchists' bomb'.[44] 'Anarchy in High Art' was how the *Tatler* announced the exhibition, and the words 'revolt' and 'anarchy' occur repeatedly in the early accounts of Post-Impressionism.[45] E. W. Cook claimed that it was 'the analogue of the anarchical movements in the political world, the aim being to reduce all institutions to chaos; to invert all accepted ideas on all subjects'.[46] Cook had expressed similar ideas about Impressionism in his book *Anarchy in Art and Chaos in Criticism* of 1904, and the knowledge that Post-Impressionist paintings sold widely in France and Germany served to intensify his francophobia. Much of Cook's writing is concerned to eulogise the idea of an English tradition (enshrined in the Royal Academy) and to warn against the influence of Whistler, the 'Anglo-Parisian-American [who] proved the evil genius of British Art and Art Criticism'[47] and who imported 'evil influences . . . from Paris, where *decadenza* was raging with especial virulence'.[48]

For several months there was almost no room for any serious art criticism in the outpouring of articles, letters, comments and remarks about Post-Impressionism. The paintings at the Grafton

Galleries were either the splendid and brilliant sign of a 'revolution in art' (the title of Frank Rutter's monograph on Post-Impressionism) or they were the symptoms of progressive disease and decay in the Western world traceable back well into the nineteenth century. The connection between art and insanity had already received expression in Max Nordau's *Degeneration* of 1895 and been elaborated in his book *On Art and Artists* (translated in 1907). Nordau exploited the relationship between cultural decadence and mental derangement in the light of Lombroso's theories about insanity, and interpreted aestheticism and expressionism as clear proof of universal decadence. For the British, the words 'alien' (i.e. foreigner) and 'alienist' (i.e. psychiatrist) were intimately connected. Were not the distortions of form and colour in Post-Impressionist art perpetrated by foreigners? Their treatment of nature and the human form was clear testimony to their insanity and did not one of them, Van Gogh, die in an asylum? Headlines such as 'Maniacs or Pioneers' or 'Paint Run Mad'[49] were commonplace in November and December of 1910, but a letter by the painter Charles Ricketts to the *Morning Post* brought together xenophobia, the fear of political unrest, and the link between art, 'egotism' and incipient mental derangement which was a prominent feature of many hostile responses to Post-Impressionism. Writing of 'the "cult" [which] has its organised headquarters in Paris, its prophets in America, and its cosmopolitan travellers in Germany', Ricketts, referring to the pictures at the Grafton Galleries, suggested how 'egotism, exasperated by opposition or resistance, has led to [these] works'. 'Morbid and suffering egotism is the spring of all anarchy in conduct, in art, as in criticism', he said; though such pictures were of no interest as art, 'they might interest the doctors of the body and the students of the sickness of the soul'.[50]

They certainly interested one such doctor – T. B. Hyslop, Physician Superintendent to the Royal Hospitals of Bridewell and Bedlam. In January 1911 Hyslop participated in an extraordinary event organised by the Art Workers' Guild. He was asked to give a lecture on the painting of the insane, and, though he claimed to have no knowledge of art and to have confined himself to 'art and degeneration in asylum practice', his lecture, entitled 'Post-Illusionism and Art in the Insane', was an extended analysis of all the categories of mental derangement hitherto discerned in Post-Impressionist art and its supporters. 'There were assembled in their hundreds the howling advocates of the tumbril and the guillotine', reported the *Pall Mall Gazette*, adding that the lantern slides were accompanied 'by roars of laughter'.[51] 'Degenerates', claimed Hyslop, 'often turn their unhealthy impulses towards art, and not only do they sometimes attain to an extraordinary degree of prominence but they may also be followed by enthusiastic admirers who herald them as creators of new eras in art'.[52] What distinguishes Hyslop's chilling exercise in defamation from the jokes and parodies of Post-Impressionism, and even from the righteous fulminations of the academicians, is its conscious perversion of language and its abuse of the terms of scientific inquiry. Hyslop used his scientific training to reinforce the prejudices of his audience by 'proving' to them that the Post-Impressionists were insane. He employs his full powers as an 'alienist' and his use of jargon anticipates the sinister terminology later employed by Soviet psychiatrists to describe the politically troublesome:

> The distorted representations of objects, or partial displacements of external facts, are known technically as 'illusions'. Their psycho-pathological significance is great, and they may arise in consequence of the fallacy of expectant attention (whereby the image of the expected becomes superimposed on that of the real) through toxic affectation of the brain cells . . . or as the result of faulty memory (paramnesia, distorted memory, whereby post-illusionism or false post-impressionism becomes manifest). Post-maniacal illusionism is almost invariably distorted, and the faulty representations bear little significance except as manifestations of disease.[53]

Hyslop makes no pretence of the fact that he believes that Post-Impressionist paintings are the fruit of diseased minds, so it comes as no surprise to find him quoting Max Nordau on the subject of primitivism in modern art. 'Retrogression to first beginnings', he says, 'and the affectation of simplicity is frequently seen in degenerates, and it has been described by Nordau as "painted drivelling or echolalia of the brush".'[54] For Hyslop the Post-Impressionists are far more dangerous to society than those under psychiatric care; at least the inmates of asylums cannot 'found so-called intellectual or aesthetic movements and by futile babbling and twaddle seek to propagate what may be, as a matter of fact, nothing else than idiocy or humbug'.[55] Hyslop concluded his talk by classing all critics, followers and admirers of modern art among

the 'rabble of hysterics, neurasthenics, weaklings and degenerates'[56] of society.

One such 'degenerate' critic was forced to be present on this
occasion, for, surprisingly enough, Roger Fry was asked to give his
own account of Post-Impressionism at the same meeting. Fry's
reaction is not recorded, though we do know that in the face of
Hyslop's pseudo-science his dignified and reasoned explanation of
modern art cut very little ice with the members of the Guild. Nor,
sad to say, was this the end of the story, for in March and April the
Art Chronicle ran a series on the art of the insane – complete with
illustrations – with the lamentable aim of demonstrating the affi-
nities between the art of Bedlam and the art of France.[57] It is small
wonder, then, that Arnold Bennett, who had sprung to the defence of Post-Impressionism soon after the opening of the Grafton
Galleries exhibition, should claim that 'the negligent disdain of
Continental artists for English artistic opinion is fairly well
founded'.[58]

Fortunately not all English artistic opinion took this perverse
form, and the year 1911 also saw the development of a debate
about Post-Impressionism which did not depend solely for its
terms on the language of pathology, or terms of abuse. Three
monographs published early in the year offered a broadly positive
view of the new art, though each was written from a different
perspective. Charles Holmes' *Notes on Post-Impressionist Painters*
explained Post-Impressionism as a reaction against 'the materialism which limited the original Impressionists to the rendering of
natural effects of light and colour' and their reversion to the
'principle of personal vision [which has] inspired all the greatest
art in the world'.[59] Holmes, the Director of the National Gallery,
had lent his personal support to the Grafton Galleries exhibition
and was most attracted to the work of Van Gogh: 'His design is
large and original, his colour powerful or refined . . . his intensity
of vision almost disquieting.'[60] He praised Gauguin's 'large primitive dignity' but felt that the paintings were really more suitable
'for a hut on a Pacific island than for any conceivable edifice in
Europe'.[61] However it was the work of Cézanne which posed for
Holmes – as it posed for most serious-minded artists at this time[62] –
the greatest problem. Cézanne, said Holmes, was 'a humbler
follower of the more famous Impressionists [whose] coarse hand-
ling is accentuated by consistent personal clumsiness of touch'.[63]

The journalistic, iconoclastic style of Frank Rutter's *Revolution in*

Art makes a considerable contrast with Holmes' measured academic prose as he calls upon the young to man the barricades and keep at bay the enemies of progress. 'The priestly caste', he said, '[is] ever warring against the prophets who keep alive the sacred fire they fain would smother'.[64] Rutter's experience of French art was extensive. He had long been art critic for *The Sunday Times* and occasionally for *L'Art et les artistes*; having witnessed the success of the two modern salons in Paris, he established the Allied Artist's Association in London. This exhibiting association operated on similar lines to the Salon des Indépendants and from 1908 put on huge shows in the Albert Hall, counting among its regular exhibitors many painters who had shown in Paris, such as Sickert, Wilson Steer, Roderic O'Conor and J. D. Fergusson. Rutter was also the first to exhibit the work of Kandinsky in London, in 1910. Rutter's recent Parisian experience had familiarised him with the paintings of Matisse – 'veritable criticisms of life, eloquently expressing in sweeping contours the joy and tragedy of human passion',[65] as he wrote in his extravagant style, but in *Revolution in Art* he also gives a brief account of Picasso's Cubist works, unusual at this time. When Cubism appeared at the Salon d'Automne of 1910 it puzzled the French as much as the English[66] and in his monograph Rutter speaks of how Picasso had recently evolved a new vision of form, building up his paintings with a series of cubes, greyish to yellow green in colour. But Rutter confesses his inadequacy: 'at the moment *je ne suis pas à la hauteur*'[67] and he offers no explanation of Cubism. Lewis Hind, the author of the third book, *The Post-Impressionists*, was also puzzled by Cubism. All through the months of 1910 he had been recounting the stages of his conversion to modern art in the *Art Journal*, the *Art Chronicle* and the *English Review*, but, when Cubism became a controversial issue in November 1911, Hind maintained an implacably hostile attitude. Nevertheless his book contains one new and prophetic note. Two chapters entitled 'The Movement in England', tracing the influence of Post-Impressionist style on English artists, accurately anticipate a French stylistic 'invasion' of England.[68] True enough, it was not long before Post-Impressionist techniques – mainly of the Fauve variety – were detected everywhere in English art[69] and prompted the remarks of P. G. Konody printed at the head of this essay.

Post-Impressionism also had its sceptical but intelligent critics, of whom Walter Sickert and D. S. MacColl were the most outstanding. They were both of Fry's generation and both were familiar with and sympathetic to the aims of French art. Nevertheless both had strong reservations about Post-Impressionism; their objections, however, were based on different premises – Sickert's on practice, MacColl's on theory.

In a lecture given at the Grafton Galleries in December 1910, Sickert justly objected to that particular group of pictures as representative of a coherent movement in art. 'As it would be impossible to establish any logical thread running through the exhibition at the Grafton, any complaints as to absentees would be beside the point. Why Manet? Why skip the other Impressionists? Since "post" is the Latin for "after", where are Vuillard and Bonnard?'[70] Sickert's view of French art history (and one which was largely promulgated in France itself) differed significantly from that of Fry. Where Fry stressed a number of criteria centred on the work of Cézanne – criteria which grew out of a reaction against Impressionism – Sickert saw this same period in terms of the work of distinguished individuals all of whom, in their various ways, were stylistically indebted to Impressionism. For Sickert, Gauguin represented 'National Gallery quality at its highest level',[71] and, though he claimed to execrate Van Gogh's 'treatment of the instrument I love',[72] he paid high tribute to the expressive power of those examples of Van Gogh's work which Fry had brought to the Grafton Galleries. Cézanne was an enigma for Sickert, and he suspected that his reputation had been inflated by French dealers. But his greatest invective was reserved for Matisse. For him Matisse was merely a *fumiste* with 'a string of property sausages trailing from the pocket of his baggy trousers' and whom nothing could induce him to 'acknowledge as next-of-kin'.[73]

D. S. MacColl also saw Post-Impressionism through the eyes of a writer deeply committed to Impressionism. Between 1890 and 1896 he had been art critic for the *Spectator*, where he had consistently championed Impressionism. *Nineteenth Century Art* (1902) was the fullest expression of his views on Impressionist painting and in 1910 those views were largely unchanged. For MacColl, Post-Impressionist art was no more than a pale reworking of many of the ideals of Impressionism – a view that he put forward in a long article entitled 'A Year of "Post-Impressionism"'. Cézanne, he said, was a minor artist who misused Impressionist techniques in a spurious attempt to generate monumental images. Gauguin too, according to MacColl, began as 'a rather dull Impressionist, in the

wake of Pissarro', and the technique of his later work was modelled on 'the drawing of Degas, [but] stiffer and less flexible'.[74]
Picasso's painting too, as it was represented at the Grafton Galleries, had for MacColl strong Impressionist qualities; he appeared
'as a Whistlerian, less certain even than Whistler in the construction of a painted figure, but with a delicate sense of colour'.[75]
MacColl could find no links between Impressionism and Fauve
painting and he likened the Fauves to 'Baal's priests, cutting and
maiming their forms in a desperate incantation of the fire that had
touched Van Gogh'.[76]

The strengths of MacColl's views as he expressed them in 'A
Year of "Post-Impressionism"' were of a negative and theoretical
kind.[77] He was very quick to point out the contradictions in the
arguments explaining Post-Impressionism as 'classical' in Maurice
Denis, but 'romantic' in the writing of Meier-Graefe. Sometimes,
as MacColl pointed out, Post-Impressionism was characterised by
a concern for abstract design; sometimes it was self-expression;
sometimes it was described as a search for an intenser view of
reality than that offered by Impressionism; sometimes it was
viewed as an effort unconcerned with mimesis except in the most
abstract way.

Both Sickert and MacColl brought to the criticism of Post-
Impressionist theory considerable knowledge and intelligence, but
neither of them offered much in the way of constructive criticism
and their views were infused with the sardonic peevishness of
men whom the world had passed by. Sickert in particular resented
Fry's championship of French painting and how 'when the whole
Continent of Europe had already been converted, [he had] become
the shaggy apostle of the *dernier cri*'.[78] For Sickert and MacColl
Post-Impressionism was a fanciful idea; for both of them it was an
historical fiction which bore no relation to their personal experience of the work of Cézanne, Gauguin and Van Gogh in Paris
many years previously. But Fry's ignorance was, in a sense, his
strength. It gave him the freedom to develop a theory about
modern art which depended more upon imaginative insight than
on historical fact. No doubt that theory, like the language which
accompanied it, was too simple and made too few discriminations
between the work of too few artists. Nevertheless, it was original.
It caused what Sickert called 'a rumpus'[79] and, by scandalising not
just the art world but the public at large, it thrust the issue of
French art into the headlines in an unprecedented manner. The

principal strength of Fry's conception of Post-Impressionism was that it commanded attention. It carried with it many of the over-tones of a cult and the public reaction was correspondingly vigor-ous. The effect on British taste was dramatic. The *Athenaeum* correctly predicted that '1910 will be remembered in our art-history as the year of the Post-Impressionists.'[80] By 1911, as P. G. Konody pointed out, 'Post-Impressionism [had] taken firm root among us.'[81] Even the *Pall Mall Gazette*, which had described the Grafton Galleries exhibition as 'the most disturbing feature in the history of British Art in 1910',[82] reviewed an exhibition of the work of Denis, Desvallières, Laprade and Serusier early in 1912. In little less than a year, said the critic, many 'scoffers have turned into admirers' and 'many of those who were most abusive and bitter in their denunci-ation have come to look with indulgence upon what only twelve months ago appeared to them intolerable!'[83]

NOTES

1. P. G. Konody, 'Art and Artists: English Post-Impressionists', *Observer*, 27 Oct 1912, p. 10.
2. Cyrena A. Pondrom, *The Road from Paris* (Cambridge: Cambridge University Press, 1974) pp. 1–8.
3. Eric Homberger, 'Modernists and Edwardians', in *Ezra Pound: The London Years: 1908–1920*, ed. Philip Grover (New York: AMS Press, 1978) pp. 1–14.
4. Judith Falkenheim points out that even in 1910 the English tended to buy Barbizon pictures from France in preference to Impressionist works. She also suggests that the humanist bias in criticism between 1905 and 1910 tended to work against Impressionism. See her *Roger Fry and the Beginnings of Formalist Art Criticism* (Ann Arbor: University of Michigan Research Press, 1973) pp. 4–8.
5. Frank Rutter, *Art in my Time* (London: Rich and Cowan, 1933) p. 111.
6. Ibid., p. 113.
7. This confession was made by Roger Fry in a review of pictures by Cézanne in 1906. See *Athenaeum*, 13 Jan 1906, pp. 56–7.
8. The title of an article by Desmond MacCarthy describing the circum-stances surrounding the first Post-Impressionist exhibition. See *Lis-tener*, 1 Feb 1945, pp. 123–4 and 129.
9. The title of an article by Clive Bell in *Art News*, Oct 1950, pp. 24–7 and 61.
10. Virginia Woolf, 'Mr Bennett and Mrs Brown', in *Collected Essays* (Lon-don: Hogarth Press, 1966) I, 320.
11. Desmond MacCarthy, 'The Post-Impressionists', in *Manet and the Post-Impressionists* (London: Ballantyne, 1910) p. 7.
12. Most recently Manet's large picture *Jésus insulté par les soldats* or *Ecce*

Homo (1865) had been shown at the spring 1910 exhibition of the International Society at the Grafton Galleries and had been the subject of considerable critical praise.

13. The term 'Post-Impressionism' seems to have been devised about a month before the exhibition opened on 8 November 1910. Frank Rutter's journal *Art News* carried an advertisement in the issue dated 15 October 1910 which read, 'The Post-Impressionists of France. Under the above title there will be held at the Grafton Galleries during November, December and January, an exhibition of paintings by Cézanne, Gauguin, Van Gogh and Henri Matisse.'

14. Benedict Nicolson, 'Post-Impressionism and Roger Fry', *Burlington Magazine*, 93 (1951) 12.

15. Ibid., p. 13.

16. His picture entitled *Rhythm* (1910) provided both the title and the frontispiece for Middleton Murry's journal which appeared in the summer of 1911 with the object of informing the British public about all that was new in art in Paris.

17. J. D. Fergusson, 'The Autumn Salon', *Art News*, 21 Oct 1909, p. 7. Fergusson had been familiar with Cézanne's work since 1905 when he settled in Paris, and on one of the visits to Paris by his friend the painter S. J. Peploe, Fergusson took him to meet Picasso. See Margaret Morris, *The Art of J. D. Fergusson* (London: Blackie, 1974) p. 45.

18. Quoted in Wendy Baron, *The Camden Town Group* (London: Scolar Press, 1979) p. 12. Sickert exhibited ten paintings at the Salon d'Automne of 1906 – one more than Matisse in the exhibition and four more than both Vlaminck and Vallotton.

19. See John Rothenstein, 'Spencer Gore', in *Modern English Painters* (London: Eyre and Spottiswoode, 1952) I, 196.

20. Ginner's picture *The Sunlit Wall* of 1908 shows very clearly the influence of Van Gogh. See Baron, *The Camden Town Group*, p. 232.

21. *Art News*, 21 Apr 1910, p. 194.

22. See Richard Shone, 'The Friday Club', *Burlington Magazine*, 117 (1975) 279–84.

23. C. R. W. Nevinson, *Paint and Prejudice* (London: Methuen, 1937) p. 9.

24. Writing from Paris in 1907 to Henry Lamb, John reported that he had met 'a young artist whose work is wonderful'. The artist was in fact Picasso, who was working on *Les Demoiselles d'Avignon*. Quoted in Michael Easton and Michael Holroyd, *The Art of Augustus John* (Boston, Mass.: David R. Godine, 1975) pp. 14–15. John's *French Fisher Boy* of 1907 combined the flat simplicity of Gauguin's colouring with the sentimentality of Picasso's so-called 'Blue Period'. See ibid., p. 59.

25. *The Times*, 2 Apr 1905, p. 5, and 9 Oct 1906, p. 10.

26. The *Tramp* for August 1910 (pp. 487–8) printed a translation of Marinetti's *Futurist Manifesto* with the comment 'it is such fun!' This was nearly two years before Futurism came to the Sackville Gallery in March 1912. The same issue of the *Tramp* printed an article by Edgcumbe Staley which referred to Cézanne as 'the maddest, far away, of all the first Impressionists'. Staley's confusion about French art verges on the comic when he speaks of Cézanne's 'cornfields . . . full of wild

red reapers: his decanters . . . bursting with raw red wine' and the way in which Cézanne 'drew and drank all along the ways about Fontainebleau and far beyond, [scattering] his sketches pell-mell over hedges and ditches' (p. 410).

27. *The Times*, 11 July 1910, p. 12.
28. *The Sunday Times*, 28 Aug 1910, p. 6.
29. *Art Journal*, n. s., 62 (1910) 296.
30. *Burlington Magazine*, 12 (1908) 374–5.
31. Ibid.
32. Maurice Denis, 'Cézanne – 1', tr. Roger Fry, *Burlington Magazine*, 16 (1910) 214.
33. Roger Fry, 'The French Post-Impressionists' (1912) in *Vision and Design*, ed. J. B. Bullen (Oxford: Oxford University Press, 1981) p. 169.
34. Ibid., p. 167.
35. Lewis Hind, 'The Consolations of an Injured Critic – V,' *Art Journal*, n. s., 62 (1910) 193.
36. Falkenheim, *Fry and the Beginnings of Formalist Art Criticism*, p. 19.
37. Julius Meier-Graefe, *Modern Art: Being a Contribution to a New System of Aesthetics*, tr. Florence Simmonds and George W. Crystal (London: Heinemann, 1908) I, 269.
38. Ibid., p. 210.
39. Roger Fry, 'The Post-Impressionists – II', *Nation*, 3 Dec 1910, p. 403.
40. Roger Fry, 'Post-Impressionism', *Fortnightly Review*, May 1911, p. 863. The word 'rhythm' became very prominent in commentaries on Post-Impressionism at this time. So, for example, it formed the title of Middleton Murry's new magazine (see n. 16). In his book *The New Spirit in Drama and Art* (1912), Huntly Carter explored the principle of rhythm as creating a link between different aspects of the modern movement.
41. Undoubtedly one of the reasons for the presence of Manet in the first Post-Impressionist exhibition was connected with Meier-Graefe's assertion that 'Manet's doctrine was the recognition of painting as flat decoration; the ruthless suppression of all those elements used by the old masters to seduce the eye by plastic illusion; and the deliberate insistence on all the pictorial elements in their stead, *Modern Art*, I, 264.
42. See Kate Flint (ed.), *Impressionists in England: The Critical Reception* (London: Routledge and Kegan Paul, 1984) pp. 8–11.
43. Holbrook Jackson, 'Pop Goes the Past', *TP's Weekly*, 16 Dec 1910, p. 829.
44. *Spectator*, 12 Nov 1910, p. 798.
45. 'The Latest Revolt in Art' (*Sphere*, 5 Nov 1910, p. 130), 'A widespread plot to destroy the whole fabric of European painting' (Robert Ross, in the *Morning Post*, 7 Nov 1910, p. 3), 'The Revolt in Painting' (*Pall Mall Gazette*, 7 Nov 1910, p. 1), 'this rotten league' (Sir William Blake Richmond, in the *Morning Post*, 16 Nov 1910, p. 5), 'the rude Jacobins of painting '(M[ichael] S[adler], in *Art News*, 15 Nov 1910, p. 13) are samples of this widespread attitude in the press. Describing what he called 'Rebels at Brighton', Frank Rutter said that, in the exhibition of

modern French art at Brighton in 1910, Cezanne and Gauguin 'are to their fellow exhibitors what Marx and Kropotkin are to the young social reformers of today'. *The Sunday Times* (7 Aug 1910, p. 4) and the *Sphere* (24 Dec 1910, p. 283) published a reproduction of a Van Gogh self-portrait under the title 'An Artistic Provocateur – Vincent Van Gogh'.

46. *Morning Post*, 19 Nov 1910, p. 4.
47. Ebenezer Wake Cook, *Anarchism in Art and Chaos in Criticism* (London: Cassell, 1904) p. 79.
48. Ibid., p. 80.
49. *Daily Chronicle*, 7 Nov 1910, p. 8; and *Daily Express*, 9 Nov 1910, p. 8.
50. *Morning Post*, 9 Nov 1910, p. 6. W. B. Richmond took a similar view when he said, 'There is no regeneration for deluded egoists. . . . They are lost morally in the inferno where Dante places the unfaithful to God and to [sic] his enemies' (*Morning Post*, 16 Dec 1910, p. 5). 'It is difficult to understand', said the critic of the *Pall Mall Gazette*, 'why pictures which, we are told, are the work of maniacs and charlatans, should have caused so vast a disturbance in the sluggish waters of British Art' (*Pall Mall Gazette*, 16 Jan 1911, p. 5).
51. 'The New Criticism', *Pall Mall Gazette*, 16 Jan 1911, p. 5. Hyslop's lecture was subsequently published in the *Nineteenth Century*.
52. Theo B. Hyslop, 'Post-Illusionism and the Art of the Insane', *Nineteenth Century*, Feb 1911, p. 271.
53. Ibid., p. 273.
54. Ibid., p. 274.
55. Ibid., p. 279.
56. Ibid., p. 280.
57. *Art Chronicle*, 1 Mar 1910, 15 Mar 1910 and 15 Apr 1910.
58. *New Age*, 8 Dec 1910, p. 135. Bennett contributed to the *New Age* under the pseudonym 'Jacob Tonson'. He had recently been staying in Paris and looking at pictures; shortly afterwards he wrote to the *Nation* in support of Post-Impressionism (see the *Nation*, 10 Dec 1910, p. 443).
59. C. J. Holmes, *Notes on the Post-Impressionist Painters* (London: Philip Lee Warner, 1910) p. 10.
60. Ibid., p. 14.
61. Ibid., p. 13.
62. For an account of the problems which British artists had with Cézanne, see John Ingamells, 'Cézanne in England', *British Journal of Aesthetics*, 5 (1955) 341–50.
63. Holmes, *Notes on the Post-Impressionist Painters*, p. 12.
64. Frank Rutter, *Revolution in Art* (London: Art News Press, 1910) p. 56.
65. Ibid., p. 53.
66. Apollinaire first used the term *cubisme* in his review of the Salon d'Automne of 1910, but the context suggests that he did not expect his readers to understand it. See 'Le Salon d'automne', (1910) in Apollinaire, *Chroniques d'art 1902–1918*, éd. L. C. Breunig (Paris: Gallimard, 1960) p. 159.
67. Rutter, *Revolution in Art*, p. 54.
68. C. Lewis Hind, 'The Movement in England: Epstein and Gill' and 'The

Movement in England: Augustus John', in *The Post-Impressionists* (London: Methuen, 1911) pp. 65–74.

69. Epstein's work was described as 'Post-Impressionist Sculpture' in the *Athenaeum*, Jan 1911, p. 104; 'Post-Impressionism', said the critic of the *Connoisseur*, was 'strongly in the ascendent at the exhibition of the Friday Club at the Alpine Gallery' (Feb 1911, p. 180). However, it was P. G. Konody who was most sensitive to Post-Impressionist influence on British art. He said of the Women's National Art Club Exhibition that 'the seed of Post-Impressionism has fallen on fertile ground' (*Observer*, 5 Mar 1911, p. 5) and that Phelan Gibb, in a one-man exhibition at the Baillie Gallery, had 'debauched his talent in the new cult' (*Observer*, 9 Apr 1911, p. 5). At the exhibition of the New English Art Club, Ethel Wright, said Konody, 'has not looked without purpose at the works of Cézanne and Van Gogh' (*Observer*, 28 May 1911, p. 16); Robert Bevan's 'unbroken primaries' at the exhibition at the London Salon betrayed the influence of 'the Matisse School' and Charles Ginner at the first exhibition of the Camden Town Group 'appears to worship at the shrine of Van Gogh' (*Observer*, 9 July 1911, p. 4). In October 1911 he pointed out that Alfred Wolmark at the Bruton Gallery had 'thrown in his lot' with the Post-Impressionists and claimed that Wolmark's conversion was 'a significant symptom of the hold the new movement is gaining on the younger generation' (*Observer*, 15 Oct 1911, p. 7).
70. Walter Sickert, 'Post-Impressionists', *Fortnightly Review*, Jan 1911, p. 89. This was the text of a lecture given at the Grafton Galleries not long before the Post-Impressionist exhibition closed. It was answered by another lecture given there by Roger Fry and published in the same journal in May (pp. 856–67).
71. Sickert, 'Post-Impressionists', *Fortnightly Review*, Jan 1911, p. 88.
72. Ibid., p. 89.
73. Ibid., pp. 79 and 89.
74. D. S. MacColl, 'A Year of "Post-Impressionism"', *Nineteenth Century*, Feb 1912, p. 291.
75. Ibid.
76. Ibid., p. 292.
77. MacColl was 'converted' to Cézanne's work in 1922. See Ingamells, 'Cézanne in England', *British Journal of Aesthetics*, 5, p. 345.
78. The words are those of Osbert Sitwell in *A Free House! or the Artists as Craftsmen* (London: Macmillan, 1947) p. xvi.
79. Sickert, 'Post-Impressionists', *Fortnightly Review*, Jan 1911, p. 79.
80. *Athenaeum*, 24 Dec 1910, p. 801.
81. In his review of the pictures by Cézanne and Gauguin at the Stafford Gallery (*Observer*, 3 Dec 1911, p. 10).
82. 'Art Notes', *Pall Mall Gazette*, 3 Jan 1911, p. 4.
83. *Pall Mall Gazette*, 15 Jan 1912, p. 4.

4

France and the Construction of the *Avant-Garde* in Britain

IAN SMALL

Concepts such as 'nationality' and the *avant-garde* need to be handled with caution when they are applied to the history of cultures. They are terms which are frequently used but only infrequently defined. That the values that they suggest, as well as the individuals or groups which they designate, might be subject to change, is an idea rarely entertained. But it seems to be the case that, while the notion of the *avant-garde* and therefore those allied concepts which define it – the provincial, the metropolitan and the cosmopolitan and so forth – were fairly stable during the last half of the nineteenth century, increasingly during this century they have lost their stability. Historically there is a very strong case for seeing the relationship between the English or British *avant-garde* and France during the last decades of the nineteenth century in terms of a natural alliance. In the years after 1860 the vanguard of the dominant intellectual, literary and artistic culture of Britain defined itself in terms of a rejection of provincial – that is, basically native – values and (in the term made famous by Matthew Arnold, one of the earliest propagandisers of France in this respect) their accompanying 'philistinism'; the natural consequence of this refusal of provincialism was the construction of a specific set of values that were exclusively 'metropolitan'. And metropolitanism, as many commentators have demonstrated, invariably involved a francophile cosmopolitanism.[1] The particular forms and dimensions of this alliance between the *avant-garde* and the metropolitan were complex; but it is a simplification, rather than a misrepresentation, to say that metropolitan London culture stood in the same relationship to provincial Britain as France was perceived to stand in relation to Britain itself.

Now, in general terms it is clearly true that the British have ascribed roles to France that are not necessarily commensurate with French perceptions of France and indeed not necessarily even consistent with each other. Only the propagandist arrogates to himself the authority to 'know' a country as complex as France. And, in a similar way, it is a fairly brave cultural historian who would claim to 'know' Britain. Which Britain? it could be asked; and which British culture? Like the concepts of foreignness and of exile, the concept of national identity – especially in its literary and artistic applications – needs to be carefully treated. To maintain that there is one simple, undifferentiated view of what constitutes a national identity, and one way in which such an identity manifests itself in cultural products, is to take as given the correctness of what are invariably partial judgements produced in the course of literary or artistic controversies. As there are, at any given historical moment, many 'Frances', so too there are many 'Englands' or 'Britains'.

Nationality and national culture were widely debated concepts in the last quarter of the nineteenth and first quarter of the twentieth century in Britain, and, as I shall show, these debates had an overt political dimension. Now, it has invariably been the case that historians of British culture – particularly historians of literary and artistic culture – have constructed their histories, and their accounts of British cultural transactions with France, in such a way as to endorse the assumptions of its main (and so francophile) protagonists. Consequently, the history of British culture becomes a normative one: the judgements of a Henry James or a Roger Fry about the relative merits of British and French artistic and literary values are usually endorsed as being correct, and as correctly anticipating the taste and judgements of posterity. However, if it is true that the whole concept of national identity is not straightforward, then it is equally true that the concept of an British national literature somehow representative of *British* national values is also a complex one. Indeed, it has been argued that the concept of a national literature commensurate with a British national culture was a specifically nineteenth century construction.[2] Before that time, the whole notion of what a 'national' culture might involve was problematic. Two examples will demonstrate how difficult that term is to define. One of the features of Walter Scott's novels was the production and articulation of a new and particularly attractive concept of Scottishness for his Scottish readers.

But Scott wrote in standard English and so his work mediated that Scottishness to an English audience by invoking a specifically non-English anthropology to emphasise the otherness of the Scots. Again, the 'Celticness' of Irish and Welsh writing and culture was a quality identified in the middle years of the nineteenth century to explain individual national differences but also to affiliate that diversity to an all-embracing concept of Britishness. The simple general point to be made from observations such as these is that notions of national identity and hence of a national literature are not necessarily historically stable ones, and that their construction (usually made by reference to accompanying ideas of 'foreignness') invariably has political implications.

The same qualifications apply in a general sense to the application of terms such as the 'provincial' and the *avant-garde*. Literary and art history still tends to written from the reassuring viewpoint of the universal historian. Literary history, despite all the recent controversies over methodology (most of which, ironically, have their origins in France), still usually invokes chronology as its organising principle. So, it is frequently asserted, national literatures are in part defined by periodicity: they begin at a certain point and progress chronologically to a certain terminus. And the *avant-garde* (the etymology of the term is interesting in this sense) is construed as a species of cultural signpost. Hence the label *avant-garde* is itself not a term used simply to designate literary or artistic experiment *sui generis*: rather it is used to describe those artistic and literary experiments that were apparently successful in determining or anticipating the future course of any particular literary or artistic history. The same is true of the term 'provincial'. That term is one uniquely applied to those whom literary history has designated as the bit-players in cultural history. Invariably larger and more challenging questions – such as what animates aesthetic or critical judgements to produce antitheses such as these at any historical moment – are passed over. It is obviously possible to name any number of revolutionary or dissenting movements within a particular national history. But, if the notion of the *avant-garde* implies successful dissent, it implies also the idea of rebellion against, or critical reaction to, the values and assumptions of a dominant culture, rather than a simple or outright rejection. In this sense, all aspects of the *avant-garde* are inescapably tied to the main culture or cultures of the society which produce it. It is in these ways, as I shall show, that the career of

John Middleton Murry is exemplary. In the first place his life demonstrates perfectly the ambivalent nature of the relationship between a main culture and its *avant-garde*. Nothing could have been easier for Murry, at certain points in his early career, to have rejected outright the dominant culture of Britain by physically 'escaping' to France permanently. He chose not to do so. His life, involving the apparent paradox of a qualified endorsement but also of an accompanying virulent condemnation of most forms of contemporary British culture, marks him out as a model in this respect. Secondly, Murry's career demonstrates how historically unstable a description the term *avant-garde* is: his intellectual career marks a precise moment when Victorian and Edwardian notions of the *avant-garde* were revised and those more familiar to the modern mind came into being.

If as I have suggested, 'nationalism' and *avant-garde* are mutually defining terms, then the relationship between both these concepts on the one hand, and 'provincialism' on the other needs to be analysed. 'Provincialism', like the other large generalisations I have mentioned, is a description that, more than most descriptions, begs questions. For example, Matthew Arnold's characteristic philistines in *Culture and Anarchy* are drawn mainly from Birmingham at a time when Birmingham and its politicians were attempting to define it in terms of its difference from London and the values of the capital. Indeed the phenomenon of large provincial centres in England (such as the one that Joseph Chamberlain was to build in Arnold's derided Birmingham) is one belonging to the last half of the nineteenth century: whether their inhabitants assented to that label of 'provincial' is a question that neither the contemporary nor the modern literary historian deigns to ask. More often than not, the term 'provincial' nowadays merely designates a literary historian's shorthand for 'non-standard' or 'non-authorised'. Considerations such as these are of considerable importance in any attempt to describe English avant-gardism and its relation to France. The first point to notice here perhaps is that it is an *English* not a British *avant-garde* that is invariably invoked by historians of culture who have tended to assume the givenness of a homogeneous, dominant national culture rather than a set or variety of national or regional cultures. Large national or regional differences tend to be subsumed under the basic metropolitan/ *avant-garde* and *avant-garde*/provincial antitheses. Secondly, and for my purposes more importantly, the concept of provincial England (or, more properly, although it is again never specifically stated as such, provincial Britain) is never analysed.

During the last decades of the nineteenth century there were two separate definitions of the 'provincial' at work, and in any account of the relationship between the *avant-garde* and France, these definitions need to be distinguished. 'Provincial', in the first and most obvious sense, designated then, as it does now, simple inferiority, a narrowness that was opposed to the alleged superiority of a 'national' or 'international' culture. In fact the term 'provincialism' is first used in this sense in the middle of the nineteenth century. The *Oxford English Dictionary* gives the following definition of the word: 'Provincial manner, fashion, mode of thought, etc. as distinct from that which is (or is held to be) national, or which is the fashion of the capital; hence narrowness of view, thought, or interests . . . (1836).'

During the following decades the term that had defined 'provincial' – 'metropolitan' – came increasingly to include or be replaced by the notion of the cosmopolitan. Here Matthew Arnold's famous exhortations against this narrowness are worth recalling, partly because he is using such a new application of the concept:

> By the very nature of things, as England is not all the world, much of the best that is known and thought in the world cannot be of English growth, must be foreign; by the nature of things, again, it is just this that we are least likely to know, while English thought is streaming in upon us from all sides, and takes excellent care that we shall not be ignorant of its existence; the English critic, therefore, must dwell much on foreign thought, and with particular heed on any part of it, which, while significant and fruitful in itself, is for any reason specially likely to escape him.[3]

Naturally (and what could be more natural for Arnold the francophile?) it was in France that the richest harvest of that 'significance' and 'fruitfulness' was to be found.

During the later decades of the century this characterisation of the 'provincial' in terms of inferiority had strong advocates, as literary and art historians have noted. Pater, Wilde and Symons (among others) all extolled in one way or another the virtues of a generous and eclectic cosmopolitanism that would in its turn animate British literary and artistic culture. In fact Symons, Wilde and others who formed this eclectic and metropolitan cosmopolitanism themselves came from the provinces. The paradox is perhaps best caught by Max Beerbohm in a cartoon depicting an angular W. B. Yeats introducing George Moore to the Queen of the Fairies. The point of Beerbohm's cartoon is that Yeats at this moment in his career was addressing a specifically metropolitan (and indeed, cosmopolitan) audience, but was doing so by producing (what was then) a particular form of contemporary British provincialism – Irish nationalism.

That matters were becoming more complex than Arnold's simple British/Continental antithesis thirty years earlier is a point that scarcely needs labouring. Here perhaps the recent literary history of France stood as a model. A whole tradition of nineteenth-century French fiction had produced a literary representation of the provinces and their relation to the centre and its values. Balzac's title *Scènes de la vie de province* is instructive in this respect; Flaubert's sub-title to *Madame Bovary* announces too that it is to be a story of 'provincial' life. This French tradition inevitably contributed to the development of attitudes to the idea of provincial life among the British literary intelligentsia later in the century. Indeed, Henry James virtually admitted as much in *A Little Tour in France*: 'France may be Paris, but Paris is not France . . . I must not speak, however, as if I had discovered the provinces. They were discovered, or at least revealed, by Balzac, if by any one, and are now easily accessible to visitors.'[4]

It is true that in the context of English literary history the metropolitan/provincial antithesis does not carry as many implications as the Paris/provincial antithesis at work in contemporary French literary culture. This may merely be testimony to the relative prestige of the particular writers involved. But it may be that in late-nineteenth-century English literary culture the provincial/metropolitan opposition is only a shorthand for representing a series of oppositions between *forms* of provincial life and *forms* of metropolitan life: Oscar Wilde's London, that of St James's and Hyde Park, is not George Gissing's north London, but neither is it George Moore's Ebury Street or Rossetti's Cheyne Walk. By the same token, Hardy's provincial life is not that of Housman, and neither have much in common with the invocation of the mythic English shires of the Georgians. Indeed, it is clear that at the end of the nineteenth century there was at work a systematic attempt to redefine or revalue what the term 'provincial' could mean, to convert it into a term not of reproach but of praise. Hardy's creation of Wessex, the significance of place in the works of nature writers such as Jefferies, the invocation of a mystical Englishness associated with the Malverns and Worcestershire in much of Elgar's early work and so on – all these are manifestations of a much larger appeal to 'Britishness' (or, more accurately perhaps in these cases, to 'Englishness') that made a virtue of the same self-absorption that the cosmopolitan francophilia of a Wilde, a Moore or a Symons had in general derided; but with the provision of course that what was once seen as provincialism and narrowness of compass was now redefined as a susceptibility to the spirit of place or to the qualities of nationality. In one sense this redefinition of the 'Englishness' of English culture has much in common with, and derived much of its impetus from, what was happening socially and economically in Britain: the literary construction of a specifically provincial 'English' set of concerns has direct connections with the construction of Chamberlain's Birmingham or the growth of the British Empire.

Indeed, our view even now of some of the mythic qualities of 'Englishness' or 'Britishness' still draws substantially upon icons and symbols produced during this period. The dog-days of the high Victorian or Edwardian summer still represent something central to most Britons' perceptions of what they hold to be essential components of British national culture. The power of this image is such that it is precisely these notional attributes of Britishness that can be easily invoked (and manipulated) in the popular imagination by advertisers and copywriters. It derives from an amalgam of manners and styles, of partial history and caricature: Lady Bracknell and the Prince of Wales, servants and aristocracy, Ascot and India are some of the constituent elements of this imagined British past.

That this particular conception of Britain is as much a product of the historical imagination as the image of 'naughty' Paris of the 1890s hardly needs labouring. That it does not correspond particularly accurately to the *facts* of social history as they are known now or indeed were known then is neither here nor there. It is an image of Britishness that was to some extent chosen to be believed then, and is still, in some ways, chosen to be believed now. It is an image that derived from the construction of a dominant national culture in order to sustain a particular bourgeois ideology. Although an account of the latter is not my present concern, it is worth noting how a whole tradition of British comic fiction and drama works in this respect. Works as varied as Wilde's *The Importance of Being Earnest*, Evelyn Waugh's comic novels (perhaps *Brideshead Revisited*, too), even contemporary television dramas such as *Upstairs, Downstairs*, have an overt political dimension to them. At times they positively revel in a nostalgia for the excesses of the British class system, the real significance of which the structures of the works in question hold in abeyance. The political dimensions of this aspect of the national culture of the last century are difficult to ignore. Class and class-bias become two of the givens of 'Britishness'. However, I am not concerned with underlying ideologies, important though they are, but rather with the mechanisms by which this notion of Britishness or Englishness was made possible. One of the most important was the construction of a set of simple antitheses that determined how both native and foreign cultures were to be viewed: home/abroad, English/foreign, provincial/ *avant-garde*, and so forth.

Many historians have described how questions of nationality became more complex just before, during and just after the First World War. Indeed, the reasons are too well known and too well documented to be rehearsed here. What I want to do is to examine one aspect of that change. It is clear that during that period the concept of a simple and undifferentiated national culture became one increasingly difficult to sustain, even at the level of symbol or icon. It was certainly increasingly difficult to assent to the particular idea of a national culture that had been current in the two decades up to the war. A growing British awareness of Germany, diplomatic and military alliance with France, the actual experience of the war by many Britons: these are the most usually adduced explanations.[5] As a consequence the accompanying and necessary concept of a simple and undifferentiated *avant-garde* ceased to have any real significance. Terms such as 'abroad', 'foreign' and 'French' could no longer act simply as invocations of otherness as they had done a generation previously.

I have suggested that the concept of the provincial and the *avant-garde* and of the foreign and the native are mutually defining binary oppositions. As the very terms 'British' and 'native' and so forth became increasingly unstable (in these senses) after the war, so the concept of the *avant-garde* itself became subject to differentiations and distinctions and took on a variety of forms: indeed, the variety of forms of the *avant-garde* answers precisely to the variety of forms of provincialism at work at the time. To make my point, I should like to examine one of these particular *avant-gardes*, that of John Middleton Murry, and compare it with that of Bloomsbury – the image of France produced by Strachey and Bell. There were of course many more varieties of the *avant-garde* at work in the years immediately following the First World War, but comprehensiveness is not my intention, for I want in particular to examine how versions of the *avant-garde* produced quite different versions of France and French culture. These versions appear at first sight to be quite incompatible with each other. It is the general implications of such incompatibilities that are important for the understanding of British uses of the image of France: in surveying the history of Anglo-French cultural relations, the modern reader tends to see as legitimate or authentic the particular construction placed upon France which coincides with those available in modern discourses about France. So at this point an important qualification needs to be made. Members of the Bloomsbury Group found in French history an idealised image of themselves; Ezra Pound found a similar image of an ideal literary culture in the France of Provence. In looking back to the varieties of artistic and literary *avant-gardes* at work in the first two decades of the century, the modern reader is in danger of reading literary history in the same way. As the idea of a national culture at any given historical moment is a construction that the contemporary historian places on the past by determining not only how evidence is to be construed but also what is to count as evidence, so also the idea of what in the first place is to be considered as a legitimate *avant-garde* is also a historical construction. To the modern reader the perception of France as the ally of the *avant-garde* in Henry James's work seems quaint; in Clive Bell's and Lytton Strachey's writing it is positively eccentric. In contrast the perception of France that we can find in John Middleton Murry's autobiography and reviews appears to have dimensions that are absent in those of his contemporaries: it touches upon nationalism, class, sexual freedom, political and literary authenticity, and so on. But in the end this is only to say that Murry's perception of France coincides more fully with modern perceptions than the France of Strachey or Bell does, and nothing more than that.

Later in this volume (Ch. 6) Ceri Crossley argues that the rediscovery of the salon life of France in the eighteenth century, particularly by Clive Bell and Lytton Strachey, was an image of

Bloomsbury life projected as it were on to the past. It stood as a moment of achieved civilisation that appeared to embody those values which Bloomsbury wished to cherish. Christophe Campos has emphasised how much this perception of the French eighteenth century was a simple misconstruction placed upon history:

> All this points to the fact that Bloomsbury was transposing into the past ideals of its own: had it really discovered the salons in reading the literature of the eighteenth century, it would have known for sure which the golden period was. The salons were a transposed ideal because of a feeling of exclusion from the present. Bloomsbury felt alien to its surroundings. . . . They preferred to move away from modern England in time as well as in space. History is at once more secure and more amenable than reality.[6]

At first sight this appears to be merely one of the many ways in which the British literary and artistic avant-garde has perceived or characterised French life. But this is not exactly the case. Campos goes on to stress how most members of the Bloomsbury group were in fact simply ignorant of many aspects of life in contemporary France. For Bloomsbury, therefore, 'France' is not a perception but a construction; it is only a point of reference which enables the members of Bloomsbury to define themselves in relation to the dominant British culture. France, like Yeats's Byzantium, or Pound's France or Italy, is a conceptual antithesis; but it is one that can operate only negatively. It is simply anti-Britain in the way that Italy in *A Room with a View* is simply an inversion of what E.M. Forster perceived to be dominant British bourgeois values. The second feature of note in the image of France produced by Bloomsbury is that it is an explicitly political one – essentially, like most of the politics of early British modernism, right-wing and hence inevitably anti-democratic. The political implications of what seem at first sight to be matters of artistic, literary or aesthetic choices might well have involved paradoxes and on occasions contradiction, as Ceri Crossley also argues; but it is not these aspects that make the politics of Bloomsbury seem distant to the modern reader. It is simply that, if modern British right-wing political thinking involves the construction of a mythical moment in the past when a truly 'civilised' culture appears to have been achieved, then it is more likely to be a more recent English past than an eighteenth-century French past. The politics may not have changed, but the manner of its representation has; and, as I argued above, it is much more likely to be in terms of an invocation of late-Victorian and Edwardian English values than a comparable period in French history. In other words, what has happened to the view of France produced by Bloomsbury is that, along with some of the politics that brought it about, it has become simply unusable. In contrast to this extravagant and clearly – to the modern British mind – quite untenable construction or perception of France, the view of a contemporary, John Middleton Murry, has in some way the appearance of what seems to be 'authenticity' or 'reality'. Murry seems to express what we now want to see as the appropriate values and the appropriate reactions to contemporary events. In particular he seems to speak of pre- and post-war France in a way in which we could comfortably imagine ourselves as doing. So, when Katherine Mansfield expressed in a letter her disapproval of Woolf's *Night and Day* for, among other things, its failure even to acknowledge the war and its consequences, Murry wrote back confirming her views: 'So few people have felt the war; and for us who have, the work of those who have not – if it pretends to be true at all – must sound a lie. And we're not arbitrary in requiring the truth from them. The War *is* Life.'[7]

To the modern reader, these comments seem somehow 'right': Murry's views about war and its cataclysmic consequences, that is, confirm us in our own partial or perceived views. Indeed, it was a fairly familiar theme with him. It is not simply the case that Murry rejected the values of his generation: in other words, it is not simply a matter of the pre-war provincial/*avant-garde* antithesis once more at work; Bell and Strachey, after all, also emphatically rejected their contemporaries, and probably, at least in the case of Strachey, with more effect. What the modern sensibility finds appealing about the version of *avant-garde* values to be found in the figure of Murry is that his rejection of his contemporaries' values confirms or tends to confirm our own preconceptions about them and about their reaction to the war. The theme was in fact rehearsed many times. Indeed, in a famous letter to Mansfield some eighteen months earlier, Murry had arrogated to his views the values of a 'real' Englishness: 'No, my darling, you and I are English, and because we are truly English we are set apart from our generation. That has gone a whoring after strange gods. . . . '[8]

'England' here has nothing to do with nationality unless it can also include New Zealand, Mansfield's birthplace. For Murry 'Englishness' and modernism and a literary and political 'realism' are mutually defining terms. This revalued notion of nationality involved Murry for the most part in an accompanying and explicit rejection of Victorian values; and, in a comparison not dissimilar in effect to those found in Strachey's and Bell's work, but totally dissimilar in intention, the rejection of Victorian orthodoxy meant embracing a 'new' France:

> It is so inconceivably hard to be fair to them [the Victorians], so hard to believe that we have profited by their victories. For if they made head on our behalf against an intellectual tyranny, it was only to impose another – the tyranny of a threadbare social conception. They deplored our provincialism, and more effectively cut us off from the world by planting the standard of 'the English gentleman' upon the ramparts than centuries of robust ignorance has done. They expounded France to us, but it was always somehow the wrong France, the Anglicised solemnity of the 'Revue des Deux Mondes' . . . instead of the epoch-making France of Flaubert.[9]

The same strategies of argument are to be found in many of Murry's reviews written at this time. The most important criteria informing his literary judgements were aesthetic and ideological (although he would have rejected both terms). A successful literary work combined realism, which he defined in familiar terms such as 'objectivity', and an appropriate set of political values. The contemporary writer who more than any other possessed these qualities in the years after the war was, typically, a Frenchman: his friend Georges Duhamel. The judgement is consistently passed that Duhamel was a writer of his time; it was he who possessed objective 'calm' – that quality which, Murry claimed, marked Flaubert's significance as a writer and which was so signally wanting in Virginia Woolf's fiction. Thus Duhamel's *Civilisation, 1914–1917*, Murry concludes in his review in 1918,

> is a book to which future generations will return with fear. It will then be either, for the many, the record of the fevered nightmare from which a pale and weak but convalescent humanity shall

have awakened, or, for the few, one of the last despairing protests of a mode of consciousness that has not survived the struggle for existence.[10]

The theme was picked up glancingly in another review, this time of Siegfried Sassoon's war poetry: 'Intellectual remoteness is not cold or callous; it is the condition in which a mind works as a mind. . . . We have read, for instance, in the pages of M. Duhamel, far more terrible things than any Mr Sassoon has to tell, but they were made terrible by the calm of the recording mind.'[11]

In fact Murry's conjunction of France and the sense of an artist's or writer's ability to find the forms appropriate to the representation of modern life wasn't particularly new; indeed it was a development of the image of the *poète maudit* of two generations earlier, but with the qualification that the modern dispossessed artist had social duties imposed upon him by the very facts of recent European history. This in fact represented a dramatic revaluation of the idea of the *poète maudit*. And it is precisely here that Murry's uses of France are different from those of his contemporaries. Murry made no attempt to redefine the modernity of France in terms of a reading of the past, in the manner of a Bell or a Strachey: he was redefining the notion of artistic and poetic responsibility bequeathed to the twentieth century by the French *avant-garde* of the nineteenth century, whereas some of his contemporaries – Yeats and Pound spring to mind – had been content simply to revive that notion, dated as it was. Murry was refashioning the image of the poet, but in terms appropriate to the second quarter of the twentieth century. All this was in a sense predictable. Murry's early career had effectively 'written' France and French writing into a role derived virtually wholesale from contemporary stereotypes. Indeed, to the modern sensibility, Murry has perfect *avant-garde* credentials, more so than any of his contemporaries, including even D. H. Lawrence. Rather than simply use French values to rehabilitate Edwardian values, Murry elected for a thoroughgoing revisionism. Indeed my main point is that some of the modern appeal of Murry (and incidentally also of Lawrence) is precisely because those credentials are so good; Murry and Lawrence fit – and, it should not be forgotten, helped to shape or define – the popular modern stereotype of what the *avant-garde* should be.

The significance of France in fitting Murry for this role cannot be underestimated: it is almost a pattern *avant-garde* pedigree in this respect. The facts of his early life are well known, but a rehearsal of some salient details will make my point. An initial desire to learn French led to a visit to Paris during his undergraduate career at Oxford. That visit led to an encounter with French café society and to an acquaintance with the Scottish painter J. D. Fergusson, and through him with Post-Impressionism, and so to the subsequent impulse to found (or part-found) the magazine *Rhythm*. Fittingly, his Parisian trip led to an affair with a French mistress – Marguéritte. Though the affair was physically and emotionally passionate, it was one which Murry was incapable of sustaining and which he could give up fairly lightly – French mistresses, but assuredly *not* French wives, in *avant-garde* mythology, being part of the young intellectual's *Lehrjahre*. The difference between Murry's Parisian affair and those now associated with the 'naughty' nineties was that the memory of his emotional failure mortified Murry. The experience, however, allowed France to be described explicitly in terms of difference in which more than the usual ingredients are to be found: a sensibility to class differences being the most prominent. Marguéritte was rejected, if we are to believe Murry, because of her inability to fit into the conventions of English bourgeois life, because of the impossibility, that is, of transplanting French experiences and values to contemporary England:

> How could she [Marguéritte] understand the complete divorce that existed between life at Oxford and the real life of England? A student in Paris was part of the living texture of the city and the nation; a student at the Oxford was secluded as by the walls of a monastery. He was not being fitted for life, he was being fitted to escape life. . . . And Marguéritte has been, and was, Life to him.[12]

It was precisely this sense of French otherness made the affair impossible to sustain; but it was also exactly this sense of difference and escape from bourgeois claustrophobia that had made Paris attractive in the first place:

> I have come to see and see clearly how living and quivering a thing is Art: here in Paris it is a Life-force you can feel – and perhaps you will find when I come back that a heresy or two has taken root in my brain on the question. At all events L'Art pour L'Art has a different but much more real meaning now to my

soul: because I have seen it lived and heard it worshipped and watched the sacrifices made for it.[13]

In his autobiography, *Between Two Worlds*, Murry is quite candid about his reasons for deserting his French mistress: he was poor and with no prospects. Simply put, he needed his degree from Oxford in order to live. To reject British society completely, that is, would involve penury, falling back into – in E. M. Forster's phrase – the 'abyss' of lower-middle-class and working-class life from which he had toiled so remorselessly to escape. It would involve, moreover, forgoing the intellectual career that he had marked out for himself. Murry's sense of the *avant-garde*, that is, involved a paradoxical acceptance and rejection of his own nationality; involved walking the highwire of being unavoidably British, but of looking always to France to catch a glimpse of how he was to achieve what he called in *Between Two Worlds* 'growing a new self'.[14]

It is not important, however, that Murry's perception of France is in any absolute sense more 'real' or 'true' than those of Bell or Strachey. But, in so far as the France of Bloomsbury involves a notion of the salon life of the eighteenth century, it now seems inaccessible. Murry's contemporaries typically saw France in familiar and established terms: of 'difference' or of 'other', as an escape from Britain, a conceptual antithesis necessarily negative in its mode of operation. But for Murry it represented too a variety of positive qualities. Murry's France involved the traditional sense of freedom from the constraints of British social and sexual mores; but it also pointed the way to the possibility of a new order in Britain. It is this element of Murry's imagined France that allows the *modern* mind to identify it as being in some way more appropriate to modern life than the France produced by his contemporaries. But perhaps all this is only asserting that one of the most powerful recent images of France and Murry's imagined France coincide at key points: that Murry's image of France anticipated the uses to which 'France' was to be put by his successors.

NOTES

1. Studies of the relationship between individual writers and contemporary French culture in the period I am concerned with are too numer-

ous to list here. The best single general account of attitudes of British writers towards France is still Christophe Campos, *The View of France* (London: Oxford University Press, 1965). Other relevant general studies include Enid Starkie, *From Gautier to Eliot* (London: Hutchinson, 1960). For a discussion of some of the issues I am concerned with, see also R. Poggioli, *The Theory of the Avant Garde* (Cambridge Mass.: Harvard University Press, 1968).

2. For a discussion of idea of the construction of a 'national' literature, see Tony Davies, 'Education, Ideology and Literature', *Red Letters*, 7 (n.d.) 4–15.

3. Matthew Arnold, 'The Function of Criticism at the Present Time', *Essays in Criticism* (1865; London: Dent, 1909) pp. 23–4.

4. Henry James, *A Little Tour in France* (Leipzig: Tauchnitz, 1885) p. 6.

5. See Campos, *The View of France*, pp. 209ff.

6. Ibid., pp. 216–7.

7. Letter to Katherine Mansfield, 14 Nov 1919. Quoted in F. A. Lea, *The Life of Middleton Murry* (London: Methuen, 1960) p. 68.

8. Ibid., p. 62.

9. John Middleton Murry, 'The Gulf Between' (1918), *The Evolution of an Intellectual* (1920; London: Cape, 1927) pp. 120–1.

10. 'The Great Hallucination', ibid., p. 66.

11. 'Mr Sassoon's Verses', ibid., p. 83.

12. John Middleton Murry, *Between Two Worlds* (London: Cape, 1935) p. 164.

13. Letter to P. Landon, Jan 1911; quoted in Lea, *The Life of Middleton Murry*, p. 20.

14. Murry, *Between Two Worlds*, p. 65.

5

Arnold Bennett and the Desire for France

NORMA RINSLER

It is common knowledge that Arnold Bennett was profoundly influenced in his development as a novelist by his acquaintance with French literature, and that he consciously or unconsciously imitated French models.[1] This generalisation, like most common knowledge, calls for some qualification. One might expect that Bennett's known familiarity with all things French, and his long residence in France, would lend authority to the images of France that appear in his fictional works; and, of course, *vice versa*. It is probable also that his immense success as a novelist and as a critic served in some measure to enhance the reputation of the French realists and naturalists who were his cheerfully acknowledged models and whose names recur so frequently in his critical writings; they in turn acted as guarantors of his status as a serious writer. There are the makings of a pair of neat critical tautologies here. I hope, however, to avoid the vicious circle in the present context, where I shall be primarily concerned not with Bennett's use of French sources and the general influence on his work of French models, but with the view of French literature, art and civilisation that he projected for an English audience in his critical writings, and with the (not always congruent) presentation of French life and manners in his fictional works.

In an interview with G. Jean-Aubry in 1928, Bennett speaks of the enormous prestige of France in the eyes of English artists and writers of the period between 1880 and 1890.[2] This ascendancy stemmed, he says, from two factors: first, the seriousness with which art was treated in France, in contrast with English philistinism; then, the freedom which French artists enjoyed to speak of any aspect of human life frankly and openly, while English writers were inhibited by the prudery and squeamishness of their public. That in France one could combine truth and art was the most impressive feature of all. The insistence on a fusion of 'art' and 'life (all of it)' is characteristic of Bennett at every stage of his career. His first novel, *A Man from the North* (1898), chronicles an initiation into the wonders of French literature. But Bennett makes it clear that Richard Larch, his hero, is not solely interested in art; his more deeply felt concern is with life, which he suspects is happening somewhere else while he is imprisoned in his restrictive northern environment. Larch escapes to London, which is to him what Paris was to others: an exciting, slightly sinful place, where artistic freedom is an offshoot of moral freedom, and sensual experience lies in wait (literally) at every street corner. Larch's literary ambition is fuelled by his reading of French literature, though at first his interest is at the anecdotal level: 'The thought of Alphonse Daudet writing "Les Amoureuses" in a Parisian garret supported him through an entire month of toil.' He acquires no real knowledge of the 'piquant field' of French fiction, but is greatly impressed by a French restaurant in Soho where the waiter is a real Frenchman who speaks French, and even more impressed by the thought that the *feuilleton* in the *Echo de Paris*, thoughtfully provided in the restaurant, was written by 'a real man' (Catulle Mendès!), who was 'no doubt eating his dinner at that moment!' Soon Larch has Zola on his bookshelves in the original French. Much later we find him still consuming French novels, now dimly aware of what he might have learned from them: 'Sometimes the French work, by its neat, severe effectiveness, would stir in him a vague desire to do likewise. . . .' He does not; and with painful truthfulness Bennett shows how Larch, through inhibition and fear, fails to achieve his own sensual and moral liberation, and thus inevitably fails as a writer. Bennett acknowledged that *A Man from the North*, published when he was twenty-one years old, owes something to his reading of Maupassant and the Goncourts, and is at least partly autobiographical. It foreshadows his mature belief that, though art is a specific activity demanding a specific vision and specific skills, it must grow out of lived experience. Moreover, the artist must be willing to encompass everything that is human if his art is to achieve greatness. As we shall see, Bennett was less certain where the models for this high conception of art were to be found. Though the great French novelists of the nineteenth century remained for him an important criterion of literary achievement, his estimate of their relative merits changed.

Like his Richard Larch, Bennett was introduced first to the work of the French naturalists, though he began by reading them in English translations. His first gods were thus Maupassant (especially), the Goncourts, Flaubert (whom he regarded at this stage as a realist) and Zola. He noted in his Journal in 1897 that the novelist must cultivate the faculty of 'seeing crudely, simply, artlessly, ignorantly'.[3] But he soon realised that there was nothing artless or ignorant about his models, and he began, perhaps on closer acquaintance with Flaubert, to speak of the 'artistic shapely presentation of truth, and . . . feeling for words as words' (11 Jan 1898). It should be noted, however, that even in what he later came to regard as his 'aesthetic' phase, it is the 'presentation of truth' that concerns him. After visiting an exhibition of Burne-Jones' paintings, Bennett noted in his Journal (3 Jan 1899): 'The sight of Burne-Jones's . . . continual preoccupation with the spiritual . . . served to complete in me a modification of view which has been proceeding now for a year or two. The day of my enthusiasm for "realism", for "naturalism", has passed. I can perceive that a modern work of fiction dealing with modern life may ignore realism and yet be great.' He adds that facts are 'of *some* importance', and cannot be ignored, but they may 'suffer a certain distortion' in order to disclose 'beauty, which is always hidden'. It may be that Bennett was persuaded to these views by events in France, where naturalism was on the wane even before Vogüé's *Le Roman russe* (1886) provided a model for the revival of a less determinist conception of the world; by 1897 the supremacy of the Russian novelists was almost unchallenged in France.[4] Bennett did not abandon his first enthusiasms, but added the Russians to his list: 'The achievements of the finest French writers, with Turgenev and Tolstoy, have set a standard for all coming masters of fiction' (3 Jan 1899). He might be describing his own evolution in his essay on George Moore: 'Steeped in the artistic theories of modern France, he contrasted the grave and scientific fiction of Flaubert and his followers with the novels of Englishmen, and he saw in the latter, by comparison, only so many fairy tales devised for the pleasure of people who would not take art seriously.' Moore's realism, in Bennett's view, though it aimed 'to reproduce life in its entirety', was a poetic realism – that is to say, not 'an unadorned recital of facts mainly sordid and disgusting', but a realism in which the artist's vision was 'combined with and superimposed upon . . . cold exactitude'. Such a combination of art and reality had a clear moral value: 'It teaches, as all true art must. . . .'[5]

Bennett had no use for mere aestheticism, still less for *fin-de-siècle* decadence. In 1901 he described Huysmans's *La Cathédrale* as 'a finicking and egotistic novel . . . in which the unsurpassed beauty of Chartres is degraded to the uses of an arena for the antics of a diseased soul'.[6] In his essay 'The "Average Reader" and the Recipe for Popularity', he rejects the notion that art is not concerned with moral values. Bennett thoroughly approves the Average Reader's preference for writers who offer 'grandeur of subject' and display those moral qualities which, he says, only 'those who are wholly preoccupied with the dandyism of technique could fail to admire'; he quotes with approval Arnold's comment on 'the subordinate character of expression'.[7] The doctrine of 'art for art's sake' was likewise meaningless to him: 'bosh' was his word for the notion that artists are inspired only by a pure disinterested love of art. Not that he thought that they should be so inspired: 'An artist', he says, ' should be a citizen before he is an artist. I esteem more highly a man who is an honest citizen at the expense of art than a man who is an honest artist at the expense of citizenship.'[8] Subtract the provocative overstatement and you still have a firm rejection of the notion that the artist is a man whose special personal experience entitles him to special consideration. Bennett's complaint about the 'deification of love in fiction' is essentially a critique of Romantic individualism; the community, he remarks, is as interesting as the individual. His prescription for narrowly repetitive English authors and the English public alike is a stiff dose of Balzac, who was rapidly taking over the whole of Bennett's pantheon. Balzac in his view is 'a valuable stimulant and corrective medicine' because of his 'faculty for portraying communities, and for describing large co-operative activities'; though love is often his subject, Balzac shows that it is not the whole of life, and that it is intimately bound up with money, ambition, the law, and any number of practical everyday considerations.[9]

At this stage in his career, Bennett is using the established reputations of French authors as standards with which, or against which, to define his own notions of what literature ought to be. He rejects the recently fashionable theories, which he correctly diagnoses as a remnant of Romanticism, of 'the brilliant decadents who have flourished (and in some ways have done so much for the novel) since Balzac died and the grand manner died with him', and he returns to a modified realism. The choice of French writers to illustrate his thesis is not mere self-advertisement. He did see essential differences between the French and the English literary traditions, especially in the novel, which was his major interest. By 1904, Bennett was boldly asserting the superiority of the French, and using them as a stick with which to beat the literary giants of the English nineteenth century. In an article self-consciously entitled 'My Literary Heresies',[10] Bennett proclaims that 'between Scott and Meredith I regard no English novelist as really great'. The only novelist of that period that he cares to read at all is Jane Austen, though he rather dims her glory when he explains that *Persuasion*, in his view, is 'the finest "minor novel" in our language'. For the rest, George Eliot is 'several miles removed from the mediocre', but nowhere near George Sand; Thackeray is soon disposed of: 'Think what a really great novel is, a novel that faces life squarely, and continually appeals to the sense of sheer beauty. Think of "War and Peace", "Père Goriot", "Madame Bovary", and then think of "Vanity Fair" '; Dickens is likewise dismissed as second-rate (in, for example, *A Tale of Two Cities* and *David Copperfield*). In Bennett's view, Dickens and Thackeray are merely 'local poets', while 'the names that shed a radiance over a whole continent', the novelists of European significance, are 'Richardson, Scott, Balzac, Stendhal, Turgenev, Flaubert, Tolstoi'.

Eventually Bennett was to remove the English novelists and Flaubert from this list, and give first place to Dostoevsky among the Russians, if not first place *tout court*. His changing view of Flaubert illustrates how his conception of the novel changed in response to French ideas and French practice. Flaubert was at first a useful ally in the attack on the traditions of the English novel, which had never been much concerned with *le mot juste* or *la Beauté*. But he was the first of Bennett's idols to be dethroned. In 1913, Bennett describes him as a classic example of 'the tragedy of the artist who repudiates the world', a response to life which is fatal to art, because it leads to 'preciosity and futility'. It seemed to Bennett that the novel had declined since Balzac's death in 1850, and was only just beginning to climb the hill again: 'It has conquered enormous territories even since *Germinal*', and was continuing to progress. The novel's great strength, in his view, is its 'inclusive and adaptable' nature, which offers the ideal form for the artist with 'the most inclusive vision'. Flaubert's weakness was his desire to exclude. He met only two of the three criteria for greatness that Bennett lists in this essay. The first of these, according to Bennett, is 'the sense of beauty'; the artist must find beauty in his material, whatever his material may be. This might be a paraphrase of Flaubert's statement: 'il n'y a ni beaux ni vilains sujets . . . le style étant à lui seul une manière absolue de voir les choses'. The second quality necessary to the novelist is 'passionate intensity of vision', so intense that the novelist is 'inconvenienced' by it, and driven to pass it on to his reader. This quality Flaubert certainly possessed, if intermittently. The final requisite is 'fineness of mind', and this, says Bennett, is almost enough in itself, while all the rest is useless without it. What is 'fineness of mind'? We can deduce what it is from Bennett's remark that Fielding is unequalled as a novelist because 'the broad nobility of his mind is unequalled'. This, I think, is the supreme moral quality that Flaubert lacked in Bennett's eyes.[11] Hence, though Bennett had little use for Henry James as a novelist, he pronounced him an excellent critic because James was 'perhaps the first important English-writing critic to deflate the balloon of Gustave Flaubert'.[12]

Though Bennett thought the English too careless of formal values, he sees form as the servant of realism. But his realism allows as much for human feeling and spiritual aspiration as for the accurate depiction of the real world. This is the blend of qualities that led Donald Fanger to describe Balzac and Dostoevsky as 'romantic realists', a term which Walter F. Wright applies to Bennett himself.[13] Provided that 'romantic' is understood not to mean 'sentimental' (Bennett loathed sentimentality), he would have been happy to accept this description. His conception of realism certainly did not exclude a romantic vision, though he is ruthlessly dismissive of the self-styled romantic attitudes of individuals. For many years he regarded Balzac as the supreme novelist, 'the mighty, all-embracing, comprehensive critic of life',[14] an object lesson for lazy and narrow-minded Anglo-Saxons, because in Balzac an exactly adequate technique is matched to heroic breadth of vision and profound human sympathy.

The regime which Bennett saw as necessary for the salvation and future prosperity of the English novel is conveniently summed up in an unpublished letter written in 1908, though all his critical writing of this period proceeds from the same assumptions: desentimentalise the English novel (and the drama); no superfluities – learn from the austere construction of the best French work; achieve a French freedom in the choice of subjects and in the manner of treating them; discover irony, though it is not popular with the English public.[15] The stress on irony suggests that there was a limit to what a theoretical naturalism could contribute to the education of English writers. The ironist is a critic (in the sense of Arnold's 'criticism of life'); his concern is not with things for their own sakes, but with the light in which they are seen. It is interesting to note that nowhere does Bennett propound a 'scientific' theory of art to match the theories of the French naturalists. Of course, this fact did not preclude the adoption of their perspective or their methods when it suited his purpose; as John Lucas points out, if Bennett was not 'the scientific naturalist that Zola saw himself as being', neither was Zola.[16]

According to Lucas, Bennett chose the Five Towns as the background to his novels and stories in imitation of the French realists' and naturalists' studies of French provincial life. Bennett's original purpose in portraying the Five Towns was not, however, simply to record, but to criticise the narrowness and aridity of the Wesleyan Methodist ethic dominating the provincial society into which he was born. Louis Tillier rightly stresses Bennett's careful selection of precisely those concrete details which will enable him to point to the moral significance of the world that he describes. If Zola is an influence at all, says Tillier, it is 'Zola le visionnaire'.[17] In fact Bennett was not very impressed by Zola on the whole; though he admired four 'tremendous affairs': *Germinal*, *L'Assommoir*, *L'Oeuvre* and *Nana*, he thought that Zola 'lacked taste', and, even worse, 'he lacked sympathy'.[18] In his view, Zola was no advance on Balzac except in logic and the capacity to plan his work, and in his sheer tenacity;[19] and, if there is a French precedent for Bennett's use of 'symbolic' description, it is probably Balzac. As time passed, Bennett began to reread Balzac in French, and to perceive the sentimentality of which Balzac could be guilty; in 1929 he confessed that he had for some time been 'tortured by frightful apprehensions' about Balzac, 'once my hero', and that he was now forced to admit to himself that 'neither of those illustrious masterpieces, *Eugénie Grandet* and *Old Goriot*, is in truth a masterpiece or anywhere near being one'. Nevertheless he believed that some of Balzac, and particularly *La Cousine Bette*, would 'victoriously survive'. He adds, 'I cling to the relics of a faith', which is sufficient evidence of what Balzac had meant to him for more than thirty years.[20]

Lucas also makes the important point that, to the English novel-reading public, provincial life was an exotic subject and the inhabitants of the Five Towns no more 'ordinary' than the inhabitants of distant foreign lands.[21] Bennett is clearly aware of this fact, and I think that he is consciously an ambassador from 'Bursley' in much of his fictional work, maintaining the ancillary fiction that he is presenting to a polished southern readership a world where life is lived somewhat nearer the bone. Very often, he uses references to France to underline the distance between the Five Towns and civilisation. This pattern occurs in two quite different modes: the serious, as in 'The Death of Simon Fuge', *Anna of the Five Towns*, the Clayhanger trilogy and the English sections of *The Old Wives' Tale*; and the comic, as in many of the short stories and in *The Card*. In neither mode, in my view, is Bennett's attitude a simple one. No doubt, as James Hall suggests, the Five Towns represented for Bennett a moral climate of solid and solidly interlocking virtues more lastingly valuable than the artistic glitter and intellectual excitement supremely represented by Paris.[22] But this, it seems to me, is only part of the truth. The virtues of the Five Towns – respect for tradition, family loyalty, thrift and dignity – had their less attractive avatars: narrow-mindedness, snobbishness, miserliness, self-satisfaction. Bennett saw vices as well as virtues in the Five Towns; but then, he saw the same ambiguities in France.

Bennett was well aware that, amongst the general public, the prestige of France and of French ideas, such as it was, had more to do with fashion than with philosophy; Paris was the place to go for both *chic* dresses and modish opinions. It was a fashion that in his own way he may have helped to foster, if the great English public, as he thought, was not very good at recognising irony. For irony is the mode in which Bennett's fictional work treats the slavish following of French fashion, and the uncritical acceptance of French superiority. The irony is obvious in the case of Vera Cheswardine's passion for a green hat ('It was Parisian. She had been to Paris – once'), or of the Fearns' French governess, 'one of the seven wonders of the Five Towns', or of Jules, the fearsome French head waiter of the Grand Babylon Hotel, who proves to be 'a Hertfordshire man born and bred' named Tom Jackson. Irony is less immediately apparent in the case of Bursley's neglect of Simon Fuge, which is contrasted with his success at the Société Nationale des Beaux Arts in Paris. True though it may be that Simon Fuge's little painting, hung in an obscure corner of the Wedgwood Institution, is a reproach to the ignorance of the Five Towns, it is also true that Bennett mocks the writer of Fuge's obituary, who regards Fuge as superior *because* he was successful in Paris. The same ambiguity is present in *A Great Man*. The hero of this novella, the

stolid and worthy Henry, discovers in himself a puzzling gift fo
the effortless production of sentimental popular novels which earr
him vast sums of money and the adoration of the English public
Henry is contrasted with Tom, the black sheep of the family, who
runs away to Paris to study art, has a sculpture in the Luxembourg
is made a Chevalier of the Légion d'Honneur and becomes 'Presi
dent of the newly-founded Cosmopolitan Art Society which was to
hold exhibitions in both London and Paris'. Henry, who has to
watch his weight and becomes President of the Anti-Breakfas
League, 'could not understand it. Tom did not even pay his
creditors.' We are certainly meant to laugh at Henry, and through
him at the undiscriminating taste of the English public. But Ben
nett holds the balance between Henry and Tom. Henry may be
naïve and rather slow-witted, but he is honest and sensible; im
pressed and excited as he is by the daring and the glamour of Paris
and Monte Carlo when he visits Tom, he is not carried away by i
all (or not more than he needed to be). Henry emerges eventually
as a rather sympathetic character. Tom on the other hand, though
he is amusing and sophisticated and has an officially consecrated
artistic reputation, has no moral existence at all.[23]

The superficial glamour of France is treated more seriously in the
Clayhanger trilogy. In *Hilda Lessways*, Hilda's frustrated impatience
with her restricted horizons traps her into believing George
Cannon to be a superior soul because he comes of Huguenot stock
and possesses, in addition to his worldly charm, volumes of Victor
Hugo's poetry. Edwin Clayhanger too, as a young man, finds
something 'extraordinarily romantic' in the fact that his friend
Charlie Orgreave is studying in a French university. Edwin reads
an English translation of *Notre-Dame de Paris*, and is both im
pressed and abashed when he sees Tom Orgreave with Hugo's
novel in the original French. When he has taught himself to read
French, he thinks Voltaire's *Contes* (his text-book) 'the greatest
stories in the world', until he is shaken by Tom's confident reserva
tions about Voltaire. Bennett does not need to describe in detail the
agonies which Edwin suffers through his uncertain taste and his
fundamental ignorance; but equally he makes it plain that Tom's
judgement has no surer foundation.[24]

In the parallel lives of Constance and Sophia Baines (*The Old
Wives' Tale*, 1908), Bennett offers his most extended and profound
comparison between the Five Towns and France. Like Hilda Less
ways, Sophia is ready to elope with an unsuitable young man

argely because he knows France. Once in Paris, Sophia's inbred
sense of proper values is aroused by what she sees as the underly-
ng vulgarity, futility and cruelty of French sophistication. Too
proud to return to Bursley when Gerald abandons her, she sets
about creating, in her boarding-house in the rue Lord Byron, an
sland of English rectitude and sound management. Grateful as
she is for Chirac's friendship, and much as she likes him, she
refuses to become his mistress – not because she is married to the
absent Gerald, but because she does not trust the sincerity of
French emotions. It sounds as if Bennett is making a case for the
moral superiority of the Five Towns; but he is more subtle than
that. When we see Sophia on her return to her birthplace, it is clear
that her northern virtues have become cold and hard; living through
the Siege of Paris has made her strong and self-reliant, but Paris
has also taught her to drive a hard bargain, both commercially and
emotionally; to her sister Constance she seems to have lived a
wasted life. Thus Bennett has given us a Five Towns view of Paris,
and at the same time he has used Paris as a distorting mirror in
which to show us the truth about the Five Towns.

All this makes it rather unlikely that, except at a very early stage
n his career, Bennett was the dupe of Gallic glamour. Even if there
s truth in H. G. Wells' assertion that 'To have a mistress in France
was, he felt, part of the ensemble of the literary artist', it is surely
overstating the case to claim, as Walter Allen does, that 'his
attitude to France seems never to have been other than that of the
English provincial'.[25] No one who was limited in his vision to the
attitudes of his place of birth (to put no more sinister construction
than that on Allen's remark) would have been capable of the
penetrating analysis of Five Towns life and values which Bennett
offers in his novels and stories; and he is equally astute in his
studies of France, despite the ambiguities which we have noted –
indeed, I would suggest that these ambiguities are evidence in
themselves of Bennett's capacity for avoiding conventional or
ready-made responses. Detachment actually made him uncertain
of his preferences. He is often as ambivalent in his occasional
writings as in his fiction about his reactions to French life and
French culture, and I find no evidence to support Lafourcade's
contention that, when Bennett criticises France or presents French
characters in an unflattering light, he is merely pandering to
English xenophobia.[26] If that were so, how could he have created
Mr Ipple, the famous drama critic, who attempts to damn a new

play by describing it as 'dangerous, unwholesome, sickly, shamelessly cynical, formless, amateurish, insidious, *continental*'?[27] Ford Madox Ford thought *The Old Wives' Tale* 'one of the best artistic representations of life in Paris that I have ever read', but he believed that Bennett 'disliked the French from whom he had learned everything'.[28] It would be nearer the truth to say that he sometimes disliked them. Certainly Bennett saw two faces of Paris: the first was the open, frank face of 'multitudes that so candidly accepted human nature as human nature is'; the other was 'meretricious', revealing 'a contented and corrupt inefficiency . . . corroding this race like a disease' and 'a refined and corrupt decadence'.[29] He worried at his divided loyalties for years, undecided whether he preferred England, 'this honest, hypocritical country of bad restaurants and good women'[30] (his summing-up of the English seaside hotel was 'Menus in French. Cooking in English'[31]) or the 'synonym and symbol of all that is luxurious, frivolous, gay, vicious, and artistic' that was Paris seen from the Sacré Coeur.[32] 'I do believe', he concluded in 1921, 'I have a kind of double mentality – one English and the other French.'[33] It was the English Bennett who looked at France, and the French one who looked at England.

What is certain is that, in Bennett's view, English writers had a great deal to learn from the French, and English life in general would benefit from an injection of French openness and moral realism, which he saw as the necessary condition of French superiority in most artistic fields (most, but not all, for he had serious doubts about the contemporary French theatre, for instance). Both before and after the Great War, in his work for the *New Age* (1908–11) and for the London *Evening Standard* (1926–31), he was a tireless interpreter of French ideas and French artistic practice, and clearly determined to bring the latest French novels, plays and essays, as well as the classic French writers, to the notice of his readers.

Many of Bennett's articles in the *New Age*, written under the pseudonym 'Jacob Tonson', were produced while he was living in Fontainebleau or staying in Paris or Switzerland. In 1917 he selected about a third of these articles for publication in volume form, thus bringing them to the notice of a wider public.[34] French literature is a constant theme. When he is not writing about a French publication or comparing French and English literary traditions, he often cites French critics' comments on English writers;

thus, for praise of H. G. Wells he turns to Maeterlinck, and for an assessment of Swinburne to Villiers de l'Isle-Adam.[35] In an article entitled 'English Literary Criticism' (3 Nov 1910), Bennett asserts uncompromisingly that English critics are 'fragmentary or provincial', and that none of them matches the 'terrific sweeping range' of Sainte-Beuve or Taine (although he did think Swinburne a great critic as well as a supreme poet). Typical of his confident presentation of contemporary French literature to readers of the *New Age* is the article entitled 'Anatole France' (29 Oct 1908). Bennett announces that Zola is going out of fashion and that Anatole France is no longer considered to be the only genius. His own judgement is that Anatole France continues to demonstrate 'his complete inability to construct a novel', and that he suffers from 'spiritual anaemia': 'one is inclined to wake him by throwing "Leaves of Grass" or "Ecce Homo" (Nietzsche's) at his head'. The man of the moment, says Bennett, is Stendhal: 'In some circles it is now a lapse from taste to read anything but Stendhal.' Bennett's tone is generally good-tempered, even when ironic, but he is firm and positive in his opinions: the Académie Française is a 'bastion of mediocrity'; the popularity of Brieux's plays in Paris suggests the imminent decadence of a once great nation; Henri Becque, on the other hand, was 'one of the greatest dramatists of the nineteenth century, and certainly the greatest realistic French dramatist', and has been shamefully neglected in England. Unexpectedly, the occasion for a rare display of critical fury is Mallarmé. In a piece entitled 'Mallarmé, Bazin, Swinburne' (17 Dec 1908), Bennett pours scorn on René Bazin, who on a visit to England had informed an English journalist that Mallarmé was a *fumiste*. Bazin, says Bennett, is 'the Mrs Humphry Ward of France' (except that he is so rude) and a 'nuncio of mediocrity and the Académie Française.' As for Mallarmé, though there may be 'two opinions as to the permanent value of Mallarmé's work . . . there cannot be two informed and honest opinions as to his profound sincerity'. Praising Mallarmé's artistic conscience and devotion to art, Bennett refers his readers to 'the Mallarmé chapter in André Gide's book *Prétextes*' for the truth about 'what is thought of Mallarmé by the younger French school'.

It is evident that in his work for the *New Age* Bennett assumes that his readers understand French, and that they might take the trouble to follow up references to French books old and new, and even to articles in French periodicals. The weekly column in the *Evening Standard* is addressed to a larger, more diverse readership.

Here Bennett's tone is informal but serious and courteous, as of one intelligent reader to another. He avoids both condescension and display, and, when he meets these faults in a book under review, he can be very funny at the expense of the pretentious writer. Even the most recondite topics are approached in a common-sense fashion; in short, Bennett knew exactly how to interest the Average Reader in above-average literature. He does not restrict himself to reviewing the week's new books, but wanders in a deceptively relaxed-seeming manner among literary topics of general interest, recollections (sparked off by current publications) of works that he has read in the past, anecdotes about authors alive or dead, and reflections on books and life. He discusses a surprisingly large number of works available only in French, giving the publisher and the price in francs in each case; if an English translation appears subsequently, Bennett will review that as well. It is impossible in the space available here to give an adequate account of the range and variety of Bennett's allusions to France in his *Evening Standard* column, but the material for a single month (selected at random) may offer at least some idea of his method. On 2 June 1927, Bennett notes the publication of some additions to Amiel's *Intimate Journal* and discusses his reputation in both France and England. Remarking that it was Matthew Arnold who introduced Amiel to English readers, he considers Arnold as a critic, then as a poet ('I would sacrifice the whole of his prose for ten of his best poems'). Returning to Amiel, he castigates English hypocrisy in the writing of biographies, and reflects on the fate of Shelley and Byron, whose work is neglected because of their private lives, and of Trollope, who recklessly admitted an interest not in sex but, which is worse, in money. On 9 June, Bennett begins with personal recollections of an essayist who has just died, then speaks of the man's quixotic attitude towards money. This allows him to continue the previous week's discussion of 'the mercantile aspects of an artistic career'; he ridicules the coy pretence, which the English public insists on maintaining, that authors do not need to eat, and finally comments on authors' stage rights, noting that they order these things better in America and France, while individualistic English authors have organised no protection for themselves against unscrupulous theatre-managers, which is bad for them, and bad for art. On 16 June, Bennett reviews recent verse: Sacheverell and Edith Sitwell, Robert Graves and Humbert Wolfe, with a passing shot at the notes provided by

Eliot to *The Waste Land* (which Bennett insists on calling *The Waste-lands*). On 23 June, he looks forward to a yet unpublished novel by H. M. Tomlinson, and discusses Virginia Woolf's *To the Lighthouse* (a discussion which ought to be quoted in full!), then three more novels by new or newish writers, assessed for professional competence and originality; he ends by denying that he admires Russian novels only because they are Russian ('Unjust! I have read quantities of mediocre Russian novels'), and by recommending two translations from Maxim Gorky. The final column of the month, on 30 June, begins with a report of a revival of Wilde's *The Florentine Tragedy*. Bennett repents his reaction after the first performance of *The Importance of Being Earnest* ('the finest comedy in English since Sheridan'); a recent revival has disillusioned him, and he is now convinced of the superior dramatic skills of Somerset Maugham and Frederick Lonsdale. Nevertheless he stresses the European significance of Wilde and recommends Gide's *Oscar Wilde – In Memoriam* (in French), which 'displays Wilde at his very best'. He goes on to reflect on mannered style, glances at Pater (who 'has gone under'), and reveals that, being tired of small works, he has been reading Gibbon, who is 'fantastically mannered', but alive and exciting. There follows a discussion of the writing of history, and of Gibbon's influence on Macaulay and Trevelyan, then speculation about whether history in the future will be written in a contemporary style. Thence to the style of Sinclair Lewis and William Gerhardi, and comments on *Elmer Gantry* and Gerhardi's latest book of stories, *Pretty Creatures*. Then back to Wilde and a reader's letter complaining that *Salomé* (in French) is not available from 'a famous and historic circulating library'. 'The price of a satisfactory circulating library', says Bennett, 'is eternal vigilance', and he adds, 'Can you imagine an important library banning an innocuous old-world trifle like *Salomé*? Well, you must.'

The ease with which Bennett moves between French and English contexts is characteristic of his literary journalism. He kept in regular touch with French publishing and the French theatre, but is never swayed by mere fashion, and invariably looks back to a tradition when he pronounces judgement. Gide, with whom Bennett corresponded for many years, was bored by some of Bennett's work (though not *The Old Wives' Tale*, which he helped to translate into French, nor *Riceyman Steps*, which he took with him to the Congo – how odd it must have seemed in that environment!); but he thought Bennett an excellent critic, welcomed his guidance in the matter of English literature, and agreed with his views on French writers.[36] It was Bennett who wrote the remarkably astute Preface to the English translation of Gide's *Dostoïevski*, thus introducing two of his favourites at once. Bennett was indeed a critic to reckon with, and his verdicts on French writers of his time now seem extraordinarily prescient (the same is true of his judgements on his English contemporaries). He thought that Barbusse's *Le Feu* had been overpraised, and that 'Its effect depended on its subject.' He regretted having himself overpraised *Les Conquérants*; reading *La Voie royale*, he thought he would have liked 'more bread and less cake', and objected to Malraux's 'overcharged style'. He refused to be carried away by the general enthusiasm for Proust, and concluded soberly that, while he was sometimes 'enchanted' by Proust's novel (and sometimes bored), its famed 'psychology' was a 'passion for . . . minutiae', and Proust's scope was very narrow. He informed the readers of the *Evening Standard* that Valéry's *Introduction to the Method of Leonardo da Vinci* was 'at least as much an introduction to the method of Paul Valéry', and, though Bennett could not understand Valéry's poems, he saw that the 'cold and pellucid waters' of the *Introduction* were the right sort of 'moral bath' for best-selling writers, French, British, or American.[37]

A. R. Orage, the editor of the *New Age*, affirmed that 'there neither is, nor has been, in English letters, Mr Bennett's parallel as a literary causeur', and Andrew Mylett adds that it was Bennett's column that kept the *New Age* alive. Mylett also notes that the circulation of the *Evening Standard* rose sharply on Thursdays, when Bennett's column appeared, and that a favourable review from Bennett was enough to make booksellers order extra copies and publishers decide to reprint.[38] His influence was enormous, and his unassailable position as the foremost journalist–critic of his day allowed him to tell the English Average Reader exactly what he should be reading, and what sort of novel and drama he should demand. In this enterprise he calls constantly on French examples, not necessarily to praise, but always to define and distinguish. Bennett calculated that notices of foreign literature (predominantly French) accounted for no more than 5 percent of his annual total of books reviewed.[39] But that figure ignores his references to French writers and French ideas in his reviews of the work of English writers. He loses no opportunity to recommend his readers to explore French literature, not only the work of established classics such as Restif de la Bretonne and Rousseau, Balzac and Stendhal, but also Maurois, Colette, Drieu la Rochelle, Léautaud, Mauriac, Julien Green, Giraudoux, Benda, Gide and many others. The French, he explained, were more professional than the English, their dramatic technique 'much better' (but not their dramatic taste), their best criticism 'superlative', the *Nouvelle revue française* the finest literary periodical in the world. Being at home in both literatures, he was able to judge each in the light of the other, and he used his thorough knowledge of English taste and English prejudices to introduce French literature in the most appropriate way, anticipating the untutored response of his readers and teaching them, not without affection, to recognise their ignorance and insularity. The un-Englishness of France, which was for him not the least of its attractions, was exactly the textbook he needed in this enterprise. His ideal, it would appear, lay somewhere in mid-Channel: 'I prefer to live in England and regret France than to live in France and regret England. . . . I suppose I have a grim passion for England. But I know why France is the darling of the nations.'[40]

NOTES

NB. Bennett invariably refers to 'English' rather than 'British' writers. For simplicity's sake, I have followed his example in discussing his work.

1. One example only: 'Arnold Bennett, as is well known, was deeply influenced by the French Naturalists . . .' – Arnold Kettle, *Introduction to the English Novel* (1953; London: Arrow Books, 1962) II, 88. See also Louis Tillier, *Studies in the Sources of Arnold Bennett's Novels* (Paris: Didier, 1969).
2. *Echo de Paris*, 10 Aug 1928. Cited in Tillier, *Arnold Bennett et ses romans réalistes* (Paris: Didier, 1968) p. 154.
3. 11 Jan 1897, *The Journals of Arnold Bennett*, ed. Newman Flower (London: Cassell, 1932–3) 3 vols. References to this edition are hereinafter given in the text by date of entry only.
4. See F. W. Hemmings, *The Russian Novel in France, 1884–1914* (London: Oxford University Press, 1950)esp. chs 2 and 3. Bennett refers to Vogüé in his essay 'Ivan Turgenev' in *Fame and Fiction: An Enquiry into Certain Popularities* (London: Grant Richards, 1901).
5. 'Mr George Moore', in *Fame and Fiction*.
6. 'The Fallow Fields of Fiction', in *The Author's Craft and Other Critical Writings of Arnold Bennett*, ed. Samuel Hynes (Lincoln, Nebr.: University of Nebraska Press, 1968).

7. Introductory essay to *Fame and Fiction*.
8. *Arnold Bennett – the 'Evening Standard' Years: 'Books and Persons' 1926–1931*, ed. Andrew Mylett (London: Chatto and Windus, 1974) pp. 297–8 (22 Aug 1929).
9. 'The Fallow Fields of Fiction', in *The Author's Craft*. See also *Bennett – the 'Evening Standard' Years*, pp. 410–12 (18 Sep 1930).
10. 'My Literary Heresies' (1904), in *The Author's Craft*, pp. 234–7. Cf. 'Meredith' (*New Age*, 27 May 1909) in *Books and Persons, Being Comments on a Past Epoch 1908–1911* (London: Chatto and Windus, 1917).
11. 'The Author's Craft' (1914; first published as 'The Story-Teller's Craft', 1913), in *The Author's Craft*. Flaubert's statement is in a letter to Louise Colet (16 Jan 1852); Bennett refers to Flaubert's *Correspondance* (which, like Gide, he preferred to Flaubert's novels) in his *Evening Standard* column for 5 July 1928 (*Bennett – the 'Evening Standard' Years*, p. 173).
12. *Bennett – the 'Evening Standard' Years*, p. 20 (27 Jan 1927).
13. D. Fanger, *Dostoevsky and Romantic Realism: A Study of Dostoevsky in Relation to Balzac, Dickens and Gogol* (Chicago: University of Chicago Press, 1967); W. F. Wright, *Arnold Bennett: Romantic Realist* (Lincoln, Nebr.: University of Nebraska Press, 1971).
14. 'The Progress of the Novel' (1929), in *The Author's Craft*.
15. Cited in Tillier, *Bennett et ses romans réalistes*, p. 153.
16. John Lucas, *Arnold Bennett: A Study of his Fiction* (London: Methuen, 1974) p. 27. Cf. V. S. Pritchett, *The Living Novel* (London: Chatto and Windus, 1946) p. 136.
17. Tillier, *Bennett et ses romans réalistes*, p. 179.
18. *Bennett – the 'Evening Standard' Years*, pp. 182 (2 Aug 1928) and 31 (10 Mar 1927).
19. 'The Progress of the Novel', in *The Author's Craft*.
20. *Bennett – the 'Evening Standard' Years*, pp. 260–1 (18 Apr 1929).
21. Lucas, *Bennett: A Study of his Fiction*, p. 27.
22. James Hall, *Arnold Bennett: Primitivism and Taste* (Seattle: University of Washington Press, 1959) p. 70ff.
23. 'The Nineteenth Hat' and 'The Death of Simon Fuge' in *The Grim Smile of the Five Towns* (1907); *The Grand Babylon Hotel* (1902); the Fearns appear in *The Card* (1911); *A Great Man* (1904).
24. *Clayhanger* (1910); *Hilda Lessways* (1911). The third novel in the trilogy is *These Twain* (1915).
25. Walter Allen, *Arnold Bennett* (London: Home and Van Thal, 1948) pp. 17 and 25. Cf. Georges Lafourcade, *Arnold Bennett: A Study* (1939; New York: Haskell House, 1971) p. 28 on 'the provincial let loose'; but Lafourcade sees 'flashes of genuine admiration and pride' in Bennett's satire of the Five Towns. See also Gilbert Cannan: 'errors of taste . . . bred out of the influence of the French novel on the Nonconformist mind' – *Manchester Guardian*, 11 Nov 1908, cited in *Arnold Bennett: The Critical Heritage*, ed. James Hepburn (London: Routledge and Kegan Paul, 1981) pp. 208–9.
26. Lafourcade, *Bennett: A Study*, p. 110.
27. 'The Mysterious Destruction of Mr Ipple', in *Elsie and the Child and Other Stories* (1924); emphasis added.

28. Cited in Reginald Pound, *Arnold Bennett: A Biography* (London: Heine-mann, 1952) p. 180.
29. 'Paris Nights' (1910), in *Paris Nights and Other Impressions of Places and People* (London: Hodder and Stoughton, 1913).
30. 'Ugliness in Fiction' (*New Age*, 9 May 1908), in *Books and Persons*.
31. *Journal 1929* (London: Cassell, 1930) p. 32.
32. *Things which have Interested Me* (Burslem: privately printed, 1908) Second Series, p. 28. See also Third Series (Burslem: privately printed, 1908) p. 24 on 'the superior advantages of London' and 'the fundamental superiority of the English character'.
33. 'The Desire for France', in *Things that have Interested Me* (London: Chatto and Windus, 1921) First Series, p. 293. See also 'French and English', in Third Series (1926) p. 232.
34. *Books and Persons*. All articles from the *New Age* cited here, by title and date, are reprinted in this volume.
35. 'H. G. Wells' (*New Age*, 4 Mar 1909) and 'Swinburne' (22 Apr 1909), in *Books and Persons*.
36. See *Correspondance André Gide – Arnold Bennett. Vingt ans d'amitié littéraire*, ed. Linette F. Brugmans (Geneva: Droz, 1964) *passim*.
37. *Bennett – the 'Evening Standard' Years* , p. 322 (14 Nov 1929, on Barbusse), pp. 443–4 (8 Jan 1931, on Malraux), pp. 27–8 and 86–7 (24 Feb and 29 Sep 1927, on Proust), pp. 263–5 (2 May 1929, on Valéry). On Proust see also 'My Literary Heresies', in *The Author's Craft*, pp. 238–41; and 'Marcel Proust', in *Things that have Interested Me* , Third Series, p. 196ff. Proust is a genius, but not 'a supreme genius'.
38. Orage, cited in Mylett's Introduction to *Bennett – the 'Evening Standard' Years*, p. xv; see also p. xxiii.
39. *Bennet – the 'Evening Standard' Years*, pp. 406–7 (4 Sep 1930); see also p. 380 (29 May 1930).
40. 'Graphic Art in Paris', in *Things that have Interested Me*, First Series, p. 308.

6

Rediscovering the French Eighteenth Century

CERI CROSSLEY

The Introduction to this volume suggested that the manner in which British culture assimilates or uses French culture is a complex process which cannot adequately be accounted for by the use of superficially attractive terms such as 'influence' and 'source'. A source can take on the dangerous prestige of a founding origin and a general designation of influences may acquire the allure of a controlling principle of explanation. It is more profitable to consider French culture as an external point of reference, as an instrument which allows the writing subject to define where he or she stands in relation to British culture. Awareness of the differentness of French culture can join with a sense of not being fully at home within the British tradition to produce a twofold movement of projection and recognition.[1] Since the middle of the nineteenth century a number of different moments in the history of French culture have been presented to the British public as possessing particular value: the France of Villon; the civilization of Provence; Renaissance France; the cultured, aristocratic society of the eighteenth century. My concern in this essay lies with the last of these.[2]

Eighteenth-century France, sophisticated and urbane, yet libertine and subversive, held an undeniable attraction for many British writers who felt constrained by the norms and conventions of Victorian and Edwardian society. It offered them an interesting alternative to another literary model proposed by French culture, that of the *poète maudit*. The latter embodied the revolt of the creative artist at odds with the values of bourgeois society. The evocation of the elegant salons of the eighteenth century added a new and important element. For, while the appeal to the eighteenth century reinforced the rejection of middle-class philistinism and narrow religious prejudice, it located the site of that rejection in a significantly different context. Here was a social group, an elite whose members placed the highest value upon intellectual and artistic accomplishments but who eschewed prudery and hypocrisy on the matter of sexual morality. My intention is to examine some examples of the way in which this image of eighteenth-century France has been used in British culture since the time of Swinburne. My argument will focus upon attitudes to Laclos's epistolary novel *Les Liaisons dangereuses* (1782).[3]

It should be emphasised that the image of pre-revolutionary France with which I am concerned did not initially arise within British culture. As a mental construct functioning within cultural discourse it was produced in France in the second half of the nineteenth century. Two studies by the Goncourt brothers were instrumental in bringing this about: *La Femme au dix-huitième siècle* (1862) and *L'Amour au dix-huitième siècle* (1875). These works encouraged a revival of interest in the eighteenth century and a general reassessment of its art and literature. Verlaine's *Fêtes galantes* popularised the picture of an elegant, artificial world whose inhabitants took delight in bittersweet sensations and transient encounters. By the turn of the century previously neglected authors were receiving critical attention. Rémy de Gourmont urged that serious consideration be given to Sade, Casanova, Restif de la Bretonne and Laclos. But the return to the libertine tradition represented more than passing literary fashion. It was felt that the time had come for human sexuality to be freed from prohibitions of a religious origin: Rémy de Gourmont challenged the basis of Christian morality by teaching the need to distinguish between the sexual and the procreative acts.[4]

The Goncourts' vision of the eighteenth century was echoed in George Moore's *Confessions of a Young Man*. Verlaine was adulated by the younger generation of English poets, in particular by Arthur Symons. Rémy de Gourmont's interest in the libertine tradition was taken up by Havelock Ellis, who wrote on Restif de la Bretonne, Alexandre de Tilly, Besenval, the Duc de Lauzun, Laclos and others.[5] However, it was one thing to express controversial views in France. It was quite another to do so in England. Victorian reviewers were not averse to denouncing the immorality of novelists such as Balzac and George Sand. Matthew Arnold warned his readers to beware of the Frenchman's tendency to worship the great goddess Lubricity. Vizetelly was put in prison for publishing Zola in England. The Victorian novel reinforced the stereotypes of submissive wife and dutiful daughter. The subversive sexuality of

Laclos's protagonists was inadmissible. What could be further removed from the Victorian moral universe than the Vicomte de Valmont and Madame de Merteuil competing in the cynical manipulation of the sexual instinct in order to further their quest for power and domination. The novel might eschew physical description but its ambiguous moral stance alone rendered it unacceptable. It was judged to be a work designed to deprave and corrupt, a work of pornography.[6]

Laclos's novel shocked French readers as well as British – it was condemned by a French court in 1865 – but the moral climate prevailing on the English side of the Channel was such that to refer to the novel amounted to making a deliberately provocative gesture. Within French culture the debate concerning the value of the libertine tradition could focus on the significance of the French Revolution. Did eighteenth-century literature depict accurately a rotten society which merited the punishment meted out to it in 1789? Or were matters more complex: did the libertines' challenge to established order pave the way for revolutionary change? 'La Révolution', wrote Baudelaire, 'a été faite par des voluptueux.'[7] Baudelaire's notes, written in 1856 but only published in 1903, foreshadowed the rather Nietzschean interpretation of the novel in vogue from the end of the century, a reading which valued the energy and will-power of the main protagonists. In England there was an added dimension: the association between libertinism and a disreputable Frenchness. But what some saw as typically French licentiousness others viewed as an admirable honesty about human sexuality. Might *Les Liaisons dangereuses* furnish a literary model which could be used to satirise British society in the nineteenth century? This step was taken by Swinburne, an author who knew his eighteenth century well (Sade, Restif de la Bretonne, Louvet de Couvray). Swinburne savoured the element of metaphysical revolt embodied in Laclos's Madame de Merteuil: 'She is a Titaness, and fights heaven . . . she is a Prometheus in petticoats, and might be put into Milton as mother of sin and death.'[8] Swinburne drew directly on Laclos in his epistolary novel *A Year's Letters* (1877). He included the character of Lady Midhurst, modelled on Madame de Merteuil, who sets about the destruction of two pairs of lovers. What interests us in particular is Swinburne's heavily ironic prefatory note (itself imitated from Laclos) which presents a patently absurd defence of conventional marriage in England:

Dear Madam,

I have read your manuscript with due care and attention, and regret that I cannot but pass upon it a verdict anything but favourable. A long sojourn in France, it appears to me, has vitiated your principles and confused your judgement. Whatever may be the case abroad, you must know that in England marriages are usually prosperous; that among us divorces are unknown, and infidelities incomprehensible. . . . I recommend you therefore to suppress or even destroy this book, for two reasons: it is a false picture of domestic life in England, because it suggests as possible that a married lady may prefer some stranger to her husband, which is palpably and demonstrably absurd; it is also, as far as I can see, deficient in purpose and significance. Morality, I need not add, is the soul of art; a picture, poem or story must be judged by the lesson it conveys.[9]

To cast doubt on the institution of English marriage can thus humorously be attributed to the effects of 'a long sojourn in France'. But is there not a danger that a writer such as Swinburne who appeals to France in order to challenge and mock British hypocrisy may in fact only serve to reinforce the simple association of France with sexuality, cultivated by those who use France in order to deplore moral licentiousness? In both cases France is being used strategically, as anti-England.[10]

It comes as no surprise to discover that the writers of the 1890s were drawn to *Les Liaisons dangereuses*. Ernest Dowson translated the novel for the publisher Leonard Smithers (1898) and Aubrey Beardsley prepared an illustration depicting Valmont to adorn the title page. Indeed, Beardsley approached his subject in a manner which caught perfectly the cerebral, analytical character of the novel: 'I have long set my heart on making some pictures for the book, not "galants" in any way but severe and reticent.'[11] Arthur Symons helped advance scholarly knowledge of Laclos by collaborating with Louis Thomas in the publication of Laclos's *Poésies* in 1908. British francophiles were alive to the reassessment of Laclos which was taking place within French culture. Arnold Bennett was impressed. He described the book as 'the only really realistic novel ever written'. In the skilled hands of a master such as Laclos '*la canaillerie* becomes beautiful'.[12] It is, however, difficult to assess the true extent of the novel's readership in Britain. Virginia Woolf read the book in 1911 'with great delight' and drew

on its characters and plot when writing *The Voyage Out*.[13] But was
the wider reading public aware of the real nature of the novel?
There is a revealing remark by Gissing: 'I have never read *Les
Liaisons dangereuses*, but have often heard of the book and its
reputation.'[14] The deliberate exclusion of the novel from George
Saintsbury's *History of the French Novel* (despite the inclusion of
references to the unambiguously libertine novels of Crébillon Fils
and Restif de la Bretonne) testified to Laclos's continuing power to
shock the British moral conscience.[15] If anything, the spirit of
eighteenth-century France was more likely to be conveyed to the
British reading public via the mediation of a later writer such as
Stendhal, in whose works the moral preoccupations of the eighteenth century were joined with a new realism and an acute awareness of social class: the young D. H. Lawrence readily identified
with Julien Sorel, the hero of *Le Rouge et le noir* (1830).[16]

Translations of eighteenth-century French works were in fact
rare in Britain before the final decade of Victoria's reign.[17] Moreover, it was the political content of Enlightenment thought which
appealed to the British public. John Morley's lengthy studies of
Voltaire (1872) and Rousseau (1873) were well received by readers
of a liberal disposition. Morley also offered a forceful statement of
Diderot's value and historical importance in the book he published
on the French thinker in 1878 – Carlyle's strictures on Diderot
could henceforth be ignored. Other writers echoed this interest in
the thinkers of the Enlightenment, and when Havelock Ellis published *The New Spirit* (1890) he elevated Diderot to the status of
cultural hero, an audacious pioneer in social, scientific and moral
questions. Diderot, wrote Ellis, 'appears before us now as a spirit
of the latter nineteenth century, at one with our aspirations today'.
This desire to ground modernity in the French eighteenth century
is a phenomenon which we shall encounter elsewhere. For Ellis,
Diderot ranks as the great precursor, the advocate of reasoned
advance joined with faith in nature and a just appreciation of
man's physicality. In this context Ellis' attitude to *Les Bijoux indis-
crets* is revealing. On the one hand it can be referred to dismissively
as 'a frivolous novel in the style of the younger Crébillon, pointless
and indecent, written, at the age of thirty-five, mainly to obtain
money for his mistress'. On the other, its value cannot be doubted:
it contains 'passages which have been considered among the finest
he ever wrote'.[18] Such judgements leave the reader wondering what
guiding principle authorises the legitimation of certain texts within

the body of eighteenth-century French writing. To what extent is value assigned to texts as a consequence of their location within a developmental philosophy of history?

It was in Bloomsbury, however, that the pull of eighteenth-century France was most strongly felt.[19] Lytton Strachey and his friends recognised themselves in the pre-revolutionary society whose memory they cultivated and whose art they admired. Eighteenth-century France came to function almost as a founding myth, legitimating many of the attitudes which members of the Bloomsbury Group placed at the centre of their own lives: a devotion to art, a delight in intellectual conversation, a sense of a shared way of living, a mistrust of conventional codes of behaviour. Might Garsington become another Sceaux? Michael Holroyd has observed that, in Lady Ottoline Morrell, Lytton Strachey 'thought he recognised an approximation to Madame du Deffand at the prime of her life'.[20] In describing the salon of Madame du Deffand, Lytton Strachey summoned up the picture of his ideal world:

> It was an intermediate period, and the comparatively small group formed by the elite of the rich, refined, and intelligent classes led an existence in which the elements of publicity and privacy were curiously combined. . . . The circle of one's friends was, in those days, the framework of one's whole being; within which was to be found all that life had to offer, and outside of which no interest, however fruitful, no passion, however profound, no art, however soaring, was of the slightest account. . . . The selfishness of the eighteenth century was a communal selfishness.[21]

In *Landmarks in French Literature* (1912) Lytton Strachey underlined the absolute centrality of the French eighteenth century for the history of the civilised world. However, it should not be assumed that his attitude was uncritical or that his views simply prefigure the thesis of Clive Bell in *Civilisation*. Strachey is concerned with mapping the general field of French literary history. He devotes sixty-six pages to the eighteenth century, which is in fact slightly less than the amount given over to the age of Louis XIV. Chapter 5 of *Landmarks in French Literature* provides an overview of eighteenth-century French literature and an assessment of its achievements. The Bloomsbury note rings out, to be sure, but

Strachey's approach is workmanlike and conscientious, drawing upon the literary histories listed in the bibliography (Petit de Julleville, Lanson, Brunetière, Dowden). The eighteenth century falls into two halves, the first being marked by Saint-Simon, Montesquieu and the younger Voltaire, the second being characterised by the *philosophes'* wish to expose the evils of the social order in the name of reason. Only those authors generally considered to be of major importance are discussed. Laclos, for example, only receives a passing mention in a later chapter: 'The culminating example of the eighteenth century form of fiction may be seen in the *Liaisons dangereuses* of Laclos, a witty, scandalous and remarkably able novel, concerned with the interacting intrigues of a small society of persons, and revealing on every page a most brilliant and concentrated art' (p. 222).[22] Laclos does not figure at all in the chronological list of authors which Strachey appended to his text. Most attention is paid to Saint-Simon, Voltaire and Rousseau. Strachey tries to present a balanced view, regretting Voltaire's inability to appreciate the beauty of religious states of mind but admiring his hatred of fanaticism and his 'passionate desire for the welfare of mankind' (p. 179). Strachey regrets that the espousal of the cause of reason by the *philosophes* was vitiated by a fondness for abstraction and system-building which he in turn associates with a reluctance to be concerned with the reality of political life. At this point we encounter an interesting comparison with the process of political change in England:

> the majority of the *Philosophes* ignored politics proper altogether. This was a great misfortune; but it was inevitable. The beneficent changes which had been introduced so effectively and with such comparative ease into the government of England had been brought about by men of affairs; in France the men of affairs were merely the helpless tools of an autocratic machine, and the changes had to owe their origin to men uninstructed in affairs – to men of letters. Reform had to come from the outside, instead of from within; and reform of that kind spells revolution.
> (pp. 157–8)

With regard to Rousseau, Strachey points to contradictions and inconsistencies. Rousseau was misguided in his direct appeal to nature: 'Nature is neither simple nor good; and all history shows that the necessary condition for the production of any of the really valuable things of life is the control of Nature by man – in fact, civilisation' (p. 188). Strachey, however, makes an important discrimination: Rousseau's critique of civilisation was really directed at 'the conventionality of civilisation – the restrictions upon the free play of the human spirit which seemed to be inherent in civilised life' (p. 188). He recognises that some find Rousseau's *Confessions* distasteful but argues for what he considers to be the book's modernity: Rousseau realised that 'the individual, now, on this earth, and in himself, was the most important thing in the world' (p. 189). The eighteenth century had invented a new secular understanding of society but it had failed to take account of man's spiritual nature. Rousseau, it would seem, restored this dimension of human experience.

In the French eighteenth century Bloomsbury discovered an image of itself, sceptical, intelligent, free of moral hypocrisy but also exclusive and self-preoccupied. Virginia Woolf's reading of Laclos has already been mentioned. Diderot found in Francis Birrell an able translator: the *Dialogues* were published in 1927. In his introduction Birrell set out to rescue Diderot from nineteenth-century commentators (Carlyle, Sainte-Beuve, Morley) and present him as profoundly human, sceptical and sane. There was more to Diderot than the architect of the *Encyclopédie* who had appealed to Morley. Birrell preferred to emphasise Diderot's writing on moral questions and his attitude towards the body: 'Diderot showers upon the body the sentiments other people reserve for the soul.'[23] In 1928 there appeared a work which more than any has served to fix for subsequent generations the image of Bloomsbury turning for inspiration to eighteenth-century France: Clive Bell's *Civilisation*.[24]

In this work Bell's thesis was that 'a Sense of Values and Reason Enthroned are the parent qualities of high civilisation' (p. 57). Civilisation is by definition artificial. To be fully civilised is to experience what Bell terms the most intense and exquisite states of mind. Civilisation, however, can only prosper within the confines of a small, leisured elite, secure in its material well-being and hence in a position to perceive that 'the true value of things is their value as means to states of mind' (p. 62). Bell sums up the civilising-process as follows: 'The richest and fullest life obtainable, a life which contains the maximum of vivid and exquisite experiences, is the end of every civilised man's desire' (pp. 97–8). Civilised individuals are permanently curious. They possess a tolerant spirit born of the power of reason to override prejudice. In conversation no topic is excluded. In life the goal is the pursuit of pleasure: 'The frank enjoyment of all life has to offer is the privilege of the completely civilised. To enjoy perfectly a man must have cleansed himself from taboos; he must be free from prudery, superstition, false shame, and the sense of sin' (p. 140). If civilised man eschews certain pleasures 'it is not because they are bad, but because their consequences are' (p. 141). Chastity, observes Bell, was of small account in the salons which welcomed Voltaire, Diderot and Helvétius.[25] Near the close of *Civilisation* Bell draws attention to the role played by the *hetairae* ('cultivated *demi-mondaines'*) in Athenian society: 'the most exquisite of human relations is the *liaison* . . . the subtlest and most impalpable things of the spirit float from one mind to another most easily on a mixed flood of sense and emotion'(p. 235).[26]

For Bell civilisation had only existed at four moments in history: in Athens from 480 to 323 BC, at Rome during the first two centuries of the Empire, in Italy during the Renaissance and in France from the middle of the seventeenth century until 1789.[27] It is, however, the latter part of the eighteenth century which most clearly corresponds to Bell's ideal (although his fullest example, that of the Hôtel de Rambouillet, is drawn from the seventeenth). Eighteenth-century society possessed intelligence and wit; it refused to be bored and judged the world in accordance with its standards. Civilised society pursued its own course, isolated from political concerns. Men and women discussed moral questions openly, without prejudice. Voltaire emerges as the true embodiment of eighteenth-century culture. At that time, comments Bell, reasonable pleasure was the end of an honest man's desire. The twentieth century has espoused different values:

> In the eighteenth century this philosophy of pleasure, under its old-world name of Philanthropy, was extremely popular. Today it is disdained as deficient in idealism, since it aims at the satisfaction of the individual rather than at the glorification of a race, a creed, or a class. It is as much detested by patriots as despised by communists, and only a few old-fashioned people still believe that there may be something to be said for it. (p. 147)

What is surprising, given the generally held view of Bell as the propounder of the cult of eighteenth-century France, is the paucity of detailed reference: glancing allusions to Voltaire, Diderot, Greuze and other figures; the very occasional quotation. The eighteenth century represented here in vague, general terms is that of Voltaire: the pursuit of pleasure under the guidance of reason. But what of the eighteenth century of Crébillon Fils, of Nerciat, of Laclos? The moral problems raised by *Les Liaisons dangereuses* are simply not addressed, despite the fact that they emerged out of the very sensationist philosophy which Bell appears to wish to make his own. In fact Bell doesn't try to assign much concrete reality to his picture of the eighteenth century. Nor for that matter does he seek to envisage any real developmental continuity between Greece, Rome, Renaissance Italy and France. The book sees no need to represent history as process, moved by an internal cultural dynamism. Instead, Bell selects those periods in which he discerns the fleeting incarnation of the ideal. No utopian future is offered as a heuristic device enabling us to deal with the present. Since the goal of civilisation is delight in the present, it is perhaps inappropriate to ask where the future lies. The civilised man is, after all, above politics and he has no regard for the politician's slogans of freedom, equality, fraternity, rights, and so on (p. 176). It is surely not without significance that for Bell the eighteenth century ended in 1789. The entire question of the relationship between the Revolution and eighteenth-century patterns of thought is elided, simply not discussed. Bell's eighteenth-century France lays little claim to historical reality since it remains in essence an imaginary world, the figure of a possible world.[28]

Bell's *Civilisation* belongs to the 1920s, a period which saw a sudden growth in the number of eighteenth-century French works done into English. Two series deserve particular attention: The Broadway Library of Eighteenth Century French Literature, directed by Richard Aldington, and XVIII Century French Romances, under the general editorship of Vyvyan Holland. The writers translated included Rousseau, Diderot, Laclos, Boufflers, Caylus, Besenval and Crébillon Fils. Among the authors of the introductions we find Aldous Huxley, Augustus John, Compton Mackenzie and Havelock Ellis. What emerges from the introductions is the feeling that French literature of the eighteenth century spoke with an uncanny immediacy to those who had survived the horrors of the Great War. The war had destroyed the optimism of the previous era, leaving in its wake moral instability and uncertainty. Hugh Walpole summed up the mood of crisis and its relation to the eighteenth century:

> The events of the last ten years have given a terrifying shock to all sense of security, and it seems a stupid impertinence for anyone to hint at an optimistic philosophy. In very much of this, in the cynicism, the scoffing and the materialism, there is justification for the belief that we are much nearer to the eighteenth-century literature than to that of any later period.[29]

Introducing Crébillon Fils' *La Nuit et le moment* Aldous Huxley reminded his readers that the image of the eighteenth century which they found appealing was in essence a response to contemporary needs and anxieties: 'The fact that we have chosen to re-create a whole historical epoch in the image of this intellectually free and morally licentious *dix-huitième* throws some light on our own problems, our own twentieth-century bugbears, our own desires.'[30] Huxley himself held the French eighteenth century in considerable affection, calling it 'this most civilised period of history'.[31] Indeed, we find characters in Huxley's novels reading libertine works such as Nerciat's *Félicia* and Crébillon's *Le Sofa*. In *Antic Hay* (1923) Mercaptan declares, 'if I glory in anything, it's in my little rococo boudoir, and the conversations across the polished mahogany, and the delicate, lascivious, *witty* little flirtations on ample sofas inhabited by the soul of Crébillon Fils'.[32] *Antic Hay*, as Huxley pointed out to his disapproving father, was a book written by a member of the war generation to be read by others of his kind who had witnessed the violent disruption of the standards and values current before 1914.[33] The analogy with the eighteenth century was closest on the question of sexual morality. In his own way Crébillon could be viewed as expounding 'the scientific truth about love – that its basis is physiological'. Love arouses intense and beautiful emotions; these, however, 'cannot be philosophically justified or explained, but should be gratefully accepted for what they are: feelings significant in themselves and of the highest practical importance for those who experience them'.[34]

The pursuit of sensual pleasure became a legitimate object of human activity once the burden of inherited values had been removed by force of external circumstance. In this wise, disillusion and disenchantment could be allied with a new consciousness of freedom. But was this freedom worth having? Or was it merely the disguised expression of the self-centredness of a privileged few? In *Antic Hay* Huxley suggested the inadequacy of the return to the eighteenth century by having Lypiatt round on Mercaptan:

> You disgust me – you and your odious little sham eighteenth-century civilisation; your piddling little poetry; your art for art's sake instead of for God's sake; your nauseating little copulations without love or passion; your hoggish materialism; your bestial indifference to all that's unhappy and your yelping hatred of all that's great.[35]

Was the morality of the eighteenth century admirable after all? Was the aim of life really to extract the greatest pleasure from transient sensations? The debate on morals which had character-ised the literature of pre-revolutionary France was carried a stage further in renewed discussion of *Les Liaisons dangereuses*.

The novel reappeared in 1925 in a new translation by Richard Aldington preceded by a lengthy biographical and critical introduction.[36] Aldington situates Laclos in the context of eighteenth-century libertine writing (Crébillon Fils, Louvet, Restif, Nerciat, Duclos, and so on), but he declares Laclos's novel to be the most modern. A sympathetic understanding of eighteenth-century literature does not stand in the way of forthright judgements on fundamental moral matters. The critic discriminates between the various authors he cites, assigning greater literary value to some than to others; all, however, represent a society which Aldington deplores. Not for him the association between libertinism and intellectual freedom or the evocation of an idealised elite. The eighteenth century stands accused of cruelty to and exploitation of women.[37] The supposed pursuit of pleasure was accompanied by an arid reasoning which destroyed spontaneous feeling; at the same time, what passed for sincere feeling was in reality artificial and excessive. Aldington makes a case for the high moral serious-ness of *Les Liaisons dangereuses*. In his view the novel is a master-piece of psychological analysis constructed with almost faultless precision. It constitutes a faithful evocation of a corrupt society, soon, thankfully, to be destroyed by the Revolution.[38] The reader is left in no doubt which interpretation of the novel is correct: 'if we are to understand Laclos' book we must perpetually keep in mind that it is an attack upon abuses inherent in the 18th century marriage system, code of morals and education of women' (p. 39). The female characters are as much the victims of society as of Valmont and Merteuil. Laclos's purpose was the denunciation of the ills of convent education and the arranged marriage: 'the social customs of the upper classes in the 18th century were such that they condemned many women almost inevitably to one or another form of unhappiness and often to "vice"' (p. 33). The men of the time viewed women with a mixture of vanity, cruelty and cynicism, and some women, like Madame de Merteuil, did indeed become seized with a corresponding desire to manipulate men and dominate them.

There is no sign here of the sneaking admiration which other critics show for Valmont and Merteuil, nor of the desire to present them as beings of superior will and energy worthy of being distinguished from the mass of their fellow citizens. In Aldington's preface the eighteenth century emerges, not as a lost paradise of civilisation, but as a cruel world marked by the oppression of women and the abuse of the innocent. We are left in no doubt as to how we should interpret any similarities with the present:

> [Laclos'] denunciation was not an unjust one. And sometimes, when we are tempted to smile at the sentiment of the early 19th century, to feel irritated at its absurd prudery, we might remember that it was a natural reaction from the rule of the Valmonts and Merteuils. That bath of sentiment had its value. It is possible that our own reaction against it has gone too far. There is something revolting in the *'goujaterie'* of a certain type of wealthy young man, which reminds one of a vulgar Valmont.   (p. 51)[39]

Aldington was also responsible for the volume *French Comedies of the XVIIIth Century* in the Broadway series. Here again he seeks to discriminate among the authors of the period. He has a particular fondness for Marivaux, who also, we are told, stood out against the cynical immorality of the marriage of convenience. The dramatist emerges as a decent man at a time of sexual licence, revolted by what Aldington describes as the hard lubricity of Crébillon Fils. Marivaux was a *grand voluptueux* who knew well that in love *volupté* was as much a matter of the heart as of the senses: grossness, cynicism and promiscuity were fatal to the pleasures of sex.[40] A further volume edited by Aldington contained the *Memoirs of the Duc de Lauzun* in a translation by C. K. Scott Moncrieff. In a brief introduction Aldington remarks that the French aristocracy of the eighteenth century is hated 'not because some of its members were licentious, but because it was a privileged class, gay, witty, rich, brave, free and superbly insolent'.[41] The nobility abdicated and was assassinated. More interesting, however, than Aldington's introduction is the fact that this volume of memoirs stimulated D. H. Lawrence to write an attack on the libertine spirit in pre-revolutionary France. In his autobiography, *Life for Life's Sake*, Aldington recounts how in the course of a visit to the Villa Mirenda in 1926 he showed the book to Lawrence and suggested that he write the introduction. The strength of Lawrence's reaction – the French aristocracy were a collection of lice – prompted Aldington to let the matter drop. Lawrence would surely write 'an improper introduction to a public which was pretty languid about the French 18th century anyhow'.[42]

Lawrence, however, had already put pen to paper, and his observations on Lauzun were discovered after his death and published in the first volume of *Phoenix* as 'The Duc de Lauzun'.[43] Lawrence, needless to say, does not mince his words. In his view the French aristocracy deserved the guillotine. Lauzun receives some sympathy since he is portrayed as being essentially a creature of his times. He had some good qualities but these were perverted by the spirit of eighteenth-century France. Lauzun fell victim to his arranged marriage, to his lack of real education and to his absorption of the vision of life purveyed by contemporary novels. For Lawrence the eighteenth century propounded two contrasting but equally false attitudes to love: an unfeelingly brutal attitude and an insincere, sickly sentimental attitude. Both were inimical to genuine feelings: 'What scope was there for a decent, manly man, in that France rotten with sentimentalism and dead with cruel callousness?' (p. 748). There are similarities with Aldington's remarks on Laclos – as when Lawrence declares, 'A mid-Victorian English sentimentalist at his worst is sincere and naïve, compared to a French romanticist of the mid-eighteenth century. One works one's way through the sticky-sweet mess with repulsion' (p. 746). The refined callousness of the period was destructive of that which is best in men. Furthermore, Lawrence cannot really bring himself to say anything in favour of the writing of the period. In 'The Good Man',[44] another essay inspired by his reading of Lauzun, Lawrence declares French literature of the eighteenth century to be depressing and dreary. The century carried to extremes the general critical tendency which marks French culture: 'The French are essentially critics of life, rather than creators of life. And when the life itself runs rather thin, as it did in the eighteenth century, and the criticism rattles all the faster, it just leaves one feeling wretched' (p. 750). France lacked the self-mocking spirit of Sterne. But there is another charge which Lawrence levels against eighteenth-century France: the period – in the shape of Rousseau and Diderot – invented the figure of the *homme de bien* and this led to the substitution of 'the reasonable social virtues' for the 'passion of life' (p. 751).[45] Seen from this perspective the eighteenth century produced both industrial civilisation and a superficial social morality. In Lawrence's eyes it had much to answer for.

Lawrence's remarks suggest that the world of the 1920s did indeed have much in common with France in the eighteenth century. But there was nothing positive in this. The two periods were alike in their cultivation of false emotion, in their failure to assign to love its true signification. For the Lawrence of the 1920s who hoped for national regeneration through phallic tenderness, the French eighteenth century seemed to embody all he deplored. In 'A propos of *Lady Chatterley's Lover*' he attacked modern sex as exhaustive and disintegrative: 'smart licentiousness' was a perversion.[46] What was taken to be sexual emancipation amounted to a denial of real emotion; the body became like a trained dog enslaved to the mind. What mattered to Lawrence was the vital connection with the universe which would produce a vast release of energy.[47] Human sexuality was nothing if not participation in cosmic activity. Lawrence raged against the betrayal of true feeling, in the past and in the present. Lawrence's adversaries in Bloomsbury could sing the praises of an idealised France; Lawrence himself did not hesitate to challenge them on their chosen ground.[48]

But what of the future? Did the analogy with the eighteenth century suggest that a new revolution would come and sweep away all that was bad in twentieth-century life? Lawrence tackles this idea directly but his use of the thematics of revolution is ambiguous. In 'The Good Man' he admits that were a revolution to take place it would nevertheless be unlikely to bring about real change. After all, the Russian Revolution had produced nothing intrinsically new: 'Bolshevist Russia, one feels, and feels with bitter regret, is nothing new on the face of the earth. It is only a sort of America. And no matter how many revolutions take place, all we can hope for is different sorts of America' (p. 753). For Lawrence, in the final analysis, the essential content of revolution is moral rather than political or social. Revolution, in the true sense, means regeneration, the birth of a new kind of man: 'a revolution is really the birth of a new baby, a new idea, a new feeling, a new way of feeling, a new feeling pattern.' Lawrence finds nothing in the present to support such an aspiration: '[you cannot] expect a revolution, because there is no new baby in the womb of our society.' In other words, the analogy between the present and eighteenth-century France, although useful up to a point, should not be taken too far. Lawrence, however, does not abandon the apocalyptic note appropriate to the rhetoric of revolution: 'The French revolution was only a bit of a brief inundation. The real deluge lies just ahead of us.' And Lawrence, despite his reservations, is not without hope: 'You who want a revolution, beget and conceive the new baby in your bodies: and not a homunculus robot like Rousseau's.' In reality the figure of the *homme de bien* bequeathed to posterity by the French eighteenth century had been destroyed by the Great War. Lawrence leaves open the possibility of regeneration, but it seems a more limited regeneration, wrought by individuals who accept to transform themselves in the face of the dissolution and general collapse of modern society:

> All that remains, since it's Louis XV's Deluge which is louring, rather belated: all that remains is to be a Noah, and build an ark. An ark, an ark, my kingdom for an ark! An ark of the covenant, into which also the animals shall go in two by two, for there's one more river to cross! (p. 754)

Lawrence's rhetoric is the rhetoric of revolution and apocalypse. But he could not fully use this rhetoric without dealing with the French eighteenth century and the myths, progressive and sexual, which surrounded it: he had to endow it with a meaning which compromised neither his views on sex nor his sense of history.

We are thus offered a number of competing interpretations of the French eighteenth century, a variety of images which carry different, sometimes contradictory, meanings. As a historical representation within British cultural discourse the French eighteenth century can be portrayed in a positive or a negative light. A process of selection determines which elements are foregrounded. Did Voltaire embody the spirit of the age? Or Diderot? Did the eighteenth century find expression in painting, literature, philosophy, or rather in a particular attitude to life and to social relations? And yet, despite the diversity of interpretation, a common set of assumptions is often in evidence. Victorian sexual morality is judged to be hypocritical; traditional forms of organised religion are refused; the optimistic philosophy of progress is considered shallow and naïve. The experience of the Great War heightened the sense of there being a common point of departure. What is at first sight surprising is the extent to which British writers who have sought a historical analogy with the present turned to the French eighteenth century. The Goncourts had made a strong case for the view that the modern age began in the eighteenth century, but they had also presented it as being quintessentially French. Our authors agreed, despite their differences, that the 'real' eighteenth century happened in France. The eighteenth century came to embody the twin attributes which British culture, especially under the influence of Arnold, assigned to French culture: intellectual prestige joined with increased freedom in matters of sexual morality. Moreover, as the case of Laclos has shown, an investigation of eighteenth-century French literature focused attention on the question of the relationship between desire and culture. The eighteenth century could be invested with different meanings, but irrespective of how it was defined or valorised its end point was not questioned: the 'real' eighteenth century ended in 1789. This meant that the reflection on the French eighteenth century was inevitably a reflection upon the relationship between ideas and action, between morality and social cohesion, between art and revolution. In the final analysis, the interpretation of the eighteenth century lay at the centre of the debate on Classicism and Romanticism. The French eighteenth century could not be ignored. Neither could it be encountered innocently. The discovery and rediscovery of its literature, particularly its more libertine literature, was a way of coming to terms with present realities and recommending alternative futures.

NOTES

1. This essay extends the argument of my paper 'Laclos et l'image du XVIIIe siècle français en Angleterre', *Laclos et le libertinage* (Paris: Presses Universitaires de France, 1983) pp. 275–87.
2. The best study of the image of France in modern English literature is by Christophe Campos, *The View of France from Arnold to Bloomsbury*

(London: Oxford University Press, 1965). See also Enid Starkie, *From Gautier to Eliot: The Influence of France on English Literature 1831–1939* (London: Hutchinson, 1960).

3. The essential work for students of Laclos is Laurent Versini, *Laclos et la tradition* (Paris: Klincksieck, 1968). An excellent English commentary is provided by Philip Thody, *Laclos: Les Liaisons dangereuses* (London: Arnold, 1970). The history of the novel's changing reputation has been charted by A. and Y. Delmas, *A la recherche des Liaisons dangereuses* (Paris: Mercure de France, 1964). For a discussion of the probable reading of Laclos by Jane Austen, see Simon Davies, 'Laclos dans la littérature anglaise du XIXe siecle', *Laclos et le libertinage*, pp. 255–64.

4. See Richard Aldington, Introduction to *Rémy de Gourmont: Selections* (1928; London: Heinemann, 1944). See D. Mossop, 'Un Disciple de Gourmont: Richard Aldington', *Revue de littérature comparée*, 1951, pp. 402–35.

5. Many of Ellis' studies are collected in *From Rousseau to Proust* (London: Constable, 1936).

6. See the views of H. S. Ashbee cited by Steven Marcus in *The Other Victorians: A Study of Sexuality and Pornography in Mid-Nineteenth Century England* (London: Weidenfeld and Nicolson, 1966) p. 44.

7. Baudelaire's notes were first published as an appendix to Laclos's previously unpublished *De l'education des femmes* (Paris: Messein, 1903). See the commentary on this text by Laurent Versini in his edition of Laclos, *Oeuvres complètes* (Paris: Gallimard, 1979). Lytton Strachey was impressed by Baudelaire's observations and he wrote to Clive Bell (9 Aug 1907), 'I've just got a book in which some notes by Baudelaire on the *Liaisons dangereuses* are printed – do you know them? They're really splendid – all his wonderful sanity, precision, and grasp of the situation are finely displayed.' Quoted in Michael Holroyd, *Lytton Strachey: A Biography* (Harmondsworth, Middx: Penguin, 1980) p. 363.

8. A. C. Swinburne, *Lesbia Brandon*, ed. R. Hughes (London: Falcon, 1952). See Davies in *Laclos et le libertinage*, pp. 259–64.

9. Quoted in Philip Henderson, *Swinburne: The Portrait of a Poet* (London: Routledge and Kegan Paul, 1974) pp. 61–2. For examples of Swinburne's use of French for satirical purposes see A. C. Swinburne, *New Writings*, ed. C. Lang (Syracuse, NY: Syracuse University Press, 1964).

10. Cf. Matthew Arnold's attitude in 'The French Play in London', *Nineteenth Century*, Aug 1879, pp. 228–43.

11. *The Letters of Aubrey Beardsley*, ed. H. Maas, J. L. Duncan and W. G. Good (London: Cassell, 1970) p. 210. The illustration, from the *Savoy*, is reproduced in Campos, *The View of France*, p. 184. It is noteworthy that Valmont becomes another of Beardsley's hermaphrodite figures, thus reinforcing in a somewhat unexpected manner the link between France and sexual aberrance.

12. R. Hughes, in his edition of Swinburne's *Lesbia Brandon* (p. 538), tells us that these words were inscribed by Bennett on his personal copy of Laclos's novel.

13. *The Letters of Virginia Woolf* (London: Hogarth Press, 1975) I, 458. See

L. A. DeSalvo, _Virginia Woolf's First Voyage: A Novel in the Making_ (London: Macmillan, 1980).

14. _The Letters of George Gissing to Gabrielle Fleury_, ed. P. Coustillas (New York: New York Public Library, 1964) p. 91. In _The Novel in France_ (London: Hamish Hamilton, 1950) Martin Turnell referred to _Les Liaisons dangereuses_ as a great masterpiece still very neglected in England.

15. George Saintsbury, _A History of the French Novel_ (London: Macmillan, 1917). The critic justifies his exclusion of Laclos in a vituperative note (pp. xiv–xv). He also shows considerable hostility towards Diderot (pp. 403–4). Campos (_The View of France_, p. 47) places Saintsbury and Dowden firmly under the influence of Arnold: the French attain great cultural and intellectual heights but the nation remains dangerously lax in matters of morality.

16. _The Letters of D. H. Lawrence_, ed. J. T. Boulton (Cambridge: Cambridge University Press, 1979) I, 262–3. In this letter to Louie Burrows (28 Apr 1911) Lawrence remarks that, having read _Le Rouge et le noir_ for four and a half hours, he naturally thinks in French. The letter ends, 'Hélas, que vous êtes loin d'ici, que votre corps loin du mien.'

17. It is also worth asking how much eighteenth-century English literature was readily available and reasonably priced. J. T. Boulton (ibid., p. 524) notes that in 1913 the only available edition of Richardson's _Clarissa_ was Mrs Humphry Ward's abridgment (1899).

18. Havelock Ellis, _The New Spirit_ (New York: Boni and Liveright, n.d.) pp. 34 and 50. The case of Ellis and his associates is a very interesting one, for it shows how the translation of works of French literature could go hand in hand with a desire to promote a serious discussion of human sexuality. Eleanor Marx translated _Madame Bovary_. Ellis translated Zola's _Germinal_ for the Lutetian Society, which 'was founded to translate works that would not generally be acceptable to Victorian readers' – Phyllis Grosskurth, _Havelock Ellis: A Biography_ (London: Allen Lane, 1980) p. 159.

19. See Campos, _The View of France_, pp. 208–37.

20. Holroyd, _Lytton Strachey_, p. 597. Unfortunately the distance separating England in 1915 from France in 1770 was such that the re-creation of the past did not prove to be an unqualified success.

21. Lytton Strachey, _Books and Characters_ (New York: Harcourt, Brace, 1922) p. 89.

22. Lytton Strachey, _Landmarks in French Literature_ (London: Williams and Norgate, n.d.). Page references are incorporated into the text. Michael Holroyd (_Lytton Strachey_, pp. 363 and 581–2) evokes Strachey's fondness for Laclos's novel.

23. Denis Diderot, _Dialogues_, tr. Francis Birrell (London: Routledge, 1927) p. 9. Birrell also translated Diderot's _La Religieuse_. See R. F. Harrod, _The Life of John Maynard Keynes_ (London: Macmillan, 1951) pp. 172–94.

24. Clive Bell, _Civilisation_ (London: Chatto and Windus, 1929). Page references are incorporated into the text. In a footnote (p. 27) Bell refers to the opinions of his friend Raymond Mortimer. As a critic Mortimer often dealt with French topics. In the Preface to his collected journal-

ism he writes, 'I have called this collection *Channel Packet* because, like the Dover–Calais steamboat, my reading runs daily between France and England; and also because these two words conjure many of the happiest hours of my life, spent on the deck of a Channel Packet anticipating the delights of being once more upon the soil of France' – *Channel Packet* (London: Hogarth Press, 1942) p. 8.

25. Cf. Virginia Woolf, *Roger Fry: A Biography* (London: Hogarth Press, 1940) pp. 235 and 251.
26. A footnote (*Civilisation*, p. 236) is worth quoting at some length, for it brings together Bell's attitudes to France, sexuality, art and civilisation:

> I once asked a French sculptor why little Toulon was such a deliciously civilised town – incidentally it supports one of the best bookshops in the world – when vast Marseille was so coarse and barbarous. He replied that an important and influential part of the population of Toulon consisted of mistresses, permanent or *de circonstance*, of naval officers who . . . demand of their mistresses – be they the mere companions of a short leave even – something better than mere physical satisfaction. It is the *hetairae* of Toulon who give that delectable little city its elegance.

27. In selecting Antonine Rome as one of his privileged ages Bell is expressing a preference widely shared in the nineteenth century and which probably derives from Gibbon. In *The Decline and Fall of the Roman Empire* Gibbon wrote, 'If a man were called to fix the period in the history of the world during which the condition of the human race was most happy and prosperous, he would, without hesitation, name that which elapsed from the death of Domitian to the accession of Commodus.' Quoted by Ian Small in the Introduction to Walter Pater, *Marius the Epicurean* (London: Oxford University Press, 1986) p. vii.
28. Some more detail is given in *An Account of French Painting* (London: Chatto and Windus, 1931). Bell appreciates Boucher and Fragonard but particularly dislikes Greuze (p. 131). He has no time for David and his political role. The eighteenth century began in 1715 and ended in 1789.
29. Stanislas-Jean de Boufflers, *The Queen of Golconda and Other Tales*, tr. E. Sutton with an intro. by Hugh Walpole (London: Chapman and Hall, 1926) pp. x–xi.
30. Crébillon Fils, *The Opportunities of a Night*, tr. E Sutton with an intro. by Aldous Huxley (London: Chapman and Hall, 1925) p. xii. Leonard Woolf later addressed himself to a related question: in *After the Deluge* (London: Hogarth Press, 1931) I, 79:

> Seeing . . . that certain ideas in the communal psychology of the eighteenth century appeared to produce the French Revolution and the wars which followed it, and that once more in 1914 in the communal psychology of twentieth-century Europe the same ideas appear in a slightly different form to cause the war and the revolu-

tions which followed it, the scientific investigator must start by comparing the communal psychology of the French Revolution with that of the early years of the twentieth century.

31. D. P. Scales, *Aldous Huxley and French Literature* (Sydney: Sydney University Press, 1969) p. 22. Scales reminds us (p. 69) that Huxley considered Proust to be 'eighteenth-century'. An extended treatment of British attitudes to eighteenth-century France would indeed need to take account of the reception of *A la recherche du temps perdu*, the representation of its author and the role of the translator, Scott Moncrieff.

32. Aldous Huxley, *Antic Hay* (London: Granada, 1977) p. 47. See the examination of *Point Counter Point* in Delmas, *A la recherche des Liaisons dangereuses*, pp. 263–4.

33. *Letters of Aldous Huxley*, ed. Grover Smith (London: Chatto and Windus, 1969) p. 224.

34. Huxley, Introduction to Crébillon Fils, *The Opportunities of a Night*, p. xvii.

35. Huxley, *Antic Hay*, p. 48.

36. Pierre Choderlos de Laclos, *Dangerous Acquaintances*, tr. Richard Aldington (London: Routledge, 1924). Page references are incorporated into the text. Dowson's translation was republished in Paris by the Black Sun Press. See H. Ford, *Published in Paris* (London: Garnstone Press, 1975). See also E. Gosse, *Silhouettes* (London: Heinemann, 1925) pp. 133–40.

37. The publication in 1903 of Laclos's treatise on the education of women lent support to those who wished to present the novel, and its author, as expressing a morally acceptable attitude to sexuality. Cf. Aldington, Introduction to *Rémy de Gourmont*, pp. 22–6.

38. See Aldington's assessment of the novel in the Introduction to *Great French Romances* (London: Pilot, 1946). See also an essay entitled 'Mr James Joyce's *Ulysses*', in which Aldington refers to Laclos's novel in a manner significantly at variance with the views he expresses in his own introduction to *Les Liaisons dangereuses*: 'Some people find Mr Joyce "indecent and repulsive"; repulsive, he may be, if you believe in human happiness, human goodness, and human relations. But not indecent in any seductive sense. He is no Laclos or Crébillon fils' – *Literary Studies and Reviews* (London: George Allen and Unwin, 1924) p. 198.

39. In a note Aldington alludes to Paul Morand's *Lewis et Irène* (1924) and, in general terms, to the work of Wyndham Lewis.

40. *French Comedies of the XVIIIth Century (Regnard, Lesage, Marivaux, Destouches)*, tr. with an intro. and biographical prefaces by Richard Aldington (London: Routledge, 1923) pp. 198–200. Aldington also wrote a biography of Voltaire.

41. *Memoirs of the Duc de Lauzun*, tr. C. K. Scott Moncrieff with an intro. by Richard Aldington (London: Routledge, 1928) p. xii.

42. Richard Aldington, *Life for Life's Sake* (1941; London: Cassell, 1968) pp. 280–1.

43. 'The Duc de Lauzun', *Phoenix: The Posthumous Papers of D. H. Lawrence* (London: Heinemann, 1936) pp. 745–9. Page references are incorporated into the text.

44. '[The Good Man]', ibid., pp. 750–4. Page references are incorporated into the text. This essay was written in October 1926. See K. Sagar, *D. H. Lawrence: a Calendar of his Works* (Manchester: Manchester University Press, 1979) p. 154.

45. In a letter to Lady Ottoline Morrell (2 Apr 1915) Lawrence had referred to his new philosophy as his *'Contrat Social'* (*Letters*, II, 312).

46. D. H. Lawrence, *Phoenix II* (London: Heinemann, 1968) p. 492.

47. 'Aristocracy', ibid., pp. 475–84.

48. On 8 April 1915 Lawrence had written to Lady Ottoline Morrell, 'I still dont like Strachey – his *French Literature* neither – words – litterateur – bore' (*Letters*, II, 315). Later, when Strachey read *Lady Chatterley's Lover*, he regretted Lawrence's moralising and expressed disapproval of 'a barbaric, anti-civilisation outlook' which he found in the novel (letter of 23 Oct 1928 quoted in Holroyd, *Lyttton Strachey*, p. 967). For a discussion of Lawrence's relations with Bloomsbury, see Quentin Bell, *Bloomsbury* (London: Weidenfeld and Nicolson, 1968) pp. 70–80.

7

A Diet of Dead Crow: Aspects of French Culture in the *Criterion* (1923–39)

VANESSA DAVIES

The First World War altered much in intellectual and cultural relationships between England and France. Normal channels for the reception of French culture were disrupted. The effect of this on the English intellect was a grievous sense of loss: Paul Fussell describes it as 'a loss of amplitude, a decay of imaginative and intellectual possibility corresponding to the literal loss of physical freedom'.[1] In the aftermath of the war, many judged it imperative that cultural links with the Continent be restored. Something had to be done to counter the feeling that, in the words of E. M. Forster, England had become 'tighter and tinier and shinier than ever – a very precious little party'.[2] Dissatisfaction was such that many English intellectuals quite simply left for France, or for another country, becoming members of what Fussell has called the 'British literary Diaspora'. For those obliged to remain, the literary review was a compensatory medium, an important instrument for the raising of cultural awareness.[3]

One of Eliot's fundamental aims in the *Criterion* was precisely to encourage an interest in foreign (and especially French) literature. He believed that reference to a foreign literature encouraged the renewal of one's own, but that this process depended on the ability of the indigenous literature both to 'assimilate influences from abroad' and to 'go back and learn from its own sources'.[4] Hence the assessment of an aspect of French culture was often achieved through comparison with English culture. Moreover, contributors to the *Criterion* held the view that 'civilisation' itself relied essentially on England and on France. Together the two nations formed the backbone of the European cultural tradition. According to Eliot, both English and French culture had their roots in classical civilisation. What mattered in the present was to bring the two traditions once again into a state of creative exchange.

The *Criterion* employed three methods of presenting aspects of French culture to its readers. First there was the publication of primary material in translation. Second, considerable space was devoted to reviews of French books and to a digest of the contents of those French periodicals with which the *Criterion* had links. The third method was the 'chronicle', in which a single critic would summarise intellectual activities and draw attention to specific works or performances. However, before examining in detail the operation of these three ways of presenting French culture, it is necessary to describe the more general ideological position adopted by the *Criterion*.

Until 1928 the *Criterion* displayed a wide range of interests and upheld a belief in the equal value of different critical positions. Indeed, Eliot was later to write that the review's aim was to maintain intellectual activity at the highest level rather than to make any particular ideas prevail. (He did, however, admit that in its later years the review did not completely manage to live up to this ideal.) In fact, only four years after the launch of the *Criterion* Eliot claimed that the review had what he termed a tendency towards Classicism. He cited six books as exemplary of this tendency. These included Hulme's *Speculations* and Babbitt's *Democracy and Leadership*. The remainder were French: *L'Avenir de l'intelligence* by Maurras; *Belphégor* by Benda; *Réflexions sur la violence* by Georges Sorel, and *Réflexions sur l'intelligence* by Jacques Maritain. As far as Eliot was concerned, the common denominator of these works was their insistence on the status of 'pure' intelligence as a tool for the criticism of society. The review grew consequently conservative in outlook and the articles became increasingly moralising in tone. At this point Eliot published in the review his own translation of work by a man whose thought had influenced him decisively: Charles Maurras.

Maurras's 'Prologue to an Essay on Criticism' appeared in the January 1928 issue. Its publication marked a watershed in the life of the *Criterion*. After that date the real commitment to French thought which the review had demonstrated at its inception gave way to a preoccupation with the writings of Maurras. The article of 1928 is a discussion of the status of criticism. It is largely descriptive and relies on inadequately defined aesthetic criteria. Maurras shared Eliot's scepticism concerning modern criticism, which he considered

insincere and incoherent. In the second half of the essay, published in the following number of the review, Maurras argued that
the concepts of taste and beauty were founded on Classicism, and
concluded that the maintenance of the exclusively French classical
tradition must remain the prime objective of writer and critic
alike.

No introduction accompanied the first publication of Maurras's
writings in the *Criterion*. However, before Eliot could publish the
second half of the essay he was forced to defend his mentor. It
should be remembered that in that very year the Vatican condemned Maurras's organisation, L'Action Française. Was such a
person a suitable contributor to the *Criterion*? Eliot's response was
to emphasise the significance of Maurras as a literary figure.
However, there can be no doubt that he considered that England
would greatly benefit from adopting the Frenchman's ideas:

> The work of M. Maurras is little known in England. . . . The
> majority of those who are in a position to advertise contempor-
> ary French literature are Liberals, horrified by such a word as
> Reaction, and by no means friendly to Catholicism; or Conserva-
> tives, indifferent to foreign thought and equally unfriendly to
> Catholicism; or Socialists, who can have no use for M. Maurras
> at all. The fact that he is also an important literary critic, and has
> written as fine prose as any French author living, makes no
> difference to his reputation. But if anything, in another genera-
> tion or so, is to preserve us from a sentimental Anglo-Fascism, it
> will be some system of ideas which will have gained much from
> the study of Maurras. His influence in England has not yet
> begun.[5]

Eliot tried to show consistency in the development of Maurras's
thought, especially in respect of his anti-Christian ideas; but he
clearly could not believe that implicit in Maurras's writings lay, at
best, class and racial antipathy, and, at worst, incitement to
hatred. In fact, Eliot did not reveal to his readers Maurras's political actions; neither did he mention his involvement in the Dreyfus
affair. Nor for that matter did he allude to his own meetings with
Maurras. Stephen Spender, who suggests that Eliot may have been
infatuated with Maurras, wonders whether Eliot recognised in the
Frenchman's views on Christianity his own developing convictions.[6]
Unfortunately, Eliot's use of the *Criterion* to expound his support for

Maurras initiated the review's decline into the politico-religious offering it finally became. The intellectual health-warning which readers of the *Criterion* were entitled to from Eliot had to come from Leo Ward, an opponent of Maurras. Describing the activities and aims of L'Action Française, Ward issued a firm condemnation of what can only be called Eliot's naïvetý in the matter. Ward argued that Maurras's theories were designed to deal with a specifically French situation and were thus inapplicable in England. Declaring himself to be a sincere friend of the *Criterion*, Ward could not be sanguine about the review becoming a refuge for moribund French philosophies.[7] Eliot did at least allow Ward's views to receive public expression. However, he was incensed by the criticisms and immediately reaffirmed his belief that the influence of Maurras's thought was in no way on the wane.

Published later in the same year, an article entitled 'The Literature of Fascism' revealed some unwillingness on Eliot's part to grasp contemporary political realities. Perhaps, as Stephen Spender has argued, Eliot sought from politics 'pure' ideas and so deemed involvement in political reality an indication of intellectual inferiority.[8] What cannot be denied is the reality of Eliot's support for Maurras. The English had much to learn from the Frenchman, even though his compatriots had not been anxious to disseminate his thought beyond national frontiers:

> Most of the concepts which might have attracted me in fascism I seem already to have found, in a more digestible form, in the work of Charles Maurras. . . . The political philosophy of Maurras is obscured from English students by the fact that . . . M. Maurras and his friends have often displayed a lamentable and even grotesque ignorance of foreign affairs.[9]

Eliot was primarily interested in those ideas which he considered had a potential for improving society. In January 1933 we see him again turning to the reflections of French intellectuals. The *Criterion* of that date included a translation of a political programme by Robert Aron and Arnaud Dandieu entitled 'Back to Flesh and Blood'. In this the authors reject both Marxist and capitalist responses to the economic crisis of Europe. They are sceptical about the politics of the modern world: 'the tardy fruits of democracy are nothing more than doubtful compensations for the all-invading tyranny of industrialization'.[10] The readers of the

Criterion are invited to collaborate in the intellectual construction of *l'ordre nouveau*. A 'commentary' of 1934 indicated the extent to which Aron and Dandieu enjoyed Eliot's support:

> The effort of some of the younger men of letters in Paris (*Esprit*, *L'Ordre Nouveau*, *L'Homme Nouveau*) shows a valuable determination not to surrender individuality to any of the prevailing tendencies of the hour, at the same time that they avoid the Liberalism that still practises its shrill choruses in England. We hope to keep in touch with such current thought in France, and present it from time to time to our readers.[11]

We may now turn to the three methods employed by the *Criterion* in order to introduce aspects of French culture to the English reading public. The first was the presentation of modern French writing in English translation. A noteworthy example was the publication in April 1924 of an excerpt from the Scott Moncrieff version of Proust. However, perhaps surprisingly, the *Criterion* did not really give prominence to the translations of work by leading French writers. A second method was contact with literary activity in France through the chronicles and the reviews. The review section included a regular assessment of the French periodical press. Often this amounted either to a list of periodicals received or to a summary of contents. However, the significance of the reviews of the French literary press for Eliot's overall design should not be underestimated. Merely by mentioning the names of the French intellectuals most active in the periodical press Eliot was fulfilling an important editorial objective, the fostering of cultural exchange between England and France. Furthermore, tangible links were forged with European editors: in 1929 a literary prize was founded with the aim of publishing the winner's work simultaneously in different countries. For Eliot such international cultural exchange was of the greatest value. In his essay 'The Unity of European Culture' he writes,

> I tried to establish relations with those literary periodicals abroad, the aims of which corresponded most nearly to my own . . . These connexions developed very satisfactorily, and it was no fault of any of the editors concerned, if they subsequently languished. I am still of the opinion . . . that the existence of such a network of independent reviews, at least one

in every capital in Europe, is necessary, for the transmission of
ideas . . . while they are still fresh. . . . Cooperation should
continually stimulate that circulation of influence of thought and
sensibility, between nation and nation in Europe, which ferti-
lises and renovates from abroad the literature of each one of
them.[12]

The *Nouvelle revue française*, the *Mercure de France* and *Europe* all
received regular notices in the *Criterion*. Readers were kept informed of the contents of the *Nouvelle revue française* and an element of comment was offered. Whether this always served the aim
of encouraging awareness of France is open to question, since
many of the reviews of French periodicals were written in great
haste or betrayed an ironic detachment from their subject. Hasty
generalisations abound, based on little concrete evidence. Having
alerted us to the publication by the *Nouvelle revue française* of
excerpts from Benda's *Fin de l'éternel* and some pages by Gide on
Valéry, the poet and translator F. S. Flint immediately drew a
conclusion of more general import:

> There is something dry, *sec*, about intelligent French writing
> nowadays. The young and the older men are analysing life, the
> world, their sensations, in the spirit of *Adolphe*, with an added
> bitterness and keenness from the war and an additional compli-
> cation from modern physics, metaphysics and psychology. The
> brain wearies of their logic. The world is not logical.[13.]

As far as reference to the *Nouvelle revue française* is concerned, the
reader cannot fail to sense the veiled resentment felt by Eliot's
reviewers at the achievement of the French journal. However, this
point should not be exaggerated. More often than not the *Criterion*
praises the quality of the contents of the *Nouvelle revue française*.
Criticism is much more frequently addressed to the *Mercure de
France*: no originality, mediocre fiction, no fresh talent. Even
greater hostility is reserved for *Europe*. On its first publication in
1923 it was greeted coolly with a deprecatory reference to it as
standing 'very decidedly to the "left" in political thought'.[14] Eliot's
journal ignored the vitality and the cosmopolitanism of *Europe*.
Romain Rolland's growing sympathy with Russia was reported
with childish glee, and *Europe*'s anti-imperialist articles were dismissed not only by the periodicals reviewer but by the editor as

well. *Europe* could be appreciated as the organ of pacifist intellectuals, but as such, it was felt, it should concern itself with France alone. The *Criterion* deals sarcastically with *Europe*'s defence of pacifism and anti-imperialism. *Europe* sensed the true importance of these causes; the *Criterion* did not. It praised the *Mercure de France* for having 'the good sense to keep clear of vociferous politics'.[15] The difficulty was that the crucial questions facing French intellectuals in the 1930s were essentially political. Eliot and the *Criterion* sought to ignore this as far as was possible and by so doing repudiated the review's original intentions of informing readers about intellectual activity in France.

We can now turn to the subject of book-reviewing in the *Criterion*. It would be tedious to detail the full extent of this activity, which accounted for some 600 pages a year. In the French field the journal published reviews of both primary and secondary material, much of the latter emanating from England. Three French writers received repeated review: Cocteau, Gide and Proust. The *Criterion* always found Cocteau difficult to situate. The eclectic nature of his creative output met with considerable resistance; his poetry and plays were ambivalently received; his art was wholeheartedly rejected. Gide met with prudish euphemism. None of his several reviewers was able to divorce Gide's writing from his homosexuality. It was held that this, together with his Protestant upbringing and the influence of Nietzsche and Dostoevsky, accounted for his view of the world. A work such as *Les Faux-monnayeurs* could be adduced as evidence that the 1920s constituted 'one of the nastiest decades in the history of literature'.[16] A critical article on Proust by Ernst Robert Curtius appeared in April 1924 and was followed in the next issue by an excerpt entitled 'The Death of Albertine'. Later reviewers were happier with reminiscences and anecdotes about Proust. When Beckett's *Proust* appeared, it was met with incomprehension.

The chronicles published in the *Criterion* often contain material relating to French culture. Here three areas of interest present themselves: an enduring conflict with some of the tendencies of modernism; a quest to establish the essentially French nature of certain aspects of intellectual activity; and an attempt to come to terms with the increasing involvement in politics shown by French intellectuals during the period 1922–39. An example of the somewhat unsatisfactory attempts to define Frenchness is provided by Roger Hinks's piece entitled 'Art Chronicle: Frenchness'. Hinks draws on Clive Bell's *An Account of French Painting* in order to put forward an interpretation of the development of French art since the Renaissance. Art is viewed as expressing national characteristics. In the 'dull and showy' canvases of Henner and Bouguereau, Hinks manages to discern 'the weakness of the French temperament, its calculating voluptuousness, its materialism, its inability to sustain from within the grand heroic mannner'. In addition we are provided with a detailed description of the French national temperament. The Frenchman, we are told, loves the good things in life in a reasonable, moderate and serious manner:

> [The Frenchman] is free, on the whole, from the passionate excesses of the inflammable southern nature and still more immune from the fantastic and neurasthenic disorders which afflict the northern imagination. He is human, sensible, and clear-headed. He knows exactly what he wants and he wants exactly what he can find in the world immediately around him. Viewed from the outside with an unsympathetic eye, there is something a little parochial about this complacent preoccupation with small profits and quick returns. But this mediocrity, called golden by the ancient sages, is despised today by those who do not happen to be French, mainly because they have lost the art of animating it with taste, reasonableness, sense and manners.[17]

Contributors to the chronicles viewed innovation in the arts with scepticism. There are exceptions – Zoë Hawley responds with enthusiasm to new ideas in the French theatre and ballet – but the general mood remained one of suspicion. There was an awareness of change in the arts in the *Criterion*, as when Walter Hanks Shaw discusses 'Cinema and Ballet in Paris', but what was lacking was a rigorous analysis of the need for new forms of artistic expression. However, while in the 1920s chronicle-writers gave a cautious welcome to some developments in the arts, by 1931, in common with other subjects treated in the review, modernist tendencies were received with hostility. In 1931 Hinks contributed a piece entitled 'Variations on a theme by Valéry' in which he deplored the emphasis which the twentieth century placed on performance. Modern art struck Hinks as both unsatisfactory and unnecessary: 'It is thin and unreal and lifeless, uninvited and unwelcome: an embarrassing intrusion. It comes without credentials, and if it disappeared, its departure would pass unnoticed.'[18] The *Criterion* also used its chronicles to keep abreast of current French writing and thus to some extent duplicated the function of the reviews. The chronicles could, however, introduce writing which had not appeared in translation either because of its narrow interest or because it had only just appeared in French. Moreover, the chronicles drew on periodicals which were not usually mentioned. In this way Drieu la Rochelle received early recognition. What impressed the chroniclers was the sheer amount of writing going on in France; this, however, did not mean that they judged that writing sympathetically. The chroniclers informed their readers of the increasing popularity of the *essai* form in France and noted the emergence of writers more concerned with Europe's underlying spiritual malaise than with the problems posed by the economic crisis. One such critic who often turned his attention to France was Montgomery Belgion. He was a conservative who looked with favour on the ideas of Massis, Aron and Dandieu. Unhappy with the direction taken by the French novel in the 1930s, he accused writers of turning to bad language, sex and violence in their frantic attempts to inject an element of novelty into their work. In a piece contributed in 1934 Belgion pointed to the increasing politicisation of writing in France. He alluded to the *roman populiste* but concentrated his attention on Céline's *Voyage au bout de la nuit*. For Belgion, Céline's novel was a success in France because it reflected the temper of the times: young people in France felt bitter and were disillusioned with existing forms of government and social organisation. Belgion clearly found Céline the most congenial among contemporary French writers and in a later issue he commented on his *Bagatelles pour un massacre*. Here, in a remarkably disingenuous passage, he described Céline's work as 'a colossal diatribe against the Jews, so dithyrambic, excessive, and in its allegations unsubstantiated, as to seem to hold up a recent recrudescence of antisemitism in France to a devastating ridicule'.[19] Once again the political naïvety of the *Criterion* was revealed. After *Kristallnacht* how could any journal with pretensions to seriousness even mention Céline's publication without making reference to the political condition of Europe in 1939?

It was ironic that the *Criterion* had entrusted the important task of keeping its readership in touch with France to a critic such as Belgion whose general attitude was one of antipathy. In such circumstances there was little hope of the review ever fulfilling its aim of presenting French culture to an English audience. Assessing the *Criterion* some ten years after it had closed, Eliot readily admitted that it had failed 'of its purpose several years before events brought it to an end'. He attributed this failure to what he called 'the gradual closing of the mental frontiers in Europe'. European creativity had been arrested by the 'cultural autarky' which inevitably followed political and economic 'autarky'. As it became more difficult for the review to secure work from Germany and Italy, the editor had to rely more on England and France, and this contributed to the review's decline. But it was the politicisation of intellectual life in France which alienated Eliot; his conviction was that 'a universal concern with politics does not unite, it divides'. Eliot claimed that the *Criterion* had 'a definite character and cohesion, although its contributors were men holding the most diverse political, social and religious views'.[20] However, the review's treatment of French culture suggests that this cohesion derived more from the fact that the contributors held very closely related views. Eliot talked of the *Criterion's* openness of mind to new ideas, but very many of the new ideas coming from France were rejected with derision or undermined by sarcasm. Work by right-wing French authors received attention in the *Criterion*; work by writers on the left, however, was largely ignored, since it was perceived as being essentially political. Sometimes the review adopted a lofty stance, disdaining all attempts at seeking political solutions. Eliot claimed that his contributors shared 'an interest, a delight, in ideas for their own sake, in the free play of intellect'.[21] Yet the *Criterion* chose to ignore whole areas of French cultural activity. As Ezra Pound put it, 'one cannot indulge continually in a diet of dead crow without it tainting the breath'. In Pound's opinion the review was preoccupied with 'dead and moribund writing'.[22] Nevertheless the review enjoyed great prestige in both English and European literary circles, and here Eliot's personal stature as one of the leading poets writing in English was certainly a major factor in its success. On the other hand, Eliot's intellectual position was also a significant factor in its final failure and this was a matter he underestimated in his retrospective assessment of the journal. Ironically, it was through its presentation of French culture that the *Criterion* contributed to that 'gradual closing of the mental frontiers of Europe' which Eliot himself so vigorously deplored.[23]

NOTES

1. Paul Fussell, *Abroad: British Literary Travelling Between the Wars* (Oxford: Oxford University Press, 1982) p. 10.
2. Quoted ibid.
3. Other reviews of note were *Art and Letters* (1917–20), *Contemporary Poetry and Prose* (1936–7) and *Babel* (1940).
4. T. S. Eliot, 'The Unity of European Culture', published as an appendix to *Notes towards the Definition of Culture* (London: Faber, 1969) p. 113.
5. T. S. Eliot, 'The *Action Française*, M. Maurras and Mr Ward', *Criterion*, 7 (March 1928) 195–203 (quotation from p. 196).
6. Stephen Spender, *Eliot* (London: Fontana, 1982) pp. 216–18.
7. Leo Ward, '*L'Action Française*: a Reply to Mr Eliot', *Criterion*, 7 (June 1928) 364–72.
8. Spender, *Eliot*, pp. 224–5.
9. T. S. Eliot, 'The Literature of Fascism', *Criterion*, 8 (Dec 1928) 280–90 (quotation from p. 288).
10. Robert Aron and Arnaud Dandieu, 'Back to Flesh and Blood', *Criterion*, 12 (Jan 1933) 185–99 (quotation from p. 187).
11. T. S. Eliot, 'A Commentary', *Criterion*, 13 (Apr 1934) 451–4 (quotation from p. 454).
12. Eliot, 'The Unity of European Culture', *Notes towards the Definition of Culture*, p. 116.
13. F. S. Flint, 'French Periodicals', *Criterion*, 8 (Dec 1928) 373–6 (quotation from p. 375).
14. R. A., 'French Periodicals', *Criterion*, 1 (July 1923) 423–4.
15. Charles K. Colhoun, 'French Periodicals', *Criterion*, 14 (Oct 1934) 175–9 (quotation from p. 177).
16. T. McG., reviewing Léon Pierre-Quint, *Andre Gide: sa vie, son œuvre* (Paris: Stock, 1934), in *Criterion* 13 (July 1934) 707–8.
17. Roger Hinks, 'Art Chronicle: Frenchness', *Criterion*, 11 (Apr 1932) 490–6 (quotation from p. 490).
18. Roger Hinks, 'Art Chronicle: Variations on a theme by Valéry', *Criterion*, 10 (Oct 1930) 315–21 (quotation from p. 318).
19. Montgomery Belgion, 'French Chronicle', *Criterion*, 18 (Jan 1939) 297–311 (quotation from p. 307).
20. Eliot, 'The Unity of European Culture', *Notes towards the Definition of Culture*, p. 117.
21. Ibid., p. 118.
22. Quoted in Ian Hamilton, *The Little Magazines* (London: Weidenfeld and Nicolson, 1976) p. 79.
23. Eliot, 'The Unity of European Culture', *Notes towards the Definition of Culture*, p. 116.

8

The Decline and Fall of Existentialism

COLIN WILSON

In his biography of Camus, Herbert Lottman tells an amusing story of how Camus, Sartre and Simone de Beauvoir spent a drunken evening in various bistros on the Left Bank. As the dawn was breaking, Sartre and Camus walked back across a bridge over the Seine, and Sartre commented, 'To think that in a few hours I'm going to talk about the writer's responsibility [at the Sorbonne].'[1]

The year was 1946, and Sartre and Camus were probably the most famous writers in France – perhaps in Europe. Both had risked their lives by working for the Resistance during the war; Camus was the editor of the Resistance newspaper *Combat*. One of his last editorials for *Combat* was entitled 'La Nuit de la verité' (25 Aug 1944); it was written as the Germans were being driven out of Paris, and it began, 'While the bullets of freedom are still whistling throughout the city, the cannon of the liberation are entering the gates of Paris amidst shouts and flowers. . . . The night is worth a world; it is the night of truth.'[2] And this helps to explain why Camus and Sartre achieved such dazzling heights of celebrity in the immediate post-war period: they were regarded as spokesmen of intellectual truth; they had become the conscience of France.

Hence Sartre's ironical remark about talking about the responsibility of the writer. He was aware of the gap that exists between the intellectual and the private man. Camus had the same thing in mind when he sighed, 'If we could write the truth!'[3] It was not – precisely – that there was some element of hypocrisy about lecturing the enthusiastic young students about the writer's responsibility; only that it meant presenting oneself as something far more abstract, far less human, than the living reality.

The point is underlined if we turn to Simone de Beauvoir's novel *Les Mandarins* (1954) – a description of Paris in the post-war years. Its two central characters are thinly disguised portraits of Sartre

135

and Camus. A stifling cloud of boredom hangs over the novel. Its characters sit around in bistros and drink and smoke too much, or crawl in and out of one another's beds like characters in a TV soap opera. What had happened to the 'night of truth?' Camus had written, '[Paris] is bursting with all the fires of hope and suffering, it has the flame of lucid courage and all the glow, not only of liberation, but of tomorrow's liberty.'[4] *Les Mandarins* makes it clear that this was pure wishful thinking.

Which is, of course, precisely what existentialism is all about. Kierkegaard had expressed it for the first time in the 1840s. Philosophy is an attempt to get at some generalised truth about the universe. But the moment the philosopher begins to generalise he immediately loses sight of the most essential element of the truth: the reality of the living individual. This is why Kierkegaard rejected the most widely acclaimed philosophical synthesis of his day, Hegel's system. Yet he rejected it to no purpose, for the philosophical writings of Kierkegaard – in particular, the immense *Concluding Unscientific Postscript* – are in no sense a valid alternative to Hegel. They amount to the repeated injunction, 'Don't forget the individual!' And, if European philosophers had felt obliged to take him seriously, they would all have blown out their brains. For philosophy, like statistics, *has* to begin by forgetting the individual. Kierkegaard's philosophical journey ended in a cul-de-sac – the same cul-de-sac that Sartre and Camus wandered into a century later. (Even their timing was precise – the *Concluding Unscientific Postscript* appeared in 1846, while the drunken evening described by Lottman took place in 1946.)

If we wish to understand the story behind the decline and fall of French existentialism, we might choose the year 1930 as a convenient starting-point, for it was the year in which the twenty-nine-year-old André Malraux published his novel *La Voie royale*. For a man whose experiences in China had already led to a commitment to communism, it is a strangely ambiguous novel. It concerns two European adventurers who search for art treasures in deserted temples along China's Royal Way. So long as they are seeking for treasure – during the first part of the novel – there are no problems; their goal endows them with a sense of direction and purpose. But once they have found the treasure, and are deserted by their helpers, the adventurers begin to experience a curious sense of futility. The Cambodian jungle has upon them the same demoralising effect as the African jungle had on Conrad's Kurtz, the hero of *Heart of Darkness*. Yet they are sustained by the thought of another man, Grabot, a fellow adventurer who has already vanished into the jungle: they feel that *he* possesses the strength to defy the universe. Yet, when they eventually find him, he has been captured by savages, blinded and tethered to a grindstone. Asked what happened, Grabot replies, 'Nothing.' He has also been destroyed by the sense of meaninglessness.

Kierkegaard had given expression to the same problem in his short novel *Repetition*:

> One sticks a finger into the ground to smell what country one is in; I stick my finger into the world – it has no smell. Where am I? . . . Who am I? How did I get into the world? Why was I not asked about it? . . . And if I am compelled to be involved, where is the manager – I have something to say about this.[5]

La Voie royale was not a particularly successful novel; it was *La Condition humaine* of 1933 that made Malraux's reputation, and also made him one of the most influential figures in French intellectual life in the 1930s. *La Condition humaine* is basically the story of the abortive attempt by Russian-inspired Communists to take over Shanghai in 1927, and their betrayal by Chiang Kai-shek. In a sense, it repeats the pattern of *La Voie royale*. While they are inspired by their determination to seize Shanghai, the central characters are magnificent. As soon as they are successful, they become the victims of their own inner weakness, and are destroyed. But Malraux ends the book on a note of uplift; in spite of this defeat, the quiet work of revolution has already begun again, and one day it will undoubtedly triumph.

What excited Malraux's contemporaries – and these included the young Sartre and Simone de Beauvoir – was not the social message but the dramatic flow of the action. Purely as a political thriller, *La Condition humaine* is a remarkable *tour de force*. The opening is deservedly famous – as the Chinese revolutionary Chen stands above a sleeping man, prepared to kill him for the sake of a document authorising the delivery of arms. 'Should Chen try lifting up the mosquito-net? Or should he strike through it?'[6] It is difficult to think of another novel that opens with such brutal immediacy. And, after keeping the reader on tenterhooks for three pages, Malraux eventually despatches the sleeper 'with a blow hard enough to pierce a plank'.[7] Then the action moves on, telling its story of violent revolution and betrayal with a cool, cinematic efficiency that is far more frightening than any attempt to make the blood run cold. Malraux may well have learned the technique from Hemingway's *A Farewell to Arms*, which had appeared four years earlier. It consists in describing events that possess a powerful emotional impact with clinical detachment, as though the author is determined to preserve total moral neutrality (a technique known in commerce as 'the soft sell') – the result, of course, being to involve the reader twice as deeply. The technique has only one minor disadvantage. To operate at maximum efficiency, it needs to describe events that take the reader's breath away. In Malraux's earlier novel *Les Conquérants* – again about the Chinese Revolution – one of the most effective scenes is a description of how the hero reaches out to close the eyes of a murdered friend, who has been left propped upright by the terrorists who killed him, and realises that the killers have removed his eyelids. In *La Condition humaine* everyone recalls the horrific scene in which prisoners are thrown alive into the furnace of a locomotive.

The problem is that, when the writer uses the same technique to describe everyday events, the result is likely to become flat and boring; the writer is obliged to look around continually for new shock effects. Malraux would encounter this problem in *L'Espoir*, and Hemingway in *For Whom the Bell Tolls*. But in *La Condition humaine* and *A Farewell to Arms* violence and revolution provide the technique with the perfect subject. As a work of art, *La Condition humaine* has two other tremendous advantages, both of which seem to lend it additional authenticity: its exotic setting, and its 'political seriousness'. I place 'political seriousness' in quotes because many of Malraux's fellow writers came to feel that he was less serious than he pretended; Lottman quotes a fellow writer of those years who later 'confided that Malraux was, quite simply, devoid of political concerns. He was verbal, without any real interest in ideas.'[8]

On 6 February 1934, France came close to revolution. A right-wing mob tried to storm the French parliament building, inspired by various right-wing extremist movements, such as L'Action Française. At the same time, Communists staged a protest against capitalism. In the clash, seventeen people were killed and more than 2000 were injured. The Radical Socialist prime minister Daladier resigned. It looked as if France was about to follow Italy and Germany into fascism. The result was an immediate alliance of the leftists, including Communists. The list of writers and artists who supported this leftist cause was impressive, including André Gide, Romain Rolland, Henri Barbusse, Louis Aragon, André Breton, Arthur Koestler, Malraux, Paul Nizan and Pablo Picasso. (Camus became a member of the Communist Party at this time, but he was still a twenty-one-year-old student in Algeria.) Sartre, oddly enough, was not among them, although Nizan was one of his closest friends; he was teaching in a *lycée* in Le Havre – although he succeeded in spending a great deal of time in Paris. Sartre and his close friend Simone de Beauvoir loathed the bourgeoisie and were pacifists, but were not active supporters of the Left. In June 1935, the Russians sponsored a congress of writers and intellectuals, which lasted for five days and had an audience of 3000 people; Pasternak and Babel were the Russian literary stars, and other speakers included Brecht, Robert Musil, E. M. Forster, Julien Benda – and, of course, Malraux and Gide (who was chairman). It was a tremendous success; but Lottman underlines the negative side of all this political activity when he observes (in *The Left Bank*) that no great literary work was produced in France during these 'political years'.

Malraux himself faded out as an artist. *Temps du mépris* appeared just before the writers' congress, but was generally agreed to be less than artistically satisfactory. It is, in fact, a propaganda novel about a Czech Communist who is arrested and tortured by the Nazis, but who is freed when another man claims his identity. Malraux obviously knows very little about German prisons, and has not taken the trouble to find out. In his preface he defends the book by asserting that it belongs to the 'passionate' tradition of Aeschylus and Dostoevsky rather than the detached tradition of Flaubert. This is disingenuous; what is wrong with *Temps du mépris* is that it is not any kind of work of art; it is journalism. Its real importance in literary history is that it probably inspired Sartre's story 'Le Mur' and Koestler's *Darkness at Noon*.

When the Spanish Civil War broke out, Malraux became commander of a squadron of planes, and wrote his largest novel, *L'Espoir* (1938), in six months. Here the technique is even more cinematic than in *La Condition humaine* (in fact, it was turned into a film almost immediately), and the reader soon becomes aware of the drawbacks of the 'cinematic novel'. It is flat, two-dimensional, like a documentary film. Chapter after chapter begins with flat statements: 'The enemy were retreating on Segovia', 'The Italians were counter-attacking towards Brihuega'; 'The Government had moved from Madrid to Valencia.'⁹ The most effective moments, as usual, are moments of violence. Malraux is particularly fond of describing men struggling against problem after problem, obstacle after obstacle. But, although the novel is undoubtedly a *tour de force* of a kind, it eventually becomes monotonous and depressing. The realism and the political commitment (whether real or apparent) that gave *La Condition humaine* its feeling of authenticity have here become mechanical gestures; one feels that Malraux has cried wolf far too often. Even the attempt to end the book on a note of uplift, with the hero on his way to a Beethoven concert, fails to carry conviction. It becomes clear that Malraux's problem is – as his unnamed contemporary remarked – that he is devoid of any interest in ideas. This immense mass of documentary material produces an effect of soullessness, as though men have no control over a destiny of futile violence.

What *L'Espoir* seems to demonstrate is the bankruptcy of the 'existentialist' ideal. The book claims to be about human existence, the human condition; it attempts to make some general statement by way of focusing relentlessly on individuals and their problems. The result is that it totally fails to make any general statement, or to give the reader that overall sense of meaning that he derives from a genuine work of art – such as a Beethoven symphony. In a sense, the book is a fake. It seems to be making the claim, 'This is not fiction; it is reality. This material has not been selected for artistic effect. It is Life. It is Truth.' But every word, every image, has been selected; it is merely masquerading as reality.

But what we can see, above all, is that Malraux is not enough of an artist or a thinker to understand where he has gone wrong. *Les Conquérants* and *La Voie royale* were attempts to dramatise the problem of individual freedom and destiny in political terms. Like Conrad, Malraux was much concerned with the problem of *identity*, and the hero's sense that he lacks any true core of identity. *La Condition humaine* is a masterpiece because it seems to present a solution to this problem. That solution is, in fact, a myth – the myth of left-wing revolutionary action that will 'save' the individual by merging his identity into the greater social whole; and, even before the end of the novel, it is fairly clear that Malraux has lost faith in it. When he tries to repeat the triumph in *Temps du mépris*, the poverty of his material underlines the fact that he has nothing positive to say. The hero is not 'saved' by his escape from his torturers; he finds himself back in a world that is just as confusing, just as ambiguous, as the world of political brainwashing. And in *L'Espoir* it becomes perfectly clear that Malraux's problem is that, in the deepest sense, he has nothing to say. He tries to conceal this by piling up the realistic detail, the obsessive documentation; but the reader never feels he is in the hands of a man who knows exactly where he is going. Someone once said of *War and Peace* that it produces an overall impression like music; this is because Tolstoy moulds his material like a man who knows his own mind. Malraux gives the impression of being a slave of his material. The attempt at an 'existentialist' work of art ends by somehow negating its own premisses.

Malraux himself seems to have recognised that he had, artistically speaking, reached the end of his tether; although he lived for forty more years – until 1976 – he wrote only one more novel, *Les Noyers d'Altenburg*, and left that unfinished. When Malraux became De Gaulle's minister of culture, most of his old left-wing colleagues felt that he had virtually become a fascist.

The significance of Malraux lies not so much in his novels as in the immense influence he exercised on a whole generation. It is only necessary to glance at almost any page in Sartre's three-volume novel *Les Chemins de la liberté* to recognise the influence of Malraux; it can also be detected in Hemingway, Koestler, Camus, even Orwell. His political influence on his contemporaries was enormous, and has been documented in Lottman's *The Left Bank*. But his real significance was in making his contemporaries aware that literature could be fashioned out of politics. In the 1930s, *La Condition humaine* seemed to be as much the authentic voice of the new generation as *Ulysses* and *The Waste Land* had been in the previous decade.

Sartre was only four years younger than Malraux; but his development had been far more slow and difficult. Sartre's father, a naval officer, had died shortly after his birth in 1905; his mother returned to Alsace to live with her family. Her father was a language-teacher, a man of passionate and histrionic temperament. Sartre was a sickly child, and was inevitably spoilt; he was also cross-eyed and ugly. He lived in a world of daydreams, and the cinema fed his intense romanticism – his autobiography, *Les Mots* (1964), is an unprecedentedly detailed description of the daydreams of childhood. He began to write as a compensation for loneliness and unhappiness, daydreaming of tremendous fame. His mother's second marriage made him miserable; then he made a remarkable recovery, became a brilliant student at school, and finally, at the age of nineteen, won a place in the Ecole Normale Supérieure, one of Paris's most select educational institutions. After five years there, he did his national service, then went to the Sorbonne. Simone de Beauvoir had become his mistress when he was still in his early twenties, and this undoubtedly did a great deal to improve his self-esteem. At this time, he was writing a novel about a love affair between Nietzsche and Cosima Wagner, called (typically) *Une Défaite*. In 1930 he read Céline's *Voyage au bout de la nuit*, and decided to abandon his highly 'literary' style for something more casual and immediate.

Since his early twenties, Sartre had been sketching out a philosophical novel on a theme he called 'contingency' – the feeling that human beings have no real importance in themselves (as religion maintains) but are totally dependent on their environment. (Sartre had been an atheist since he was about ten.) It is, in fact, precisely what Malraux was writing about in *Les Conquérants* and *La Voie royale* – the feeling that man possesses no real 'inner identity'. We have seen that the theme can be traced back to Conrad's *Heart of Darkness*, in which the Victorian idealist Kurtz is undermined by the futility of life in the jungle, and becomes the worst kind of sensualist. (Maugham's *Rain* is a variation on the same theme; so is Golding's *Lord of the Flies*.)

Everyone is familiar with this feeling; most of us experience it as children in the form of homesickness: that curious feeling of losing one's identity when away from familiar surroundings. When a child is at home, he is quite unaware that his identity depends on his surroundings. So it comes as a shock to be away on holiday – an experience that ought to be entirely delightful – and to feel like a fish out of water. In a child as intelligent and sensitive as Sartre, it clearly engendered a feeling of self-mistrust.

As an oversensitive individual, Sartre was also much preoccupied with the *apparent* strength and independence of other people, and he soon reached the conclusion – perhaps based upon his observation of his rather overpowering grandfather – that such 'strength' is based upon stupidity and self-deception. Every sensitive child who has ever existed has probably felt much the same. (We find it recorded, for example, in the writings of Thomas Mann and Hermann Hesse.) If 'character' is a form of dishonesty or self-deception, then a totally honest man would be a 'man without qualities' (to borrow Musil's phrase). And such a man would recognise that most of us are far more dependent on 'objects' than we realise.

In 1933, Sartre became immensely excited when he heard about the ideas of Edmund Husserl – the philosophical method known as phenomenology. Husserl had stated that, whenever we think we are perceiving something objectively, our perceptions and prejudices are actually distorting it. In order to perceive anything 'without prejudice', we must make a certain act of detachment, which Husserl called the *epoché*. Sartre's friend Raymond Aron told Sartre and Beauvoir about phenomenology over a drink. He pointed to the cocktail glass. 'You see, my dear fellow, if you are a phenomenologist, you can talk about this cocktail and make philosophy out of it!'[10] Beauvoir recalls that Sartre turned pale with emotion. He went into the nearest bookshop and bought a book on Husserl. He was downcast when he discovered a reference to contingency – which he regarded as his own discovery – but decided that Husserl didn't mean quite the same thing after all.

Beauvoir describes how Sartre sketched out the broad principles of Husserlian phenomenology to her in Easter 1935:

> He had always been repelled by the idea of '*la vie intérieure*'; according to him this faculty was wholly eliminated as soon as the rational mind came into existence, which it did by continually leap-frogging over itself towards some specific object. Everything possessed an external situation and actuality: physical objects, statements of truth, emotions, meaning, even the self; it followed that no subjective factor could modify the truth concerning the world as it was presented to our senses.[11]

In short, Sartre, like Malraux, longed to escape the uncertainties and ambiguities of his own inner world; he longed for objective certainty and clarity in the way that a man who has burned his hand longs to hold a piece of ice.

Now the very essence of Husserl's philosophy is the recognition that perception is *intentional*. When I look at something, I am inclined to believe that it walks in through my eyes and imprints itself on my retina. But Husserl showed that this view is naïve. When I look at something, I *fire* my attention at it, like an arrow. If, for example, I go to a picture gallery, and my mind is on something else, then I shall not really 'see' the pictures. Moreover, the more energy and concentration I put into looking *at* them, the more I shall grasp their meaning.

Now, if my attention is like an arrow, this clearly implies that 'I' am the archer. When I speak of 'I', I do not refer to the person who goes under my name, for he changes continually from birth to death. My personality is not 'the real me'. But, according to Husserl, there *is* a 'real me' somewhere inside my head – the 'archer'. He called this 'the transcendental ego'.

Sartre would have none of it. According to him, Husserl had simply failed to grasp his own premisses. 'I' *am* my personality. And, if that means that I do not have any real, permanent existence, then so be it. Sartre expressed these views in his earliest philosophical essay, *La Transcendance de l'ego*, published in 1936.

It was in the February of this year that Sartre had one of the most crucial experiences of his life. He decided to take a mescalin injection, to study its effect on his imagination. The result was disastrous. Sartre had a classic 'bad trip', and hallucinated skeletons and leering faces. He thought he was being followed by an enormous lobster. For some time after this, he became depressed and was afraid that he was going insane. Again and again, he experienced the typical phenomenon of depression, the sense of 'inner collapse', sudden loss of interest in the world, the sense that life is a meaningless repetition of futilities, 'vanity of vanities'. (One might call it the 'Ecclesiastes effect'.) But at least it provided the stimulus to finish the almost-forgotten novel about contingency. He called it *La Nausée* (1938) – the word he appropriated to describe this sudden sense of total contingency, entrapment in a world of objects. The hero, Roquentin, is an adventurer and scholar who is writing a biography of a French diplomat. To write such a work, one must have a feeling that the man's life had some meaning in its historical context. But Roquentin keeps experiencing this sudden appalling sense of futility, the 'Ecclesiastes effect', when his own life and that of his diplomat seem equally meaningless.

What Sartre's position amounts to, of course, is the belief that free will is an illusion. Man is a passive object; he can be acted upon, but he cannot really act. He is merely a witness, an observer, of his own life. He thinks he has free will, as the tide might believe it had free will if it was conscious of its movements; in reality, he is pulled into activities by forces outside himself. Roquentin's experiences of 'nausea' give him a glimpse of his own nonentity.

How could anyone accept such an obviously nonsensical position? In the case of various philosophers of the nineteenth century, it came about by pursuing the arguments of scientific rationalism to their logical conclusion. But, in the case of Sartre, it was clearly an expression of a fundamental craving to escape the messy, personal world of self-doubt and self-contempt, and to take his stand on a kind of Hegelianism: the real is the rational and the rational is the real. All human beings are divided by passion and reason; we all have to learn, to some extent, to overrule our emotions in favour of what we *know* to be true. But few of us feel such a painful craving for reason that we want to deny the validity of all emotion, all feeling, everything that springs from personality.

Sartre's position is, in fact, an absurdity. Husserl says that perception is intentional, fired like an arrow at its object – and that therefore, there must be an archer. Sartre replies that our perceptions are not fired like an arrow, but *pulled*, like the tides. There is no 'real you'.

But this fails to explain the most obvious fact about perception: that we can vary its intensity at will. I may read a book so half-heartedly that I hardly take in a word; but I can *decide* to focus my full attention, and grasp far more of its significance. If our 'gaze' is an arrow fired at its object, then *meaning* depends on how far you pull back the bowstring. Or, to use another image, if our gaze is a spear thrown at an object, then meaning depends on how hard you choose to throw it. In any case, the meaning is, to some extent, within our control. This is a basic part of our experience of consciousness. If, for example, we are having some enjoyable experience – anything from sex to eating a good dinner – we are aware that we possess the power to vary its intensity by an act of focusing (intentionality). If I eat my dinner while reading a novel, I shall simply not enjoy it as much as when I give it my full attention. According to Sartre, consciousness possesses no such power. Clearly, there is something wrong with his reasoning.

We must be quite clear about this. *La Nausée* is not an intellectual presentation of existentialism, like Kierkegaard's *Concluding Unscientific Postscript*. It does not ask the question, 'Is an existential system possible?' Like Malraux's novels, it is an 'instinctive' presentation of the existential problem. Roquentin examines his life through a magnifying glass, finds each detail meaningless ('There are no adventures'), and decides that, even if he could look at it from a divine standpoint, it would still be meaningless.[12] So he has, in effect, decided that an existential system is impossible.

Or almost. Towards the end of the book, he contradicts himself. When Roquentin listens to a record of a negress singing 'Some of these Days', he is overwhelmed by a sense of meaning – immediate (existential) meaning. And he wonders whether it might not be possible for him to create some work that would have the same effect on other people – a novel, perhaps. So the experience of the gramophone record convinces him that there *is* meaning after all. But perhaps he is deceiving himself. On this note of ambiguity, Sartre ends the book.

It is, of course, basically a question about *freedom*. The argument of *La Nausée* is that people only think they are free; in reality, their freedom is limited by objects as a train's freedom is limited by railway lines. Without freedom, of course, there can be no morality, for morality is a belief about what we should do with our freedom; a train cannot be moral or immoral. 'Some of these Days' makes Roquentin feel that perhaps freedom *does* exist after all. Yet Sartre's whole philosophy, as developed in works such as *La Transcendance de l'ego*, *Esquisse d'une théorie des émotions* and *L'Imaginaire*, flatly denies this. And his major philosophical work, *L'Etre et le néant* (1943), is a protracted demonstration that our feelings are all delusions, that it is meaningless that we live and meaningless that we die.[13]

But by the time *L'Etre et le néant* appeared, Sartre was already doing his best to retreat from this nihilistic position. The Germans had occupied Paris, and Sartre was in the Resistance. Clearly, it was an absurdity to say that freedom was a delusion and morality an impossibility. Besides, as Sartre later remarked in an article on the Resistance, 'We were never more free than under the German occupation.' The threat of being arrested and shot at any moment created a deep sense of the meaning of freedom, just as Nazi propaganda and censorship made Sartre feel that thinking was really worthwhile, because 'each accurate thought was a victory'.[14]

By 1943, Sartre's position as the most interesting member of the younger generation was already being challenged by a young newcomer, Albert Camus, eight years Sartre's junior. Camus had been much influenced by *La Nausée*, and by Sartre's concept of 'the absurd' (another name for contingency). Camus had arrived at an 'instinctive existentialism' by a quite different route from Sartre. Brought up in Algiers in the household of a dominant grandmother, Camus was told at seventeen that he had consumption and had not long to live. The result was that he began 'living in the present', appreciating every moment of his life in the sun-drenched Mediterranean. He rejected religion and abstract philosophical systems, not because he saw life as meaningless and boring, but because he saw immediate reality as so overwhelmingly fascinating. Although he recovered from the consumption, the vision never left him. He joined the Communist Party, dramatised Malraux's *Temps du mépris*, broke with the Communists (who denounced him as a Trotskyite) and became a journalist. When the war came, he moved to Paris. In 1942, his first two books appeared: *Le Mythe de Sisyphe*, a grim little meditation on suicide and 'absurdity', and *L'Etranger*, which might be regarded as Camus's own version of *La Nausée*. The hero, Meursault, is a man who lives contentedly in the present like a lizard basking in the sun. Religion and morality seem to him self-evidently meaningless because they attempt to remove from man's shoulders the weight of his own life.

But Meursault's honesty backfires. He accidentally kills an Arab in a shooting, and his inability to shed tears of remorse or put on a show of injured innocence costs him his life. Camus always had a curiously fatalistic streak, reminiscent of Thomas Hardy, an obscure conviction that the gods enjoy doing us down. It is illustrated by an anecdote – included in *L'Etranger* and reworked in the play *Le Malentendu* – about a sailor who returns home to his poverty-stricken family after many years, with a fortune in his pocket, but decides not to reveal his identity until the next morning; in the night, his family murder him for his money. In one breath, Camus is telling us that the universe is meaningless; in the next, that it is actively malevolent. Like Sartre, he has obviously failed to think out his position.

Le Mythe de Sisyphe again insists that the basic reality of life is meaninglessness. Only a kind of blindness allows us to live our repetitive lives without succumbing to despair. Some men 'wake up' to the meaninglessness; as they plod through their dreary lives they ask 'why?': 'one day the "why" arises and everything begins in that weariness tinged with amazement'.[15] Once this vision of futility has been clearly recognised, it can never be forgotten; we keep glimpsing 'the absurd' under the face of everyday life – for example, watching a man in a telephone booth, his face expressing all kinds of emotions while his voice remains inaudible.

It is this image that gives the game away. If a man in a telephone booth seems absurd, it is because some essential element of *meaning* – the sound – has been *removed*. A lip-reader would not experience the sense of absurdity under these circumstances because he would be capable of *penetrating deeper into the reality* of what is going on. This ability to 'penetrate deeper' is what Husserl meant by intentionality. Sartre's nausea and Camus's absurdity are – to put it crudely – a form of mental feebleness. Maupassant has a story about a man who has pursued a girl for a long time; finally, he lures her into his room and persuades her to undress. As she does so, he sees a patch of black hair on her back, and it completely 'turns him off', so he becomes impotent. His sexual intentionality has been destroyed; the arrow falls feebly out of the bow at the feet of the archer. But it would obviously be absurd to regard this 'impotent' consciousness as somehow deeper, truer, than the desire it has replaced; it is merely weaker.

All of us are prone to experiences in which some intended act suddenly seems futile. It happens more to children than to adults, more to undisciplined people than to disciplined ones, more to neurotic weaklings than to people who know their own mind. The 'Ecclesiastes effect' is not a glimpse of a profounder reality; it is a confidence trick played on us by our emotions. The belief that 'nausea' is a glimpse of 'truth' is a schoolboy howler.

During the war, neither Sartre nor Camus were under any necessity to think out their philosophical position to its logical conclusion. Resisting the Germans provided them with a sense of purpose. But – as we have seen – the end of the war brought them once again face to face with this fundamental problem. Was life really meaningless and absurd? If so, it made no real difference that the Germans had been defeated. And both could recognise the absurdity of this position. In fact, their philosophy of meaninglessness left them in a thoroughly vulnerable position. There is an amusing story of Sartre lecturing at the Sorbonne and telling his audience, 'You are free! Dare to make use of your freedom!' The students were deeply inspired. But, when some of them asked Sartre, 'What should we *do* with our freedom?' and he replied, 'Anything you like', their enthusiasm evaporated.

Sartre and Camus were now regarded as the intellectual spokes-men of their generation. Simone de Beauvoir describes the result in *Les Mandarins*. Both Camus and Sartre became successful play-wrights. And in their discussions they returned again and again to the question of 'commitment' to communism. Having decided – with some reluctance – that man *is* free, Sartre now found himself facing the same problem as his students. How should he use his freedom? Sartre's decision was, perhaps, inevitable. Ever since childhood, one of his strongest emotions had been hatred of the bourgeoisie. In the 1930s, he had been unable to commit himself to communism because he felt that this would be a form of self-deception (*mauvaise-foi*). Now he seems to have decided that com-munism was the only belief into which he could pour all his energy of conviction.

The long novel *Les Chemins de la liberté* (1945–7) shows us the circuitous route by which he came to this conviction. Its hero, Mathieu Delarue, is a schoolmaster who lacks any form of deep conviction, but who, like his creator, detests the bourgeoisie. He envies his friend Brunet – a Communist – his intellectual convic-tion; but Mathieu's intelligence is too balanced and too active to swallow any 'ism'. He spends most of the first volume, *L'Age de raison*, in pursuit of the money to enable his mistress to have an abortion. He feels trapped in triviality, yet unable to surrender himself to any 'greater purpose'.

The second and third volumes, *Le Sursis* and *La Mort dans l'âme* describe the coming of war, the political betrayal of Munich. But this faced Sartre with the problem of how to describe European events without taking the position of a 'god-like' narrator. He had always believed – as a good existentialist – that events must be shown through the eyes of individuals, and in *L'Age de raison* he had succeeded in sticking to this basic rule. But how could be describe the coming of war without sounding like a historian? His solution was to combine the techniques of *La Condition humaine* and the novels of John Dos Passos (whom he had once described as the greatest novelist of the age). The narrative moves without warning from description of what is happening to his leading characters to slices of historical exposition. And the result – as with *L'Espoir* – is practically unreadable. The reader simply loses all sense of conti-nuity, and probably begins to skip through the book in an attempt to get back to the thread of narrative that has captured his interest.

Now it must be clearly understood that this failure is not simply a matter of novelistic technique. It arises – once again – as a result of a false 'existential' philosophy. We have already encountered the problem in Malraux. *La Condition humaine* is a fine novel because Malraux has succeeded in presenting historical events in terms of individuals; we become interested in the individuals, then become aware that there is a bigger, 'overall' meaning. But, when Malraux tries to repeat the trick in *L'Espoir*, he fails to arouse our interest in its characters as individuals, so the book becomes merely a dramatised documentary. Sartre's *La Nausée* focuses on one individual; and, although it has little or no plot, it holds the interest because the reader becomes interested in that individual. *L'Age de raison* focuses on several individuals, but always one at a time, so that we have time to become involved in each one's problems. But that book ends before the outbreak of war. Sartre's problem was how to present historical events as well as individual destinies. He fell into the same trap as Malraux, and turned it into a dramatised documentary. The aim was laudable enough – to present a kind of mosaic, the literary equivalent of pointillism. But we can look at Seurat's *Baigneurs* as a *whole*; with a novel, this is impossible. So once again, the attempt to create an 'existential system' – to create a 'large' sweep of events entirely in terms of individual moments – is a failure. Sartre was sufficiently aware of this to decide to leave the fourth volume unfinished.

But in the fragment of the fourth volume, which appeared in *Les Temps modernes* as 'La Dernière chance', we encounter Mathieu in a German prison camp. His Communist friend Brunet is also there. Mathieu joins an organisation for helping prisoners to escape, and takes part in the execution of a suspected traitor; Brunet thoroughly approves of this conversion to 'commitment' and action. The moral also seems quite clear. If more people like Mathieu had joined with Malraux and his friends in the 1930s, Hitler might have been stopped, and all this would never have happened. (In fact, we now know that, if France had challenged Hitler's occupation of the Rhineland, Hitler would have withdrawn.)

Sartre accepted his own logic, and in his post-war essays made it clear that he was a Marxist. Simone de Beauvoir makes it clear in *Les Mandarins* that there was a great deal of heart-searching, since Sartre had shared the French distrust of the Soviet Union since the Nazi–Soviet pact. But for the remaining three decades of his life – he died in 1980 – Sartre remained a committed leftist.

This 'solution' strikes British and American readers as rather simplistic – not to say downright silly. Our inclination towards democratic politics means that we inevitably think of revolution as a form of extremism that is foreign to common sense. Moreover, anyone who has followed Sartre's philosophical progress from *L'Imaginaire* to *L'Etre et le néant* is bound to feel that his 'solution' is as unacceptable as becoming a born-again Christian. Communism is so obviously *not* the answer to the problems of the central characters of *Les Chemins de la liberté*; they would certainly not feel wildly happy in a Communist state – or even in some ideal Marxist society that had achieved a totally fair distribution of income. Mathieu often talks about his goal as 'salvation', and it is quite clear that he does not mean becoming a proletarian revolutionary; the very idea has a touch of bathos.

However, Sartre decided that he had made his bed, and had better lie on it. Beauvoir's memoirs of his last years – *Adieux* – make it quite plain that he found no real satisfaction in Maoism, and that his involvement with the young comrades cost him a great deal of moral energy. The Sartre of these final years is not a particularly dignified figure. In Beauvoir's portrait, we see him drinking too much, accepting the sexual services of a crowd of female 'groupies', and generally feeling sad and dissatisfied. His autobiography *Les Mots* confesses his sense of failure. 'My retrospective illusions are in pieces. Martyrdom, salvation, immortality: all are crumbling; the building is falling in ruins . . . for about ten years I have been a man who is waking up, cured of a long, bitter-sweet madness . . . and who no longer has any idea of what to do with his life.'[16]

Camus, predictably, chose a different course. For about a decade after the war, he seemed a symbol of literary integrity. In *L'Homme revolté* (1951) he turns his back firmly on all leftist myths and ideologies, and points out that 'revolt' has always ended in tyranny. He dismisses most rebels as 'jejeune' and infantile.[17] The gesture cost him his friendship with Sartre, although it probably contributed to the Nobel Prize he received in 1957; in the same year, he denounced the Soviet occupation of Hungary, comparing it to the Fascist takeover in Spain. Yet, unlike Sartre, he never found a sense of direction. He never committed himself to rightism in the way that Sartre committed himself to leftism. The Nobel Prize led to accusations of selling out to the 'establishment', and these hurt Camus so much that they brought him close to nervous breakdown. In January 1960 he was killed when the car in which he was returning to Paris swerved off the road and struck a tree, hurling him through the rear windscreen; he died instantly. He was forty-six years old, and his death seemed as 'absurd' as that of his own Meursault.

In retrospect, it seems clear that Malraux, Sartre and Camus were all defeated by that problem of creating an 'existential system'. That problem, stated simply, is how the individual can move from individual truths to some general Truth. All three began by rejecting general Truth in its most widely accepted form: religion. All three took the next step into a 'religion of humanity'; yet all three found themselves unable to commit themselves to this religion in a way that would satisfy the emotions. Sartre's cousin Albert Schweitzer had no such problem; but Sartre lacked either the heroic or the saintly temperament. At least Sartre committed himself to a political system. Malraux and Camus – perhaps more honest, perhaps less courageous – simply became uncommitted rightists. French existentialism died with Sartre; but in truth it had eclipsed itself by demonstrating its own absurdity as long ago as 1936, when *L'Espoir* appeared.

Is there any solution to the problem? I personally have never doubted it. To anyone who grasps the true meaning of Husserl's phenomenology, it is almost obvious. If our gaze is a spear thrown towards its object, then meaning depends on how hard you throw it. That is to say, we are in control of meaning. Dr Johnson grasped the same point when he remarked, 'when a man knows he is to be hanged in a fortnight, it concentrates his mind wonderfully.' Sartre himself glimpsed his own version of this solution when he observed that he had never felt so free as under the German occupation, when he was likely to be arrested and shot at any time. The crisis caused a certain *focusing of the will*.

Our problem is that most of us are inclined to carry out this 'focusing' activity quite unconsciously. And we 'defocus' in the same way. This unconscious defocusing causes boredom, the 'Ecclesiastes effect'. The continued crisis of being in the Resistance prevented this unconscious defocusing, and so kept Sartre at a higher level of vitality than usual.

We can see that Sartre, Camus and Malraux made the identical mistake: *they left the mind itself out of account*. In Sartre's case, this was not simply an inability to reason analytically: he deliberately created a philosophy that excluded the mind and free will. Where Sartre *is* to blame is that, when he saw clearly that this philosophy was self-contradictory – it was apparent even in the final pages of

La Nausée, long before the war made him aware that 'Man is free' –
he made no attempt to rethink his ideas; he merely tried to graft his
new doctrine of commitment on to the old philosophy of nihilism.
The result, predictably, was self-contradiction, leading eventually
to philosophical impotence. Maoism, unlike the Nazi occupation,
failed to 'concentrate Sartre's mind wonderfully', and he drifted
into the boredom and dissatisfaction of his last years. But he still
failed to see the obvious conclusion: that, if the answer lies in
'concentrating the mind wonderfully', then the question of *what*
concentrates the mind – leftism, rightism, upsidedownism – is
irrelevant; the answer lies in *the mind itself*.

NOTES

1. Herbert R. Lottman, *Albert Camus: A Biography* (London: Weidenfeld and Nicolson, 1979) p. 404.
2. Albert Camus, 'The Night of Truth', in *Resistance, Rebellion and Death*, tr. Justin O'Brien (London: Hamish Hamilton, 1961) p. 29.
3. Lottman, *Camus*, p. 404.
4. Camus, 'The Blood of Freedom', in *Resistance, Rebellion and Death*, p. 28. First published as 'Le Sang de la liberté' in *Combat*, 24 Aug 1944.
5. Søren Kierkegaard, *Repetition*, tr. Howard and Edna Hong (Princeton, NJ: Princeton University Press, 1983) p. 200.
6. André Malraux, *Man's Estate*, tr. Alastair Macdonald (Harmondsworth, Middx: Penguin, 1961) p. 5.
7. Ibid., p. 7.
8. Herbert R. Lottman, *The Left Bank: Writers, Artists, and Politics from the Popular Front to the Cold War* (London: Heinemann, 1982) p. 99.
9. André Malraux, *Days of Hope*, tr. Stuart Gilbert and Alastair Macdonald (London: Hamish Hamilton, 1968) pp. 345, 417 and 258.
10. Simone de Beauvoir, *The Prime of Life*, tr. Peter Green (Harmondsworth, Middx: Penguin, 1966) p. 135. First published as *La Force de l'âge* 1960.
11. Ibid., p. 187.
12. Jean-Paul Sartre, *Nausea*, tr. Robert Baldick (Harmondsworth, Middx: Penguin, 1965) p. 213.
13. See Jean-Paul Sartre, *Being and Nothingness: An Essay on Phenomenological Ontology*, tr. Hazel E. Barnes (London: Methuen, 1969).
14. Jean-Paul Sartre, 'La République du silence', in *Situations, III* (Paris: Gallimard, 1949) p. 11. First published in *Lettres françaises*, 1944.
15. Albert Camus, *The Myth of Sisyphus*, tr. Justin O'Brien (Harmondsworth, Middx: Penguin, 1975) p. 19.
16. Jean-Paul Sartre, *Words*, tr. Irene Clephane (Harmondsworth, Middx: Penguin, 1967) p. 157.
17. See Albert Camus, *The Rebel*, tr. Anthony Bower (Harmondsworth, Middx: Penguin, 1971).

9

French Film Culture and British Cinema

JILL FORBES

We knew we had an authentic British tradition; we hated it.
Ben Brewster

I taught myself French by reading Cahiers du cinéma.
V. F. Perkins

BAZIN. *En quoi, d'après vous, la médiocrité du cinéma anglais est-elle exemplaire?*
RIVETTE. *Cinéma anglais, c'est-à-dire cinéma de genres sans que ces genres aient une nécessité profonde. D'une part il n'y a pas, comme à l'intérieur du cinéma américain, des genres ayant leur justification propre comme le western, le policier . . . d'autre part, ce n'est pas non plus un cinéma d'auteurs, puisque personne n'a rien à dire. C'est un cinéma boiteux, un cinéma entre deux chaises. Un cinéma purement fondé sur l'offre et la demande. . . .*
(1957)[1]

One is hard put to find, in the whole British cinema, any real 'authors of films', total creators capable of moulding a subject after their own personal vision and of looking at the world and its people with fresh eyes: like a Jean Renoir, a René Clair, a John Ford, an Orson Welles, an Eisenstein, a Dovjenko. The only true 'revelations' of the British cinema since 1945 have either been

154

> *silenced, for all practical purposes, by the hostility of the British film industry or have departed to America.*

Louis Marcorelles (1957)[2]

By the end of the 1950s it was a truth as widely acknowledged in Britain as in France that British cinema was moribund, and it was from that time onwards that film culture in Britain began to take its lead from France. The French influence was felt on film criticism, film theory and, to a degree, on film exhibition and production. It was partial at first but, thanks to the activities of the journals *Movie* and *Screen*, it had become widespread by the middle of the 1970s and was no longer confined to the cinema but embraced the fields of politics, literary criticism and education. However, the French influence was always felt selectively and usually used polemically: as frequently seems to have been the case in Britain,[3] groups of intellectuals exploited France and the French tradition to point up what they most disliked about their own culture and what changes they wished to bring about. This means that the impact of French film culture in Britain cannot be properly understood without some knowledge of the British cinema in the immediate post-war years.[4]

The British film industry was revived by the war. Cinema-going reached a peak and the volume of film production increased. More important, the war permitted the creative fusion of the two domestic traditions of film-making – what Grierson had called the 'working clothes' and the 'knee-breeches' schools. At Ealing ('the Studios with team spirit') Michael Balcon explicitly set out to contribute to the war effort by 'projecting Britain and the British character', and his best-known production, *Passport to Pimlico* (1947), is a good example of the successful, if short-lived, marriage of the documentary and the nostalgic romantic feature film.[5] By 1945 Dilys Powell noted that the prospects for authentically British features were excellent: '[the war] has set the English [*sic*] film on the path in which masterpieces may be created; it has established precisely what was lacking in the English cinema before 1940, a traditional English style'.[6]

The creation of a national cinema, however, posed complex political and economic problems. At the end of the war the central preoccupation of the major European film-producing countries, with the exception of Germany, whose film industry was dismantled by the Allies, was how to strengthen film production in the face of stiffer American competition. American film exports were targeted on Britain in particular, since the country had the biggest domestic market and was English-speaking. American films were very popular and the so-called 'Bogart or bacon' debate arose when it appeared that the post-war sterling crisis could only be resolved by limiting the import of Hollywood film.[7] The debate also raised important questions of national and cultural integrity. If the war had revealed the cinema's capacity to influence hearts and minds, this only made the task of comprehending and criticising popular culture more urgent; and, if the war had introduced a 'new realism' into the cinema, this only rendered the creation of an independent national cinema more necessary, for Hollywood films, particularly in circles influenced by the pre-war documentary movement, were often seen as the agents of capitalism and American domination, as well as a drain on national resources.[8]

I SEQUENCE

In 1946 a group of Oxford undergraduates which included Lindsay Anderson, Gavin Lambert and Penelope Houston founded the journal *Sequence* and set out to investigate the related questions of realism and popular culture with the hope of creating a genuinely British cinema.[9] Film criticism had encountered an apparently insoluble intellectual difficulty: a revitalised national cinema must appeal to the mass of people or else it could not be national. However, the popular cinema – and this was particularly true of the sound cinema – was generally dismissed with contempt, while critical approval was reserved for certain kinds of silent films (especially those of the Soviet school) that were considered to be 'art'.[10] The question therefore was whether it would be possible to produce popular sound films which were nevertheless 'art'.

Initially *Sequence* suggested that film could be considered 'art' on condition that content and form, or what it called the 'thematic' and the 'aesthetic', were judged separately.[11] This meant that the thematic could provide the requisite dose of realism while the aesthetic provided the art. Crude though it may have been, the attempted distinction is important, since it was carried over into British film-making a decade later and, as a subsequent generation of critics gleefully pointed out,[12] it continued to inform some of

Sight and Sound's less cogent criticism for many years. *Sequence* itself soon came round to a more considered view with a series of articles explicitly or implicitly devoted to the British cinema.[13]

Lindsay Anderson noted that 'the impact of the documentary school on feature films has resulted in nothing more than a string of well-intentioned failures',[14] and launched an appeal for new directors and above all new writers for the cinema.[15] But *Sequence* also supported the position, defended by Thorold Dickinson in *Sight and Sound*, that a director was far more crucial to the success of a film than a writer. Gavin Lambert deplored the lack of 'sustained imaginative power'[16] in British cinema, whilst Lindsay Anderson was convinced that 'a good film must draw its inspiration from a script; but it may grow to full creative life through various patterns and degrees of collaboration. And the fact remains . . . that the man most in a position to guide and regulate the expressive resources of the cinema is the director. To that extent it remains, and will remain, a director's medium.'[17] For Anderson, the 'first duty of an artist is, not to interpret, not to propagandise, but to create'.[18] This is not far short of designating the director as *auteur*, and it is not surprising, therefore, that the discussions in *Sequence* paralleled, and indeed in some cases prefigured, those conducted in *Cahiers du cinéma* in the 1950s.[19]

II 'THIS IS THE WORLD'

These ideas were soon put to the test. Lindsay Anderson made a series of short, independently financed documentaries of which the best known are *O, Dreamland* (1952), *Thursday's Children* (1952) and *Everyday Except Christmas* (1957). Some of his films, together with works by Karel Reisz, Tony Richardson and Lorenza Mazzetti, were presented in a series of screenings at the National Film Theatre under the general title 'Free Cinema'. This is how Anderson described the objectives of the Group:

The programme is presented not as an achievement but as an aim. We ask you to view it not as critics, nor as a diversion, but in direct relation to British cinema, still obstinately class-bound; still rejecting the stimulus of contemporary life as well as the responsibility to criticise; still reflecting a metropolitan, Southern English culture which excludes the rich diversity of tradition and personality which is the whole of Britain. . . . Our aim is first to look at Britain, with honesty and with affection. To relish its eccentricities, attack its abuses, love its people. To use the cinema to express our allegiances, our rejections and our aspirations.[20]

Critics were quick to situate the group within a tradition of social and cultural criticism going back to D. H. Lawrence which sprang from 'non-conformism, impatience with convention, sadness about urban life, a sense of isolation from the main social and artistic development . . . a desire to regain contact with a more vital individual force'.[21] In addition (and this is suggested by Anderson's oblique reference to *Listen to Britain*), the members of Free Cinema hoped to recapture the 'atmosphere of purpose and meaning' and the sense of community that they felt had characterised the documentaries of the war years, especially those of Humphrey Jennings. Their enterprise was generally well received on the Left: John Berger thought it a marvellous programme of documentaries and described Anderson's films as 'like daylight after formalised dreams',[22] while Richard Hoggart praised Reisz's *We are the Lambeth Boys* as 'immensely tougher, more honest and sensitive, and more intelligent than commercial cinema' and as having 'dispelled a lot of the suffocating fog of phoney sentiment and false observation'.[23]

But there were some inherently unsatisfactory aspects to the Free Cinema enterprise. What had made the documentaries of the 1930s so extraordinarily moving was that they were literally a revelation to a society unused to self-examination and lacking the technology and even the techniques of social research. Their success may be judged by the creation of Mass Observation, which was, in part, the child of the thirties documentaries. In the inter-war years, a documentary film had been a voyage of discovery for both film-maker and audience in a way that could hardly be repeated in an age of television. The war had added a unity of purpose, the Lawrentian 'sense of oneness' which had also dissipated subsequently. No reference to Jennings could therefore disguise the fact that the Free Cinema films were effectively class-based in that they required the film-maker to observe from a position of exteriority a sub-culture or social group deemed to be of interest because previously unobserved.[24] It was a rather naïve notion of realism that did not consider the position of the observer to be problematic.

Free Cinema had other shortcomings that were only too well recognised by its members. Its films were all independent, low-budget shorts, some of which were privately financed and some made with the aid of the Experimental Film Fund. It consequently had no impact on a film industry in which both the trade union (ACT) regulations and the policies of the distributors served to discourage the making and viewing of similar films. Free Cinema films were not features, so that, whatever their excellent qualities, and however much they took ordinary people and everyday events as their subject, their audience would not be the mass audience to which the film-makers aspired but would remain an elite minority. Hence the striking contrast with other European countries, particularly Italy, but increasingly France, where a cinematic revival was taking place within the structure of the national film industries.

III   THE ABORTIVE RENAISSANCE[25]

But a 'New British Cinema' rapidly came into being, thanks, in no small part, to the association between Tony Richardson, Lindsay Anderson and the Royal Court Theatre.[26] Richardson's career had begun in the theatre: in 1955 he became Assistant Artistic Director of the English Stage Company, for whom he directed John Osborne's *Look Back in Anger* in 1956 and *The Entertainer* in 1957. With Osborne he set up Woodfall Films in 1958, and the first features he directed were translations from the stage (*Look Back in Anger*, 1959, and *The Entertainer*, 1960). Richardson went on to direct Shelagh Delaney's *A Taste of Honey* on stage in 1960 and on film in 1961 and a film adaptation of Stan Barstow's novel *The Loneliness of the Long Distance Runner* in 1962. Anderson, meanwhile, made his first feature, *This Sporting Life* (from David Storey's novel), in 1962, while Karel Reisz directed *Saturday Night and Sunday Morning* (from Alan Sillitoe's story) in 1960. With Jack Clayton's film version of *Room at the Top* (1958) and John Schlesinger's *A Kind of Loving* (1962) and *Billy Liar* (1963), these films made up the 'New Cinema'. The extent to which the renaissance depended on an existing renaissance in the novel and the theatre is obvious, though it is probably true that only Richardson was more committed to the theatre than the cinema. However, adaptation in itself was not necessarily a bad thing and it in any case reflected the difficulty of raising film finance in Britain as well as the independent producers' need to sell confirmed successes to the distributors.

What is more interesting is the extent to which these films match Anderson's Free Cinema prescriptions. Their protagonists are a factory worker, a borstal boy, a pregnant teenager, an ambitious working-class boy, a lower middle-class angry young man, and so on. These were not *auteur* films, in the sense that none was a personal statement; instead, all observe from the outside characters and locations (often in contrived dramatic situations) which had not previously merited, or so the argument ran, attention from the knee-breeches school of film-making. All evinced the passionate concern that had been the strength of Free Cinema;[27] few exemplified the talent that at least some of these directors demonstrated later in their careers. Karel Reisz, in particular, went on to make more interesting films, such as *Morgan* (1965) and *Isadora* (1967), and, while the question of Lindsay Anderson's talent remains controversial, it is undeniable that *If ...*, *O, Lucky Man* and especially *Britannia Hospital* all reflect his personal preoccupations to a greater degree than his earlier films.

There was therefore something almost perverse about the New British Cinema. On the one hand, the decline in the popular audience (from attendances of about 27 million a week in 1950 to about 12 million in 1959) had led to the closure of many independent houses and a reinforcement of the power and conservatism of the distribution monopolies. On the other hand, these independent film-makers seemed determined to break into a market which was increasingly closed to them, and attempted to do so with films which were didactic to the point of being patronising. In their choice and treatment of subject matter, their styles of acting and their academic approach to narrative, these films emerged as bastard descendants of Grierson documentaries rather than the legitimate offspring of the plays and novels from which they were adapted.

Reviewing this cinema in 1963, Peter Graham was quite clear that its failure was indeed one of realism, but not as identified by Anderson. The failure derived from the fact that the *mise en scène* of this group of British directors was vitiated by a tradition of moralising didacticism. Graham criticises Schlesinger's *A Kind of Loving* in these terms:

> After showing Vic and Ingrid kissing, Schlesinger pans right, excluding them from frame, and shows some incriptions carved into the wall ('I love Adam' etc) and a notice about the wilful destruction of park property. Had these details simply been left in the background, they would have made a discreet, instead of ham-fisted, comment upon the action. Here, as in the rest of the film, the deeply ingrained convention in British films that any detail of special importance must be specifically thrown into relief seems to have been at work.

In an analysis directly inspired by André Bazin, Graham condemns Schlesinger for 'needlessly breaking up the physical continuity of the scene' by cross-cutting, for his use of a 'watered-down version of classical montage' and for 'allowing only one version of reality which is the director's, thus excluding ambiguity'. 'A more comprehensive style, characterised by composition in depth within the frame, an emphasis on the physical presence of actors in a decor, and continuity of action, allows the spectator to interpret what he is shown in a number of ways all of which are valid, the correlative of this style is real life itself.'[28] Thus the new British cinema-directors were not authors of films but, as it were, observers of life through the proscenium arch; their *mise en scène* was academic, their film language was stilted and as a result they were entirely lacking in the moral force that they thought to achieve through subject matter alone.

IV   A NEW REALISM

Peter Graham is representative of a new generation of film critics who graduated from Oxford and Cambridge in the later fifties and early sixties.[29] They contributed to *Oxford Opinion, Universities and Left Review* (later *New Left Review*) and to *Motion*, but attacked *Sight and Sound* bitterly, and some of them later founded the journal *Movie*. They drew their inspiration partly from André Bazin, but mainly from *Cahiers du cinéma*, of which Bazin was joint editor until his death in 1958.[30]

Since Bazin's writing is so much better known today than it was in 1960, a brief summary will recall why it proved so illuminating not just to critics in Britain but, initially, to a younger generation at *Cahiers du cinéma*. Broadly, his project was to reconsider film as an art in terms of its realism. According to Bazin, the photographic image is 'objective' and thus provides what Western art has sought for centuries – namely, a reproduction of the real which is permanent and not distorted by human intervention (since it is 'mechanically' reproduced). Film shares these properties with photography and adds the dimension of time.[31] Hence the crucial characteristic of cinema is its capacity to show reality, but this is also where its aesthetic possibilities reside: 'Ce ne sera pas . . . le moindre mérite du cinéma italien que d'avoir rappelé . . . qu'il n'était pas de "réalisme" en art qui ne fût d'abord profondément "esthétique" . . . Quand l'invention et la complexité des formes ne portent plus sur le contenu même de l'oeuvre, elles ne cessent pas pour autant de s'exercer sur l'efficacité des moyens.'[32]

The implications of this thesis are enormous. Traditionally (up to and including Malraux),[33] the aesthetic possibilities of film were held to lie in what was sometimes called its 'grammar' – that is, in the combination and juxtaposition of shots – so that the cinema of montage, the pre-war *avant-garde* cinema, the Soviet cinema and the German expressionist schools were most highly regarded. Bazin now suggested that films with more naturalistic sets, acting-styles and camera work might equally, indeed preferably, be considered art, with his own admiration going to Dreyer, Murnau and Stroheim among pre-war directors and Renoir, Welles, Wyler and the Italian neo-realists among his contemporaries.

In some respects Bazin did no more than bring film aesthetics into line with actual film production. Montage, as practised by Eisenstein, is not immediately suited to the kind of narrative cinema that sound had made possible and which tends to require naturalistic acting and locations and a minimum degree of continuity.[34] But Bazin challenged not just Eisensteinian montage but conventional *découpage* as well, arguing (particularly in his essays on Welles) that, by, as it were, preselecting the significant elements of a scene on behalf of the spectator, *découpage* amounts to directing a spectator to a point of view. The use of deep focus permits a film to be constructed in sequences. This offers continuity of action and creates an ambiguity about what is or is not important that is somehow closer to 'reality'.[35]

Bazin's theories have an obvious ideological undertow which may be explained as a response to the war and its aftermath and which was almost entirely lost on his first British readers.[36] For his colleagues at *Cahiers du cinéma*, however, his criticism proved liberating not least because it allowed attention to be concentrated firmly on the American cinema. Though Bazin himself remained sceptical,[37] his work was an important contributory factor in the development of a new critical approach at *Cahiers* which became known as the *politique des auteurs*.[38] It is important to emphasise that for *Cahiers* the *politique des auteurs* was a twin offensive providing, on the one hand, the means for a fresh look at narrative cinema (primarily though not exclusively American), and on the other the ammunition for an attack on existing French cinema and the creation of a new cinema in France. When the *politique des auteurs* travelled abroad, as it rapidly did, it lost the creative dimension that had originally rendered it so persuasive in France, where most of the critics who contributed to it and who most strongly condemned the 'cinéma de papa' were also the film-makers who belonged to the *Nouvelle Vague*.

Besides responding to the conspicuous need to develop a theory which could embrace the sound cinema, the *politique des auteurs* owed much to the special circumstances of Paris after the war:[39] the sudden release of previously barred American films and the eclecticism of Henri Langlois, who ran the Cinémathèque, meant that large numbers of American films were viewed in no particular order or hierarchy by a youthful audience that was fascinated by the United States.[40] At its simplest, the *politique des auteurs* offered a critical path through a mass of undifferentiated material and taught the critic to back his personal preferences and trust his judgement. There was an irony, however, in searching for *auteurs* in the output of the most rigidly organised studio system, and an important aspect of the *politique des auteurs* was that it served as a rite of initiation offering the critic who practised it a secret knowledge hidden from the vulgar and profane,[41] But it also allowed both continuities and similarities to be observed in the work of a given director and individual creativity to be detected, primarily by focusing attention on *mise en scène*, since it was there, rather than in subject matter, that a studio director had an opportunity to exercise his individualism.

The most obvious consequence of what *a priori* appeared to be an insistence on the primacy of individual taste was the development of a new canon. The American output of directors who had emigrated to Hollywood (Hitchcock, Lang, Renoir and, later, Sirk) was preferred to the same directors' pre-war films, against received opinion; the B-picture or genre movie was prized often because its formulaic qualities obliged the *auteur*, if he was one, to make his mark against the odds,[42] and, if such films were right-wing, as was often the case, this merely strengthened the often-expounded view that ethics had little to do with subject matter and everything to do with *mise en scène*.[43] In addition to the establishment of a 'pantheon', the *politique des auteurs* demanded frequent viewing of films, more difficult in the pre-video age, together with detailed discussions with film-directors in which points of technical interest were raised and questions concerning the genesis of a project and the constraints it suffered from were invariably put. *Cahiers du cinéma* published several special issues devoted to individual directors, the best known of which is the Hitchcock number,[44] and it was ultimately responsible for proving, contrary to the common wisdom, that films repay close watching. The 'close reading' of films, and, indeed, academic film study today, owe a great deal to this pioneering example.

For all that it was expressed as a 'Blast' and 'Bless' grid rather like the one devised by Wyndham Lewis, the *politique des auteurs* had method. There were underlying points of community between, say, Cukor, Hawks, Hitchcock, Mann, Minnelli, Ray, Preminger, and a few others, which dictated that they should have been elected and others rejected. In view of their later reputation, it is perhaps a paradox that what the *Cahiers* critics admired in the Hollywood cinema was its classicism. 'Je veux, pour citer Fénelon, "un sublime si familier que chacun soit tenté de croire qu'il l'aurait trouvé sans peine"', wrote Godard.[45] The cinema they liked combined economy and elegance, and was not ashamed of the simplicity which derived from universal pretensions and a moral approach to narrative. So far from being unusual or offbeat, this was a cinema which took both itself and the human predicament seriously and which had a confidence uncomplicated by the self-doubt of modernism: 'Oublie-t-on', wrote Godard again, 'que l'aisance des cinéastes d'Outre-Atlantique trouva autrefois son écho en notre aimable et malheureux dix-huitième siècle?'[46]

The *politique des auteurs* has been criticised as 'a justification, couched in aesthetic terms, of a culturally conservative, politically reactionary attempt to remove film from the realm of social and political concern in which the progressive forces of the Resistance had placed all the arts in the years immediately following the war'.[47] However, such an accusation (though perhaps true of the *politique* as it was interpreted in Britain and the United States in the 1960s) misses the original thrust of an approach which posited a continuity between man and his environment that cannot admit a distinction between the individual and the collective. The *Cahiers* critics showed a predilection for the *mise en scène* of moral solitude, of which the *locus classicus* is Nicholas Ray's *In a Lonely Place* (the 'place' being both the protagonist's mind and his physical surroundings). Indeed, the reason why the cinema, rather than the theatre or the novel, was seen as central to certain kinds of moral preoccupation – and ultimately why it had to be taken seriously – was that the medium is predicated on a body–mind continuum and represents moral significance through spatial relationships. In this, *Cahiers* did no more than follow the direction of contemporary philosophical and psychological research; as Merleau-Ponty wrote: 'le cinéma ne nous donne pas, comme le roman l'a fait longtemps, les *pensées* de l'homme, il nous donne sa conduite ou son comportement, il nous offre directement cette manière spéciale d'être au monde. . . . Le cinéma est particulièrement apte à faire paraître l'union de l'esprit et du corps, de l'esprit et du monde et l'expression de l'un dans l'autre.'[48] As for the accusation that *Cahiers* was culturally conservative, a particular interpretation of 'progressive' is required for this to be accepted, since events suggest, rather, that the journal's approach to cinema prepared the ground for an upsurge of creative activity at the end of the 1950s.

V   NOUVELLE VAGUE

Godard, Truffaut, Rivette, Chabrol and their contemporaries did not necessarily want to make films that were imitations of classical Hollywood cinema, but they had ambitions for the same degree of cultural centrality and, just as important, authenticity. If one recalls Truffaut's celebrated attack on the *tradition de qualité* which was characteristic of the French cinema of the early fifties,[49] it can be seen that his objection was to a cinema that was doubly inauthentic. It was dominated not by writers with a personal statement to make, but by adapters whose task was the *mise en forme* of existing literary successes (the best-known scriptwriters were Jean

Aurenche and Pierre Bost, whom Bazin called 'les Viollet-le-Duc de l'adaptation'). Their technique, moreover, was based on a principle of 'fidelity to the spirit', rather than the letter, of the original which allowed them systematically to take liberties that traduced the work adapted. Examples cited by Truffaut are the introduction of spurious realism into the dialogue (through the use of slang and colloquialisms) and of anti-clerical or anti-military sentiments designed to appeal to a particular sector of the audience. Not only was the *tradition de qualité* not personal, it was positively contemptuous in its approach to the cinema.

The *Nouvelle Vague*, on the other hand, 'se définit en partie par ce nouveau rapport entre fiction et réalité . . . nous parlons de ce que nous connaissons . . . nous cherchons à voir la France'.[50] No longer was the film-maker obliged to seek a subject of obvious social and moral significance; instead, as Chabrol pointed out, his subject matter took on the significance he gave it.[51] Ironically enough, social significance is not absent from *Nouvelle Vague* films (both Chabrol's *Le Beau Serge* and *Les Bonnes femmes* may be read as criticisms of a class society), but it is never the point of them. If the corpus as a whole is considered,[52] it becomes clear that these films frequently combine the *mise en scène* of the existential predicament, for which examples abounded in the Hollywood cinema, with elements of the nascent youth culture. It is easy to see why Nicholas Ray was such a favourite *auteur* (with films such as *Johnny Guitar* and *Rebel without a Cause*), for if not exactly 'progressive' the *Nouvelle Vague* achieved a different verisimilitude that combined immediacy with energy. So, far from being *avant-garde*, it was in step with its time and this was the source of its strength.

Its other virtues were that it offered a solution to the crisis of production and exhibition in the post-war European cinema. In representing the interests and values of a new class of young people,[53] it enabled the French film industry to cope with Hollywood's increasing investment in spectaculars and with the gradual loss of domestic audiences to television. It also took advantage of new technologies which enabled films to be made more cheaply. Indeed, *Nouvelle Vague* films are perhaps more united in their production histories than in any thematic resemblance: they were invariably low-budget features made by inexperienced directors using cameramen, such as Henri Decaë and Raoul Coutard, who were used to working in the difficult conditions of army film units in Indo-China. Lighter cameras and faster film permitted shooting with smaller crews, inside and outside and on location rather than on sets, while the use of unknown actors also kept costs down.

Although the *Nouvelle Vague* had probably ceased to be a defined group by the middle of the 1960s, its effects on the French film industry had been very beneficial. The fact that unknown directors and actors in small-subject, low-budget, independently produced features could be commercially viable, both nationally and internationally, encouraged other producers to take risks and led to the creation of structures of state aid, based on the *prime à la qualité* and the *avance sur recettes*, which made pre-production finance more readily available.

Nouvelle Vague films were popular in Britain. Together with the new Italian cinema, particularly the films of Antonioni, they helped to create a climate in which young, middle-class audiences respected the medium. This was well understood by the film critics. Welcoming the new decade in *Sight and Sound*, Penelope Houston wrote,

> The interest is already in a cinema less sweeping, closer to the novel in the intensity of its preoccupations, the amount of meaning it can isolate in one limited area of experience. Essentially the problems are those of the individual confronting himself: not concerned with social conditions, nor with issues demanding big decisions, but with the complicated business of living. . . . The artist, whether it is Alain Resnais . . . or Bergman . . . or Chabrol is turning inward rather than outward.[54]

Similarly, a brilliantly premonitory essay on *L'Avventura* by Geoffrey Nowell-Smith suggested how even an avowedly Marxist filmmaker was concerned to invent a new approach to cinema:

> *L'Avventura* is not a film without content. It has theme . . . a clearly defined background and beyond that a richness of suggestion rare in the cinema. . . . But what is remarkable . . . is the rigorous connexion of image and idea. . . . For *L'Avventura* the dichotomy of form and content does not exist. For the old fallacious idea of the film as a bastard art, with intellectual content dressed up in cinematic form, it substitutes a new conception of cinematic content; and the means of its expression is precisely a new language.[55]

The contrast between the new European and the new British cinema could not have been more striking, but what producers and exhibitors who attempted to exploit the new mode did not understand was that without the crucial moral dimension the *auteur* film was no more guaranteed to succeed than the average British potboiler.

VI   THE CROSBY–COCTEAU LINE

The *politique des auteurs* and the *Nouvelle Vague* had an important, and lasting, effect on film exhibition in Britain. With the post-war contraction of the mass audience, the circuits were trapped in a spiral of diminishing returns and confined their screens to American films. There simultaneously grew up an informal parallel circuit consisting of the surviving independent houses, the Classic and Gala chains, together with the Regional Film Theatres which the British Film Institute (BFI) supported. These 'art houses' (often significantly named 'Continental') were serviced by specialist distributors such as Contemporary, Gala and, increasingly, the BFI itself[56] and ventilated non-family (i.e. X-rated) films made in languages other than English and shown in the original version with sub-titles. Their audience was primarily young and middle-class.

What became known as the Crosby–Cocteau line dividing these films from others marked distinctions which were both real and imaginary and which were really commercial but were expressed as aesthetic.[57] Such distinctions included those between 'art' and 'entertainment', between 'quality' and 'popular', and indeed (as in the celebrated trial of *Lady Chatterley's Lover*) between a legitimate eroticism and pornography. They had more to do with the characteristics of the consumer than the nature of the product consumed. Thus the art movie was born. Whereas the influence of the *politique des auteurs* on the *Nouvelle Vague* meant that the art movie was morally and aesthetically distinctive (though as Hollywood production changed throughout the 1970s it became less so), the crucial point is that in Britain it is a term which relates purely to *exhibition*; on the other hand an apparently comparable classification, such as the French *film d'art et d'essai* is a *production* category. Thus the crisis of both production and exhibition in the domestic industry, the fact that 'art' films could be conveniently defined as 'non-English-language', and a peculiarly class-bound approach to culture all contributed to the success of what was, at the outset, nothing more than distributors' shorthand. The sobriquet 'art' served both to sanitise and render marginal a whole branch of film exhibition in Britain, and this meant that educationalists began to direct their attention away from this branch of the entertainment industry and to devote their thoughts to the evil effects of television.

Film-producers in Britain, however, have always been nostalgic for the *Nouvelle Vague*. The Interim Action Committee on the Film Industry, which was set up in 1977, the Association of Independent Producers and indeed the technicians union, have all at one time or another recommended forms of state aid similar to those obtaining across the Channel, in the mistaken belief that the failure of the independent feature in Britain is a purely financial matter. Finally, when Channel Four television was set up in 1982 it reserved its *Film on Four* slot for the kind of feature (both in terms of budget and type of subject) which had been successful in France twenty years earlier and, sometimes with the BFI Production Board and sometimes independently of it, used the best part of its features budget for those kinds of films.

VII MOVIE AND THE PUBLISHING REVOLUTION

The first issue of *Movie* came out in June 1962, edited and designed by Ian Cameron in association with Paul Mayersberg, V. F. Perkins and Mark Shivas. The editorial group had first come together as undergraduates at Oxford, and the new journal was a continuation, in more professional form, of their contributions to *Oxford Opinion* and *Isis* in 1960 and 1961. Though *Movie*'s unbroken run was short (June 1962 to Summer 1963), and, although it was by all accounts a hand-to-mouth affair financially, these limitations were reflected neither in its physical appearance nor in the influence it had, and continues to have.

A glance through the back issues of *Movie*[58] demonstrates that one of its strengths was the shared views of the editorial board. Indeed, when the group dispersed, *Movie* ceased to appear regularly and its cutting edge was lost. This being the case, it might seem invidious to distinguish the contributions of individuals, but it is interesting to do so in the light of their subsequent careers. Schematically, there does appear to have been some division of labour between Ian Cameron, whose financial acumen kept the journal afloat and who had a strong interest in design, and V. F. Perkins, whose contribution was of a much more intellectual and theoretical kind. Today Cameron is a publisher who, with hindsight, can be said to have created cinema publishing in Britain and, both with *Movie* and with the Movie Paperbacks and Studio Vista imprint, to have effected a dramatic change in the design of books and magazines. *Movie* was printed on glossy paper, which allowed excellent photographic reproduction and greater typographical variation than was then customary. It used bold type and capitals a great deal, and adopted a three-column layout that exploited its format, cutting down the margins and making the eye work to encompass the page as a whole. The contrast with *Sight and Sound* or *Films and Filming* in the same period is remarkable. For Movie Paperbacks Cameron took over the characteristically small, square shape of the Seghers *Cinéma d'aujourd'hui* series, but updated the graphics and improved the quality of the paper and reproduction to give something much more visually attractive and less academic. Many, though not all, of the Movie Paperbacks were monographs,[59] but the secret of their success was that they all combined an auteurist approach to cinema, supplying in handy form the kind of information that was otherwise only available in *Cahiers du cinéma*, with ease of reference and clarity of presentation.

Movie's opening statements, written by Perkins on behalf of the board, was ostensibly an attack on the new British cinema. As befits such manifestos, it was heavy with irony:

Five years ago the ineptitude of British films was generally acknowledged. The stiff upper lip movie was a standard target for critical scorn. But now the British cinema has come to grips with Reality. We have had a breakthrough, a renaissance, a New Wave. . . . All we can see is a change of attitude, which disguises the fact that British cinema is as dead as before. Perhaps it was never alive. Our films have improved, if at all, only in their intentions. We are still unable to find evidence of artistic sensibilities in working order. There is as much genuine personality in *Room at the Top*, method in *A Kind of Loving* and style in *A Taste of Honey* as there is wit in *An Alligator named Daisy*, intelligence in *Above us the Waves* and ambition in *Ramsbottom Rides Again*.[60]

Movie particularly rejected the equation between 'quality' and 'problem picture' that it attributed to the *Sequence* generation:

'These pictures are particularly offensive in assuming that their holy platitudes are too loftily intellectual to be accepted by audiences unless the pill of wisdom is sweetened by spurious excitement', and it was clear that the *Cahiers* prescription for the reform of British cinema was correct: 'What the British cinema needs is not new subjects but new ideas about direction.' Both Mark Shivas and Ian Cameron had already mounted a spirited defence of the 'commercial' cinema in the pages of *Oxford Opinion*. Shivas stated, 'To left wing writers, films stressing an immediate social problem, in a rather sooty black and white, embodied all that cinema should aspire to; "Glossiness", denoting technical skill or clear images and an appearance of expense, became a deadly word.' Cameron suggested, 'We are . . . attacking two aspects of film criticism in Britain: the pallid philanthropy that has always provided its criteria for evaluation, and the falseness of the implicitly accepted distinction between art and commerce.'[61] But the closing pages of Perkins's statements make clear that *Movie*'s major concern is not, as might have been imagined, film-making in Britain but film criticism, and indeed that the failure of British films is to be laid at the door of the critics: 'We shall be on the way when British film enthusiasts are prepared to distinguish rigorously between the "haves" and the "have nots" of talent, to champion the artists they respect, and to shout loud the names of the hacks they despise. But until it is accepted that style is worthy of passionate feeling and detailed analysis there will be no change.'

Not surprisingly, the first issue of *Movie* provoked consternation among the newspaper critics, especially Derek Hill of the *Financial Times*. The objections were answered in Cameron's 'Films, Directors and Critics':

The motive for interviewing directors at all is to see how far their ideas of their aims square with the critics' rationalisations from the films. . . . The alternative which we find elsewhere is the *gestalt* approach which . . . usually results in giving almost no impression of what the film was actually like. . . . Everyone accepts the cinema of directors for France, Italy, Japan, India, Argentina, Sweden and Poland – everywhere in fact that the Art is easily identifiable. . . . It is only over American movies that the trouble starts and reviews are likely to end with a desultory 'George Cukor directed efficiently.'[62]

As its title indicates, *Movie*'s principal objective was the defence of a certain kind of American cinema previously dismissed or underrated by British critics. The techniques used were clearly similar to those of *Cahiers du cinéma*, if not directly inspired by them, and thanks to *Movie* it now seems so self-evidently interesting to interview American film-directors that the extent to which the journal innovated may not be apparent. Many of the directors *Movie* admired coincided with the *auteurs* acclaimed by *Cahiers*, and it printed interviews with Minnelli, Preminger, Fritz Lang, Hawks, Hitchcock and Nicholas Ray.[63] By contrast, *Movie* devoted relatively little space to the new European cinema. It liked Chabrol, reprinting his 'Big Subjects, Little Subjects', reviewing *Le Beau Serge* and devoting half the June 1963 number to a study of his work. It reviewed Rivette, Rozier, Varda and Bresson, but was divided about Godard[64] and did not mention Truffaut. *Movie* betrays no sense that this would be the cinema of the future. As for the British film, it was constantly disparaged in passing, but only Joseph Losey was treated as an *auteur* and he was in any case an expatriate American.

Movie made no attempt to be comprehensive or even, necessarily, to preview what was about to open in London, although its contributors did attend major film festivals. It pursued its tastes and prejudices rather than attempting to influence institutions, and this may well have been one source of its success: *Sight and Sound*, the film critics of the quality press, and the programmes of the National Film Theatre all began to reflect the *Movie* line and to explore the work of the American directors it admired.[65] On the other hand, *Movie* had no impact on film production in Britain and little on film exhibition.

The explanation is undoubtedly to be found in the fact that *Movie*, and especially V. F. Perkins, who was its intellectual force, did not share the concern for social responsibility that informed British film criticism and film-making in general, and only very partially accepted the moral framework which underpinned the *Cahiers* criticism of the 1950s. Perkins clearly had a better grasp of what lay behind the *politique des auteurs* than almost any other writer on film, and in the *Movie* editorial board's 'Discussion' of April 1963 appeared to be defending the kind of classicism that was sought by the early *Cahiers*. Many of Perkins's remarks and strictures are based on a notion of what is inherently appropriate to the cinema: 'Film is the art of *showing*; it seems a contradiction to use it in order not to show';[66] similarly, his favourite terms of dismissal, 'silly' and 'ridiculous', are, when due allowance is made for the conversational register, terms which censure excesses of any kind. Thus he dislikes the early Godard films because of their propensity to exaggerate and for what he considers their bombast. But, when it comes to the relationship between body and mind, there is the suggestion that, where *Cahiers* posited an ideal continuity in film between the physical and the intellectual, Perkins prizes the cinema for its emphasis on the physical. When he refers to 'the old heresy – which the cinema was virtually invented to disprove – that the intellect is superior to the body' he suggests a hedonism that British criticism has always found hard to accept.

Recalling his early childhood,[67] Perkins explains that his involvement with the cinema came from being 'star struck': 'I saw myself as the next James Mason.' He also points out that his background was one in which he did not realise 'it wasn't done to take movies seriously', and that he grew up admiring not just 'film society films' but also with a passion for *Johnny Guitar* and Ava Gardner. It is perhaps also significant that he was a student at Oxford rather than Cambridge and that even there he read history rather than English, which was the discipline that traditionally nurtured British cultural critics. Thus Perkins claims to have discovered Leavis through what others were writing about the cinema. In his book *Film as Film*, much of which was written in the mid sixties,[68] Perkins makes clear his distaste for the Film Appreciation school:

> The creative cinema of America, says Dr Manvell, 'was destroyed by the need to please continuously the demands of an international audience of a low quality of emotional understanding'. The belief that popularity and excellence are incompatible dies hard. It survives in the pejorative undertones of the word 'commercial', and in the equation of significance with solemnity and obscurity.

Perkins would perhaps have been more influential if the emphasis on enjoyment in *Film as Film* had been couched in the psychoanalytic terms that were becoming fashionable by the time the book was published, if his display of taste had been backed up by erudition, and if his diverse and pluralistic views had not appeared in a period which sought simple prescriptions. As it was, Robin Wood, who came later to *Movie* from Cambridge, attempted to marry a Leavisite concern with the good and an auteurist admiration for the beautiful, and more easily reached a public educated to appreciate moral theses. But by 1968, when it resumed publication, *Movie's* moment had passed. In addition to the dissolution of the original editorial group, two factors made its positions untenable: one was that the Hollywood films it most admired were ceasing to be produced; the other was that the escalation of the Vietnam War meant that, even for individuals who had not previously been concerned with politics, any unqualified admiration for American products became problematic.

VIII   BACK TO FIRST PRINCIPLES: *SCREEN*

If *Movie* marked an attempt to get away from the British tradition, *Screen*, which took over as the major film journal of the seventies, represented an attempt to change it from within, though if anything it relied more heavily than had its predecessor on *Cahiers du cinéma* and French theoretical writing in general. *Screen* has attained considerable notoriety for a number of interlinked reasons. It featured as a point of reference in the 1980–1 Cambridge English controversy because Stephen Heath and Colin MacCabe were members of its editorial board between 1973 and 1981; it also published translations of work on semiotics and psychoanalysis that were often the first versions of French texts to be available in Britain. In this way it became essential reading for students in other fields, such as literary and social studies, who had no particular interest in the cinema. Finally, it was throughout the 1970s a symbol of the dissatisfaction with the BFI (its funding body) felt by some governors and by many people outside the Institute. Sometimes these issues became hopelessly entangled in the minds of ill-informed commentators. Thus, in an article more typical in its spleen than its accuracy, Lindsay Anderson complained of 'the maintenance far beyond public use or demand of subsidised magazines like *Sight and Sound* and *Screen'*. He continued: 'It is significant that there should be a close link between Marxism and this new aesthetic party line . . . the results in practice are rather similar: depersonalisation, pretension and platitude in place of meaning, self-righteous dictation in place of argument. . . . The stables need a good cleaning. Sooner rather than later.'[69]

Ben Brewster, editor of *Screen* between 1973 and 1977 claims that despite well-publicised resignations from the editorial board[70] and a highly litigious board membership, the editorial policy of *Screen* was consistent throughout the seventies.[71] If true, this suggests that though *Screen* took on the important role of naturalising certain, mainly French, approaches to cultural forms and signifying-systems, it remained a journal devoted, as the name of its parent organisation the Society for Education in Film and Television (SEFT)[72] indicates, to education in Britain. This is substantially different from the function its critics attribute to it, and in order to understand *Screen*'s activities it is essential to bear in mind what the BFI was (and was not) doing at the time.

Speaking to the National Union of Teachers' special conference 'Popular Culture and Personal Responsibility' in 1960, Raymond Williams used the example of the supposed relationship between the 1870 Education Act and the rise of the Northcliffe Press to challenge widespread assumptions about mass communications.[73] However, the conventional association between popular education and 'works of low quality' was responsible, among other things, for the creation of the BFI in 1933, since a need was felt for a body able to educate tastes to enjoy 'art' films and reject 'commercial' films.[74] This was the origin of the Film Appreciation school presided over by Manvell and Lindgren, whose preferences ran almost exclusively towards the silent cinema rather than sound films from Hollywood. By the 1960s, the BFI had, in Stanley Reed, a Director whose background was in popular education in the East End of London.

Originally *Screen* was a journal intended to assist schoolteachers who wished to teach film appreciation. However, its intellectual leadership lay in the BFI Education Department, headed from 1957 to 1971 by Paddy Whannel. He is generally credited with having invented the term 'film culture' (as a substitute for 'appreciation'), which comprehended both the making and viewing of films and all that related to the cinema within the context of culture as a whole. Author, with Stuart Hall, of *The Popular Arts* (1964), Whannel always held a position distinguishable from both the right-wing Leavisites and the traditional Marxists. While these two schools of thought both accepted that some forms of culture were 'higher' than others, and simply argued about how to persuade people of that fact and about the numbers of people who had access to the 'higher' forms, for Whannel the 'popular arts', and the popular cinema *par excellence*, could be good and interesting in themselves.

Unlike Richard Hoggart, for example, he was not primarily concerned with the 'how to make bus conductors enjoy Beethoven' debate, but unlike the Marxists he did not accept that the popular arts were capitalist and therefore to be rejected. The 'Whannel position' may well have been reinforced by the social origins of those who propounded it, for if they did not wish to submit to the acculturation so graphically described in *The Uses of Literacy*, the study of the cinema offered a way of not denying their origins.[75]

Whannel's programme was essentially pragmatic: it consisted in integrating film education into the secondary-school curriculum. He argued that this required a process of filtering-down from higher education. One way in which this was done was through 'pump-priming' university lectureships in film;[76] the other was the development of theory, since if film were to become established in higher education it would require a 'substantial theoretical background'. However, theory was also necessary to break up the consensus upon which liberal education was based, since without this film studies could not progress, and here the *politique des auteurs* initially proved useful but, increasingly, came under pressure.[77]

This was evident in an article entitled 'Robin Wood's Criticism' that Alan Lovell published as early as 1969.[78] It served to bring to a close the decade dominated by *Movie* by questioning Wood's Leavisite orientation. Lovell quotes Perry Anderson's seminal attack on Leavis in 'Components of the National Culture', where Anderson suggests that the crucial precondition for the Leavisite 'epistemology' is a 'shared, stable system of beliefs and values' but shows that 'if the basic formation and outlook of readers diverges, their experience will be incommensurable', and Lovell goes on to suggest that the requisite shared system of beliefs and values 'is missing from film criticism. There is no agreement as to who are the important artists, no consensus about critical methods, no agreement about the crucial relationship between the artist and the industrial system of which he is part.'

Of course, this was less a criticism of Robin Wood than a statement of the radical possibilities of film studies and a programme of action for the future. The argument conducted in the pages of *Screen*, and often referred to by its proponents as well as its detractors as an argument about 'theory', was really, as Ben Brewster points out, an argument about the nature of liberal education in general:

Whether you took a Leavisite position with its emphasis on the high culture tradition or whether you took an ultra-liberal position, with its emphasis on individual child response, what was common to both was the unargued nature of the critical position and the *unarguable* nature of it . . . and what educationalists felt was that however much you disclaim it you are bound, in effect, to produce an authoritarian educational context by doing that. . . . The solution was to have some much more rational and objective knowledge of the objects you were considering, which was in some sense shared by teacher and student.[79]

There was clearly a contiguity between the interests of the *New Left Review*, and journals such as *Theoretical Practice*, on the one hand, and *Screen* on the other. There was also some overlap of editorial board membership and a shared view that much of the most interesting and innovative work in the humanities was, at that time, being published in France.[80] However, crucial differences remained in the nature of the audiences addressed: whereas the *New Left Review* remained distantly patrician, *Screen's* constant concern, even at the time when it was most under attack for sterile theoreticism, was to engage with practice. Brewster would not agree, but there was a sense in which the study of film was conceived as strategic: as Alan Lovell's article had made clear, it offered a standpoint from which to criticise other disciplines, especially the dominant one of English Literature, and above all to change the nature of liberal education from within. This, ultimately, is the significance of *Screen* and the growth of film studies in the 1970s.

However, there was another aspect to *Screen's* commitment to 'theory' that is self-evident to those concerned with cinema but rarely discussed outside such circles. *Movie*, it will be recalled, lost ground as much because of changes in the film industry as for any other reason. Conscious of the need for change, SEFT appointed Sam Rhodie to edit *Screen*. His inaugural statement, though concerned with the development of theory, makes clear the urgent need to come to terms with modernism:

What has happened, is happening in film? *Auteur* criticism culturally is not an isolated phenomenon. Since its appearance (but not necessarily due to that appearance) an extraordinary emphasis has been placed within film-making on individual creativity and expression, on formal structure rather than on social communicability and comprehension. Whether it is mainstream, underground, or somewhere-in-between cinema, continuous narrative structures have been broken, made more elliptical, surface values have come to the fore, an older previous naturalist convention has been thrown over. Films are increasingly more difficult to comprehend. Emphasis is less on presenting some sort of reality than in presenting perspectives on reality and on modes of perceiving. Film has become more personal, more private, more subjective. . . . What is it all about?[81]

Such a description would fit not just Godard's films after 1968 but much of the new French cinema, much new American cinema and some British and German cinema as well, whilst the narrative modes of mainstream cinema were forced to respond indirectly to this *avant-garde* (a director such as Robert Altman interestingly straddles the line between classicism and the *avant-garde*). In coming to terms with the new cinema, and particularly in its investigation of the works of Godard, Straub and Oshima, *Screen* now had also to come to terms with the *avant-garde*, which had previously been thought marginal to its projects for change. In a certain sense all film-viewers, not just those who contributed to *Screen*, were forced to return to the issues raised by *Sequence* in the 1940s: What is the nature of film realism? What is the role of the author, and of the spectator?

In choosing the problems of signification and subjectivity as its terrain, in seeking out the chinks in the consensus, the interstices or 'spaces' through which to drive the wedge of counter-cultural practice, *Screen* strongly resembled *Tel quel*. *Screen* was not the first film journal to take account of the revolution of the human sciences in France: that honour must go to the Cambridge undergraduate journal *Cinema*.[82] Nor did it provide the first attempt to apply the lessons of the *sciences humaines* to the cinema, for this was contained in Peter Wollen's *Signs and Meaning in the Cinema* (1969). But with hindsight it is apparent that it opted, in fact, for a much more direct approach to the questions of realism.

Screen in the 1970s seems, at first glance, to have followed the evolution of the debates about the cinema that were being carried on in France. Having set itself to translate a certain amount of new

French material (and this was an explicit project), it provided in 1973 a special issue entitled 'Cinema Semiotics and the work of Christian Metz',[83] which gave a brief guide to the semiological work of the 1960s in France. It then followed *Cahiers* through a period in which materialism and ideology, following 1968, were the issues of close concern. It reprinted parts of the debate from *Cahiers* in 1969 and 1970, but without the serialisation of Eisenstein's writings and without fully relating this debate to Bazin's discussions of technology. The seminal text of this period is 'Young Mr Lincoln'.[84] Finally, it followed the upsurge of interest in psychoanalysis and the cinema which had given rise to a special issue of *Communications* (no. 23, 1975) including Metz's seminal text 'Le Signifiant imaginaire'.[85] One only has to look at the shift from Marx to Freud in French writing of the period, not just texts devoted to the cinema, to understand what *Screen* was about, though without that information it might not always have been obvious.

Alongside this logic, however, there was another which brought out considerable scepticism about the possibilities of the modernist text. The most frequently cited articles from the *Screen* of this period are Colin MacCabe's 'Realism and the Cinema: Notes on Some Brechtian Theses' and Laura Mulvey's 'Visual Pleasure and the Narrative Cinema'. This is partly to be explained by the fact that each succeeds in putting over interpretations of French material in accessible form. But it is also because each addressed the problem of realism in a way which related directly to the traditions of British criticism and the concerns of practising film-makers in the period. Thus, although Mulvey's article is inspired by Lacan's description of the mirror phase and is entirely concerned with the creation and representation of identities, it appealed to a self-evidence which was capable of being received quite simply because it discussed women. Similarly, MacCabe's article draws on a body of work represented in France by Pierre Macherey, Renée Balibar and Michel Pêcheux (whom he cites), as well as the discussions by Sartre, in *Qu'est-ce que la littérature?*, and Barthes, in *Le Degré zéro de l'écriture*, of the possibilities of revolutionary writing. But MacCabe poses a central question:

> One could say that the revolutionary artist may practise certain strategies of subversion but must finally content himself with the production of a progressive realist text. The question I want to raise here . . . is the possibility of another activity which rather

than the simple subversion of the subject or the representation of different (and *correct*) identities, would consist of the displacement of the subject within ideology – a different constitution of the subject.[86]

Every film-maker could aspire to produce a progressive realist text, and one or two, such as Ken Loach, succeeded in the seventies. Every trade unionist and every woman could engage with the representation of *correct* identities. Indeed, many trade unions and women's organisations set up media-studies groups in the late seventies for just that purpose. But when it came to 'the displacement of the subject within ideology', the journal reached an intellectual impasse. Stephen Heath's series of articles exploring Lacanian psychoanalysis were challenged by a section of the editorial board who felt that the material was obscure, uncritical of Freud and unhelpful to practising teachers.

Since that time[87] *Screen* has apparently lost its appetite for innovation and has reverted to the earlier, more pragmatic and less interventionist approach to film education. But this does not mean that the activities of the seventies were without lasting effect. The study of mass culture and mass communications has been permanently changed by semiotics from France, while the reading of Lacan, initiated by Stephen Heath, continues in different arenas. Where *Screen* did fail was in paying too little attention to British film-making, which was, after all, the staple viewing of the audiences with which it was concerned. One only has to consider what passes across our screens in any given week to realise that modernism might as well not exist for all the effect it has had on British realism. The agenda drawn up by *Sequence* after the war remains on the table.

NOTES

Earlier versions of part of this essay were given as lectures at the British Institute in Paris and to the Political Studies Association. I am most grateful to Ben Brewster, Alan Lovell and V. F. Perkins for agreeing to recall the past and to Mandy Merck and Vincent Porter for the loan of rare documents.

1. 'Six personnages en quête d'auteurs: débat sur le cinéma français', *Cahiers du cinéma*, May 1957, pp. 16–17, which may be translated as follows:

BAZIN: What can be learned from the mediocrity of the British cinema?

RIVETTE: British cinema is a *genre* cinema but those genres spring from no deep necessity. On the one hand, the genres do not have an inherent justification as the Western and the thriller do within the American cinema . . . on the other hand, it is not an *auteur* cinema since no one has anything to say. It is a cinema which limps along and falls between two stools. A cinema which is exclusively based on supply and demand.

2. 'What's Wrong with British Films?', *Film*, 14 (Nov–Dec 1957).
3. Cf. Christophe Campos, *The View of France from Arnold to Bloomsbury* (London: Oxford University Press, 1965).
4. This account owes a great deal to Margaret Dickinson and Sarah Street, *Cinema and State: The Film Industry and the Government 1927–84* (London: British Film Institute, 1985).
5. Cf. Charles Barr, *Ealing Studios* (London: Cameron and Tayleur, 1977); and John Ellis, 'Made in Ealing', *Screen*, 16.1 (1975) 78–127.
6. Dickinson and Street, *Cinema and State*, p. 150.
7. See Simon Hartog and Margaret Dickinson, 'Interview with Sir Harold Wilson', *Screen*, 22.3 (1981) 9–22.
8. A fascinating article by Luc Boltanski, 'America, America. Le Plan Marshall et l'importation du "management" en France', *Actes de la recherche en sciences sociales*, 38 (May 1981) 19–41, documents the mistrust in which the United States was held in France in the early 1950s and serves to correct Jim Hillier's view in his introduction to *Cahiers du cinéma: the 1950s* (London: Routledge and Kegan Paul, 1985) that America was almost universally well regarded. British intellectuals were more pro-American than the French were.
9. Gavin Lambert and Penelope Houston subsequently edited *Sight and Sound*. Houston still does.
10. This was the position of the Film Appreciation school, whose *maître à penser* was Roger Manvell, and it was reflected both in the programming of the National Film Theatre and in the work of the BFI Education Department. There were, of course, technical reasons why early sound cinema should have appeared naïve and clumsy. Cf. Jean-Pierre Jeancolas, *15 Ans d'Années Trente* (Paris: Stock, 1982) pp. 52–5. André Breton's opinion, shared by many artists, was that sound cinema represented 'une régression désolante vers le théâtre'.
11. Cf. John Boud, 'Film among the Arts', *Sequence*, 1 (Dec 1946) 1–3.
12. See, for example, Ian Cameron, 'Films, Directors and Critics', *Movie*, 2 (Sep 1962) 4–7; and Raymond Durgnat, 'Standing up for Jesus', *Motion*, 3 (Autumn 1963) 25–8 and 38–41.
13. Lindsay Anderson, 'Angles of Approach', *Sequence*, 2 (Winter 1947) 5–8; Gavin Lambert, 'British Films: Survey and Prospect', ibid., pp. 9–14; Lindsay Anderson, 'British Cinema and the Descending Spiral', *Sequence*, 7 (Spring 1949) 6–10, and 'The Director's Cinema?', *Sequence*, 12 (Autumn 1950) 6–11 and 37.
14. Anderson, 'British Cinema and the Descending Spiral', *Sequence*, 7, p. 8.
15. Ibid., p. 11.

16. Lambert, 'British Films: Survey and Prospect', *Sequence*, 2, p. 14.
17. Anderson, 'The Director's Cinema?', *Sequence*, 12, p. 14.
18. Anderson, 'Angles of Approach', *Sequence*, 2, p. 8.
19. Cf. François Truffaut, 'Une certaine tendance du cinéma français', *Cahiers du cinéma*, 31 (Jan 1954) 15–28, where an attack on the pre-eminence of screenwriters is launched. Other similarities between *Sequence* and *Cahiers du cinéma* might be observed in the close attention paid to how films are made. Cf. Lindsay Anderson, *Making a Film: The Story of 'Secret People'* (London: Allen and Unwin, 1952).
20. Lindsay Anderson, 'Free Cinema', *Universities and Left Review*, 1 (1958) 51–2.
21. Gavin Lambert, 'Free Cinema', *Sight and Sound*, Spring 1956, p. 173.
22. John Berger, 'Look at Britain', *Sight and Sound*, Summer 1957, pp. 12–13.
23. Richard Hoggart, 'We are the Lambeth Boys', *Sight and Sound*, Autumn 1959, pp. 164–5.
24. It is interesting that the grotesque plays an increasing role in Anderson's œuvre until, in *Britannia Hospital*, it becomes the dominant mode. Schlesinger, though with less wit and no finesse, shows the same tendency in, for example, *Sunday, Bloody Sunday*.
25. Title of a pamphlet by Peter Graham (London: Axle Publications, 1963).
26. Cf. Richard Findlater (ed.), *At the Royal Court* (Ambergate, Derbys: Amber Lane Press, 1981).
27. Cf. Penelope Houston, 'Room at the Top', *Sight and Sound*, Spring 1959, p. 51.
28. Graham, *The Abortive Renaissance*. This is, of course, taken almost directly from André Bazin's essay 'Le réalisme cinématographique et l'école italienne de la Libération', repr. in *Qu'est-ce que le cinéma?*, édition définitive (Paris: Eds. du Cerf., 1975) pp. 257–85.
29. In view of the so-called Cambridge English controversy associated with the journal *Screen* in the 1980s, it is perhaps of some sociological interest that almost all of the early British disciples of *Cahiers*, including contributors to the *New Left Review*, came out of Oxford.
30. Bazin's collected essays were published as *Qu'est-ce que le cinéma?*, 4 vols (Paris: Eds. du Cerf, 1958–61), and it was probably this edition that was read in England. The collection should not be confused with the less complete so-called 'édition définitive' (see n. 28), which is by no means definitive. Dudley Andrew, in *André Bazin* (London: Oxford University Press, 1978) provides no bibliography, so that any scholarly approach to Bazin would begin by first collecting what he wrote. By all accounts his output was voluminous.
31. Cf. Bazin's 'Ontologie de l'image photographique', *Qu'est-ce que le cinéma?*, édition définitive, pp. 9–17.
32. Bazin, 'Le réalisme cinématographique et l'école italienne', ibid., pp. 267–9, which may be translated: 'Not the least of the Italian cinema's merits is to have reminded us that all "realism" in art is in the first place profoundly "aesthetic" . . . and even when invention and formal complexity do not affect the very content of a work they still influence how effective it is.'

33. The exception being Roger Leenhardt, whose essays on film technique, published in *Esprit* in the 1930s, earned him the role of spiritual father to the *Nouvelle Vague*. See Roger Leenhardt, *Les Yeux ouverts* (Paris: Seuil, 1979).

34. These conventions were, of course, totally disrupted by Godard in films such as *Lotte in Italia* and, most recently, *Passion*. The observation nevertheless remains true for the 1950s and most of the 1960s.

35. Cf. *Qu'est-ce que le cinéma?* It is not difficult to refute Bazin. Both in Renoir's *La Règle du jeu* and Wyler's *The Best Years of Our Lives*, films which he particularly admired, deep focus is a device which creates ambiguity in order to heighten dramatic tension, while in *Citizen Kane* the photography is almost expressionist. But, of course, the debate was not really about the technical resources of the cinema.

36. Bazin was nothing if not a Cold War critic, hence his extravagant claim in *Cahiers du cinéma*, Feb 1948, p. 70, that 'la profondeur du champ de William Wyler se veut libérale et démocratique comme la conscience du spectateur américain et les héros du film' ('William Wyler's depth of field aspires to be liberal and democratic, like the mind of the American viewer and the heroes of the film'). Inexplicably, however, Gérard Gozlan's attack on Bazin's Catholicism and 'Manichean world view' published in *Positif* (1962) appears as 'In Praise of Bazin' in Peter Graham (ed.), *The New Wave* (London: Secker and Warburg, 1968) pp. 52–72.

37. Cf. André Bazin, 'Comment peut-on être Hitchcocko – Hawksien?', *Cahiers du cinéma*, Feb 1955, pp. 17–18, and 'La Politique des auteurs', *Cahiers du cinéma*, Apr 1957, pp. 2–11.

38. Quite the best account of the *politique des auteurs* is to be found in Peter Wollen, *Signs and Meaning in the Cinema* (London: Secker and Warburg, 1969). The American critic Andrew Sarris popularised as *'auteur theory'* a version which consisted in the selection of so-called 'pantheon directors'. There is a considerable difference between the two.

39. Wollen, *Signs and Meaning*, pp. 74–5.

40. Cf. Eric Rohmer's claim that 'Le visage de la France a fort peu changé depuis 20 ans . . . il ne s'est rien passé de nouveau dans les mœurs, sinon ce qui nous vient de l'Amérique' ('The face of France has altered very little over the past 20 years . . . nothing has changed in the way we live except what has come to us from America') – 'Six personnages en quête d'auteurs', *Cahiers du cinéma*, May 1957, p. 19. Fascination did not mean total approval, however.

41. Peter Wollen, in *Signs and Meaning*, emphasises the importance of the surrealist heritage in the elaboration of the *politique des auteurs*.

42. Sam Fuller was an *auteur* who was typically held to have made his mark despite the studio system.

43. Godard famously remarked that 'Les travellings sont affaire de morale', which, since he was referring specifically to shots in *Hiroshima, mon amour*, gives 'the tracking shots are a question of morality'. He is frequently misquoted as having said, 'La morale est affaire de travellings.' Nevertheless, the point is made. See *Cahiers du cinéma*, July 1959.

44. This caused a furore which prompted Bazin to defend his young colleagues thus: 'De ce que leur érudition n'est pas fondée sur les

mêmes critères de valeur que celles des critiques chevronnés ou
anglais n'enlève rien à leur efficacité' ('Their effectiveness is not
impaired just because their erudition is not based on the same criteria
of value as those of established or English critics') – 'Comment peut-on
être Hitchcocko–Hawksien?', *Cahiers du cinéma*, Feb 1955, p. 18. The
Hitchcock interviews were also published in book form: Eric Rohmer
and Claude Chabrol, *Hitchcock* (Paris: Editions Universitaires, 1957).

45. 'Défence et illustration du découpage classique', *Cahiers du cinéma*, Sep
1952; repr. in Jean Narboni (ed.), *Jean-Luc Godard par Jean-Luc Godard*
(Paris: Pierre Belfond, 1968) p. 29. The passage may be translated thus:
'To quote Fénelon, I seek "a sublime so familiar that everybody might
be tempted to think he could have achieved it without effort."'

46. Ibid., p. 33, which may be translated thus: 'We should not forget that
the facility of transatlantic film-makers echoes that once found in
France in the delightful but unfortunate eighteenth century'.

47. John Hess, 'La Politique des auteurs', *Jump Cut*, May–June 1974, pp.
19–22, and July–Aug 1974, pp. 20–2.

48. Maurice Merleau-Ponty, 'Le cinéma et la nouvelle psychologie', *Sens et
non-sens* (Paris: Nagel, 1966) pp. 104–5. This text was originally delivered
as a lecture to the Institut des Hautes Etudes Cinématographiques in
1947. The passage may be translated thus: 'the cinema does not give us
man's *thoughts*, as the novel did for so long, it gives us his conduct or
his behaviour, it provides us directly with this particular way of being
in the world. . . . The cinema is particularly well-suited to bringing
out the union of mind and body, of mind and world, and how the one
is expressed in the other.'

49. 'Une certaine tendance du cinema français', *Cahiers du cinéma*, Jan
1954, pp. 15–29.

50. Narboni, *Jean-Luc Godard*, p. 315.

51. Claude Chabrol, 'Petits sujets, grands sujets', *Cahiers du cinéma*, Oct
1959; tr. in Graham, *The New Wave*, pp. 73–8.

52. See Claude Brémond, Evelyne Sullerot and Simone Berton, 'Les Héros
de films dits "de la Nouvelle Vague"', *Communications*, 1 (1961)
142–77.

53. Cf. Edgar Morin, 'Conditions d'apparition de la "Nouvelle Vague"',
ibid., pp. 139–41.

54. Penelope Houston, 'Into the Sixties', *Sight and Sound*, Winter 1959, pp.
5–6.

55. Geoffrey Nowell-Smith, 'A New Cinematic Language', *Oxford Opinion*,
45 (1960) 24–6.

56. Cf. Allen Eyles, 'Focus on Exhibition', *Motion*, 2 (Winter 1961) 13–19
and 38. Artificial Eye, Cinegate and the Other Cinema are all distribution companies which came into being as a result of this shake-out in
film distribution, and each specialises in one section of the art market
(e.g. new German cinema, new American cinema, Latin American
and Third World cinema).

57. Cf. Mark Shivas's contention that 'in the face of the only tenable
division, talented and untalented, British writers on the film resolutely
continue with their distinction between art and commerce – 'The

Commercial Cinema: A Few Basic Principles', *Oxford Opinion*, 38 (1960) 38–9.

58. June 1962 to July–Aug 1963 (monthly): Spring to Autumn 1965 (3 issues, quarterly); Spring 1968; Winter 1968; 1969 to present (annually). See also Ian Cameron (ed.), *Movie Reader* (London: November Books, 1972).

59. See I. and E. Cameron, *The Heavies* (1969); I. Cameron and R. Wood, *Antonioni* (1968); R. Wood, *Arthur Penn* (1968); I. and E. Cameron, *Broads* (1969); I. Cameron (ed.), *The Films of Robert Bresson* (1969), and *Second Wave* (1970); R. Wood, *The Apu Trilogy* (1972).

60. *Movie*, 1 (June 1962) 3–7.

61. Mark Shivas, *Oxford Opinion*, 38 (Apr 1960) 38–9; and Ian Cameron, *Movie Reader*. p. 36.

62. Ian Cameron, 'Films, Directors and Critics', *Movie*, 2 (Sep 1962) 4–7.

63. Respectively, *Movie*, 1 (June 1962) 25–7; 2 (Sep 1962) 28–30; 4 (Nov 1962) 4–6; 5 (Dec 1962) 19–20; 6 (Jan 1963) 8–12; 9 (May 1963) 26–7.

64. Cf. V. F. Perkins: 'This is my criticism of Godard – he has to use too much to get what a really fine film-maker could achieve without this extreme technical device' – 'Movie Differences: A Discussion', *Movie*, 8 (Apr 1963) 28.

65. Thanks to Richard Roud, who was sensitive to *Cahiers du cinéma* and to *Movie*, the National Film Theatre mounted seasons on 'The Western' and 'American Thrillers' (1961), 'Fritz Lang' and 'Vincente Minnelli' (1962), 'Howard Hawks' (1963). In February 1964 Ian Cameron was asked to offer a 'Critics' Choice' and proposed *Adieu Philippine*, *Angel Face*, *Diary of a Chambermaid*, *It's Always Fair Weather*, *The Left-Handed Gun* and *Viaggio in Italia*.

66. Perkins, 'Movie Differences', *Movie*, 8, pp. 23–34.

67. Conversation with the author, June 1985.

68. V. F. Perkins, *Film as Film* (Harmondsworth, Mddx: Penguin, 1972).

69. Lindsay Anderson, 'A Critical Betrayal', *Guardian*, 2 Mar 1981.

70. Cf. Ed Buscombe, Christine Gledhill, Alan Lovell and Christopher Williams, 'Why We Have Resigned from the Editorial Board of *Screen*', *Screen*, 17.2 (1976) 106–9; and B. Brewster, E. Cowie, J. Halliday, K. Hanet, S. Heath, C. MacCabe, P. Willemen, P. Wollen, 'Reply', ibid., pp. 110–16. Brewster was unofficially editor from 1973 and officially from 1974.

71. Conversation with the author, June 1985.

72. A body in receipt of a grant-in-aid from the BFI.

73. Typewritten transcript available in the British Library.

74. Cf. *The Film in National Life: A Report of the Inquiry Chaired by Sir Benjamin Gott* (London: Allen and Unwin, 1932).

75. Personal testimony by Alan Lovell.

76. This policy has been extremely successful. Currently there are film-studies departments at Canterbury (headed by Ben Brewster), Warwick (headed by V. F. Perkins) and East Anglia, all of which have been aided by the BFI, as have the Institute of Education in London and the Universities of Essex and Stirling.

77. Cf. Sam Rhodie's comment that 'Work must now be devoted to the

auteur theory, on the *auteur* theory and not the *auteur* theory used as a means to do work on film' – 'Education and Criticism. Notes on Work to be Done', *Screen*, 12.1 (1971) 9–13.

78. *Screen*, 10.2 (1969) 42–55.
79. Conversation with the author.
80. In addition to the many ties of personal friendship, Jon Halliday was for a while a member of both boards; Peter Wollen, employed in the BFI Education Department, had contributed to the *New Left Review* under the pseudonym 'Lee Russell' and was on the *Screen* board; Ben Brewster was one of the founders of *Theoretical Practice* and later editor of *Screen*; Alan Lovell had contributed to the *New Left Review* and was on the board of *Screen* as well as being employed in the BFI Education Department.
81. Rhodie, 'Education and Criticism', *Screen*, 12.1, pp. 11–12.
82. In *Cinema*, 3 (1968), Mike Wallington published an article on Pasolini which referred to Barthes, Althusser and Lacan. Sam Rhodie, who was responsible for bringing Stephen Heath onto the board of *Screen*, was also a contributor to *Cinema*.
83. *Screen*, 14.1–2 (1973). This was, of course, a very partial view of Metz and took no account of most of the material in *Essais sur la signification au cinéma*.
84. Essentially Narboni's and Comolli's 'Cinéma/Idéologie/Critique', repr. with 'Young Mr Lincoln' in John Ellis (ed.), *Screen Reader*, 1 (London: Society for Education in Film and Television, 1977).
85. *Screen*, 16.2 (1975) 14–76.
86. Laura Mulvey, 'Visual Pleasure and the Narrative Cinema', *Screen*, 16.3 (1975); Colin MacCabe, 'Realism and the Cinema: Notes on some Brechtian Theses', *Screen*, 15.2 (1974) 22.
87. After the publication of Heath's prophetically entitled 'Difference', the attempt to work through Lacan seems to have come to a full stop. See *Screen*, 19.3 (1978), 51–112.

10

Althusserian Materialism in England

SUSAN JAMES

Hearing that I was about to write this essay, a friend recently remarked to me that he no longer felt ashamed at not knowing about the work of Louis Althusser – a reaction which has become, I think, quite common among English and American philosophers and social scientists. During the 1970s, when Althusser was a star of the kind that shines only from Paris, many intellectuals were excited by his brilliance, and ignorance was a source, if not of shame, at least of regret. Some people studied his views and others did not; but for all of them his reputation stood high, and he was acknowledged as the author of a serious and important contribution to the interpretation of Marxism. Now that the star has waned, however, the name of Althusser is no longer one to conjure with. In France and elsewhere his claims have been criticised on both philosophical and political grounds, so that his period of popular fame is sometimes represented as nothing but a season's fancy, without lasting consequences for either the theory or the practice of Marxism.

Twenty years on, it is of course true that Althusser's work is neither so fashionable nor intellectually novel as it was, and self-avowed Althusserians are hard to come by. Nevertheless, a dismissive response to this state of affairs, which looks only superficially at the contours of Althusser's public career, is deeply insensitive to the ways in which his views have moulded the character of much recent social theory and changed the direction of current debate. His startling claims about the emergence of Marx's ideas have provoked a rejuvenating, hermeneutic interest in Marx's own texts.[1] And his insistence on the need for a materialist interpretation of these ideas, allied to an appreciation of their consequences for many of our everyday conceptions of society, has inspired a new fascination with the relation between 'structure'

187

and 'agency' in social explanation, evident in the work of Marxists and non-Marxists alike.[2] Althusser's significance as a social theorist is therefore not in doubt, and he has duly taken his place in the textbooks. But, to understand why his ideas have been at once so influential and so little accepted on their own terms in the English-speaking world, one must first learn a little about them.

I

Louis Althusser, who was born in Algeria in 1918, has spent his life as an academic. Trained as a philosopher, he taught until 1980 at the Ecole Normale Supérieure, from where he published a series of essays on Rousseau, Montesquieu and Hegel,[3] and where he also pursued a deep interest in the work of Spinoza. In 1948 he joined the French Communist Party, and gradually became known as one of its most distinctive and outspoken intellectuals. His great reputation, however, is founded on two collections of essays which unite these scholarly and political commitments. The first – *Pour Marx* – appeared in 1965,[4] signalling, among other things, the emergence of a comparatively relaxed attitude to intellectual debate on the part of the French Communist Party. For at a time when the Party officially expounded a 'humanist' brand of Marxism, Althusser began to outline a strongly contrasting materialism, at once stimulating and heretical. The dissonance between his position and the Party line grew still sharper later in the same year, when Althusser gave a series of seminars with Etienne Balibar on the text of *Das Kapital*; in these papers (which were published in 1968 as *Lire le Capital*[5]) he laid out in detail a series of radical interpretative and philosophical claims about Marx's *magnum opus*, portraying Marx himself as the stumbling but triumphant discoverer of the science of historical materialism.

It may at first seem curious that Althusser chose to present his ideas in the form of a commentary on a particular text; yet this approach is in fact an integral part of his project. Only by cleansing our minds of Marx*ism*, he suggests, and looking afresh at what Marx actually wrote, can we hope to appreciate his unprecedented but obscured originality, and understand the development of his thought.[6] This last point is important to Althusser, as he uses his study of *Capital* to provide further support for an earlier claim, originally made in the essays in *Pour Marx*, that there is an epistemological break in Marx's writings, a particular point, marked by *The German Ideology* of 1845, when Marx shuffled off the coil of Hegelianism and started to formulate historical materialism proper.[7] More generally, however, Althusser's reliance on the text also fulfils the function of underpinning his radical interpretation of this very theory.

Althusser offers an account of historical materialism which is designed to avoid two unsatisfactory extremes. On the one hand, he wishes to clear Marx of the charge of holding the crude and implausible belief that the base determines the superstructure; on the other he obviously eschews the non-Marxist view that the superstructure is no more dependent on the base than the base is on it. To steer between these dangers, Althusser attributes to Marx a sophisticated and flexible account of society as 'a complex whole, structured in dominance', made up of 'practices'. Practices, the basic building-blocks of Marx's theory, are themselves complex entities modelled on the analysis of the economic mode of production given in *Capital*. Like the economic mode of production, they are seen as processes comprising raw materials, means of production and products. But, in addition to economic practice, Althusser identifies politico-legal practice, ideological practice and – in his earlier work – theoretical practice.[8] These *ensembles* are said to be found in all societies and, importantly, are invariably interdependent. For example, Althusser points out that among the relations of production of capitalist societies are the buying and selling of labour power by capitalists and workers. These relations, which are part of economic practice, can only exist in the context of a legal system which establishes individual agents as buyers and sellers. And this arrangement, in turn, may have to be maintained by political or ideological means. Certain aspects of economic practice therefore depend upon the so-called superstructure, as well as the other way round, and Althusser emphasises that it is a serious mistake to neglect this aspect of Marx's theory. 'The whole superstructure of the society considered is thus implicit and present in a specific way in the relations of production, i.e., in the fixed structure of the distribution of means of production and economic functions between determinate categories of production agents.'[9]

Societies are therefore to be seen as 'complex wholes' constructed out of interdependent practices; but, if Althusser's model is to be able to explain social change as well as social structure, some more elaborate account of the relations between practices will be needed. For this, Althusser relies on the notions of contradiction and non-contradiction, which are, he claims, in turn illuminated by the notion of the complex, structured whole. Contradiction and non-contradiction are themselves ideal types, standing at opposite ends of the spectrum of possible relations between practices, so that practices are contradictory when they grate on one another, so to speak, and non-contradictory when they are mutually supporting.[10] Althusser is not in the least apologetic about describing these relations metaphorically. Philosophy, he believes, is bound to be metaphorical, since this is the only way of breaking the bounds of established usage and grasping ideas which are not already intuitively familiar.[11] He does, however, throw a little more light on the notions of contradiction and non-contradiction, while at the same time doing obeisance to Lenin, by showing how they are incorporated into the latter's analysis of the Russian Revolution.

Lenin wished to explain why it was that, although the 'peaceable mask' of capitalism had been torn off in all the countries of Western Europe by the end of the nineteenth century and popular discontent was widespread, it was only in Russia that a successful revolution occurred. He suggests that this was due to the fact that Russia was the 'weak link' in a 'collection of imperialist states', by virtue of the fact that it contained 'all the contradictions which were then possible within a single state'. The explanation of the Revolution is consequently traced to two sets of circumstances. The first are conditions within Russia, such as large-scale exploitation in cities, suburbs, mining-districts, and so on; the disparity between urban industrialisation and the medieval condition of the countryside; and the lack of unity of the ruling class. The second deals with the relation of Russia to the rest of the world, and includes the existence of an elite of Russians, exiled by the Tsar, who had become sophisticated socialists, as well as those aspects of foreign policy which played into the hands of revolutionaries.

Althusser uses this case to support his claim that Marx held a complex view of social change, and did not regard it as the outcome of a single contradiction between the forces and relations of production.[12] He appeals to the differences between events in Russia and those in Western Europe to show that, while a contradiction between the forces and relations of production may be a necessary condition of a situation in which revolution is 'the task of the day', it is clearly not sufficient to bring about a revolution proper:

> If this contradiction is to become *'active'* in the strongest sense, to become a ruptural principle, there must be an accumulation of 'circumstances' and 'currents' so that whatever their origin and sense (and many of them will *necessarily* be paradoxically foreign to the revolution in origin and sense, or even its 'direct opponents'), they *'fuse'* into a *ruptural unity*: when they produce the result of the immense majority of the popular masses *grouped* in an assault on a regime which its ruling classes are *unable to defend*.[13]

And then he claims that the list of circumstances above were among the factors needed to produce the revolution in Russia. Furthermore, these circumstances are said to be essentially heterogeneous, so that they cannot be seen as aspects of one large contradiction; each is a contradiction within a particular social totality:

> If, as in this situation, a vast accumulation of 'contradictions' comes into play *in the same court*, some of which are radically heterogeneous – of different origins, different sense, different *levels* and *points* of application – but which nevertheless 'merge' into a ruptural unity, we can no longer talk of the sole, unique power of the general 'contradiction'.[14]

Althusser therefore concludes that Marx's concept of contradiction is inseparable from that of a social whole, and borrows a Freudian term to describe the relations between various states of affairs. Changes in social structure are said to be *overdetermined* by numerous contradictions.[15]

This reading, if it is correct, certainly demolishes the charge that Marx is a vulgar materialist. As it stands, however, it is equally destructive of the claim that he is any kind of materialist at all, since there is so far no suggestion that economic practice has any special role to play. To correct this impression, Althusser introduces the idea that the complex whole is 'structured in dominance'; one of its practices dominates the others, in the sense that it has more effect on them than they have on it, and therefore stands out as being of particular significance. This most prominent aspect of society (which is held to be religious in feudal formations and economic in capitalist ones) is called the 'dominant instance', and Althusser argues that it is in turn determined 'in the last instance' by the economy. That is to say, the economic practice of a society determines which other aspect of it dominates that society as a whole.[16]

The idea of determination in the last instance is therefore vital to Althusser's analysis of historical materialism, but one may still wonder why there must always *be* a dominant instance determined by economic practice. The answer is to be found, I think, in the underlying belief that any mode of production which distributes wealth away from its producers will not survive unless it can somehow be made acceptable. The *dominant* instance of a society is then that aspect of it which sustains the existing economic system by controlling and justifying its allocation of income and resources. And, granted that particular modes of production will be more effectively legitimated by some practices than by others, the exact character of an economy will determine which instance is dominant.

According to Althusser, the analysis of society as a complex whole was one of Marx's greatest achievements. To appreciate its significance, however, it is not enough to regard it, as we have so far done, as a relatively straightforward account of social organisation and change; instead, one must look more deeply into the epistemological assumptions underlying it. For the extraordinary innovativeness of Marx's insights only becomes clear once we realise that he constructed a theory quite unlike those of his predecessors and of a kind of hitherto unknown, a science of historical materialism comparable in originality to the mathematics of Thales or the cosmology of Galileo.[17]

Althusser's discussion of the birth of historical materialism and the analogy he draws between Marx and these mathematical and scientific geniuses owes a good deal to the work of one of his teachers, Gaston Bachelard. Himself an extremely eminent philosopher of science, Bachelard held that a scientific theory proper emerges out of a collection of pre-scientific techniques and beliefs, and incorporates its own epistemological standards – a set of criteria for testing and judging propositions, on the basis of which some are regarded as known to be true. These standards change with the theories of which they are a part: modern science, for

instance, relies on mathematical techniques, and, as these develop, new ways of expressing and testing them have to be found.
The epistemological criteria used to generate scientific knowledge
are therefore not fixed, but are at any time a function of a particular
set of theories.[18]

When Althusser argues that Marx transcended the 'pre-
scientific' assumptions of classical political economy to institute, in
historical materialism, a science of history, he conceives this transition along roughly Bachelardian lines. As a new *science*, historical
materialism will not merely be a modification of earlier economic
theories. It will bring with it its own conception of knowledge and
how to get it. This attempt to formulate the philosophical and
methodological precepts on which *Capital* is founded is not in itself
new. Korsch, Lukács, Marcuse, della Volpe, Sartre and Adorno
had all pointed to the need to extract a method from Marx's works,
which could then be applied and refined.[19] Althusser's attempt to
do this is unusual, however, in its scope and boldness, characteristics which have bred both intense excitement and genuine perplexity. The claim that Marx was a thoroughgoing materialist was a
heady antidote to the prevailing humanism. Yet what *was* the vast
epistemological change that Marx had wrought?

Althusser's reply to this central question begins by enumerating
what Marx is not: he is *not* an empiricist, an idealist or a pragma-
tist. Of these demons, the most insinuating is empiricism (a term
which Althusser employs in an unusually broad sense). The empiricist conception of knowledge, he says, presupposes the existence of a subject and an object, and regards the subject as gaining
knowledge of the object by extracting its essential from its inessential properties. The function of knowledge is thus to 'separate, in
the object, the two parts which exist in it, the essential and the
inessential – by special procedures whose aim is to *eliminate the
inessential real . . .* and to leave the knowing subject only the
second part of the real which is its essence, itself real'.[20] Once the
problem is set up in this way, the task of epistemology is to offer
some sort of guarantee that the object of knowledge corresponds to
the real object, that its essence has been successfully extracted, and
Althusser argues that the major traditions of modern philosophy,
however disparate they appear, should all be seen in this light.
Like the eighteenth-century tradition 'from Locke to Condillac',
the idealist solution of identifying the real object with the thought
object is 'in principle simply a variant of the confusion which

characterises the problematic of empiricism', as is pragmatism when it offers practice as the criterion of knowledge.[21] All these traditions make the same mistake: they address a 'problem of knowledge' which is presented as a genuine quest for enlightenment, but is actually limited by the need to maintain the pre-established categories of subject and object. Anything that is to count as a solution to the problem must leave these intact; yet this requirement may render it – in another sense – insoluble.

By the standards of most twentieth-century philosophy, this analysis appears monstrously unfair and shockingly ignorant. To flatten out the differences between opposed schools, to suggest that idealists and empiricists are both committed to the categories of subject and object, is enough to make one a laughingstock. Althusser is of course aware of this, and lumps such a broad spectrum of epistemological positions together the better to contrast them with Marxism. For the innovativeness of Marx's view is said to consist precisely in his break with the categories of subject and object, on the one hand, and with the idea of identifying some sort of process guaranteed to produce knowledge, on the other.

Of these two connected ideas, the abandonment of the notions of subject and object – the abolition of the subject, as Althusser calls it – is the most fundamental. What Marx means to transform here is our everyday conception of the human agent (the subject) whose desires, motives and beliefs are cited as the explanation for social events and states of affairs. Rather than being regarded as actors who make their own history, individuals are to be seen as the 'supports' of social practices which maintain and reproduce them. As Althusser puts it,

> The structure of the relations of production determines the *places* and *functions* occupied and adopted by the agents of production, who are never anything more than the occupants of these places, insofar as they are the 'supports' (*Träger*) of these functions. The true 'subjects' (in the sense of constitutive subjects of the process) are therefore not these occupants or functionaries, are not, despite all appearances, the 'obviousness' of the 'given' of naïve anthropology, 'concrete individuals', 'real men' – but *the definition and distribution of these places and functions.*[22]

This is not to deny, of course, that individuals are causal subjects: they fill various social roles, engage in the work of production, and thereby bring about changes in the social world. But their intentional properties are to be regarded as consequences, rather than causes, of social practice.

The view that individuals are determined by social practice is, of course, familiar enough, but it remains to see how Althusser fills it out. First of all, because conditions vary from society to society, the social practices in which particular individuals engage will depend on time and place. This much is uncontentious, and provides a defence of the claim that the properties of individuals are not constant, so that – as Althusser puts it – each class has 'its' individuals, whose beliefs and behaviour are founded upon their experiences.[23] However, Althusser also argues that not only do the manifestations of subjecthood change from society to society, but the concept of subjecthood itself changes. What it is to be an individual subject fluctuates from ideology to ideology:

> Where only a single subject (such and such an individual) is concerned, the existence of the ideas of his belief is material in that *his ideas are his material actions inserted into material practices governed by material rituals which are themselves defined by the material ideological apparatus from which derive the ideas of that subject*. . . . It therefore appears that the subject acts insofar as he is acted by the following system: . . . ideology existing in a material ideological apparatus, prescribing material practices governed by a material ritual, which practices exist in the material actions of a subject acting in all consciousness according to his belief.[24]

A central part of our common-sense view of individual agents is our conviction that there is an explanatory link between belief and action. But Althusser argues that this, too, is the fruit of practice:

> The ideological representation of ideology is itself forced to recognise that every 'subject' endowed with a 'consciousness' and believing in the 'ideas' that his 'consciousness' inspires in him and freely accepts, must *'act according to his ideas'*, must therefore inscribe his own ideas as a free subject in the actions of his material practice. If he does not do so, 'that is wicked'. . . . In every case, the ideology of ideology thus recognises, despite its imaginary distortion, that the 'ideas' of a human subject exist in his actions, or ought to exist in his actions, and if that is not the

case, it lends him other ideas corresponding to the actions (however perverse) that he does perform.[25]

Within bourgeois society the human individual is generally regarded as a subject with a certain range of properties, including that of being a self-conscious agent. However, people's capacity for perceiving themselves in this way is not innate; it is acquired within a framework of established social practices which impose on them the role (*forme*) of a subject. Each set of social practices not only determines the characteristics of the individuals who engage in it but also supplies them with a conception of the range of properties they can have, and of its limits. For example, individuals brought up in a truly Marxist society would presumably not regard themselves as the subjects of history, whereas those in bourgeois society believe that they are intentional agents.

Having established history as a process without a subject, Marx has, in Althusser's view, got free of empiricist epistemology and its search for guarantees. Instead, Marx asks what mechanism enables the process of knowledge, which takes place entirely in thought, to produce the cognitive appropriation of its real object, which exists outside thought in the real world?[26] But how, one might ask, does this search for a mechanism differ from the old search for a guarantee? (Indeed, might not the discovery of a mechanism *be* such a guarantee?)

The difference between the two approaches is said to lie in the fact that Marx sees knowledge as the outcome of a production process which unites raw materials, means of production, and so on, instead of as a relation between a subject and an object. Knowledge therefore has to be seen as the product of a structure, and it is only by studying the characteristics of this structure that we can come to know what knowledge is. The change is from 'things as they are' (their essences) to things as they are *produced*.[27]

Althusser originally argued that Marx's historical materialism had not only shaken off empiricist epistemology, but had at the same time got free of ideology and established a new science. Whereas ideologies were illusory representations, designed to sustain a particular theoretical account (as bourgeois epistemology sustains the categories of subject and object) and are thus arranged to produce an answer known in advance, scientific inquiry is genuinely open and critical. Sciences are also able, so Althusser originally argued, to tell you what the world is really like; historical materialism, as well as being revolutionary, is also *true*.[28]

This distinction between realist science and illusory ideology is, needless to say, extremely crude, and it is unsurprising that Althusser later abandoned it in favour of a more complex analysis of the relations between science, ideology and the subject. Rather than being straightforwardly a source of illusions, ideological practice (itself composed of ideological state apparatuses or ISAs) has an important role to play in constituting subjects:

> [It] 'acts' or 'functions' in such a way that it 'recruits' subjects among the individuals (it recruits them all), or 'transforms' the individuals into subjects (it transforms them all) by that very precise operation which I have called *interpellation* or hailing, and which can be imagined along the lines of the most commonplace everyday police (or other) hailing: 'Hey, you there!'[29]

The 'precision' of this mechanism leaves something to be desired. But Althusser elaborates it a little, using the example of Christianity, where the religious practice is said to 'hail' the individual and provide him with his status as a subject:

> It [Christian religious ideology] says: I address myself to you, a human individual . . . in order to tell you that God exists and that you are answerable to Him . . . This is your origin, you were created by God for all eternity, although you were born in the 1920th year of Our Lord! This is your place in the world! This is what you must do! . . . God thus defines himself as the Subject *par excellence*, he who is through himself and for himself ('I am that I am'), and he who interpellates his subject.[30]

This case is supposed to show not only how Christianity works as an ideology, but how ideology works in general, and Althusser denies the need for a more detailed account on the grounds that, 'as the formal structure of all ideology is always the same, I shall restrict my analysis to a single example, one accessible to everyone, that of religious ideology, with the proviso that the same demonstration can be produced for ethical, legal, political, aesthetic ideology, etc.'[31] With this reassurance he moves on.

II

Quite apart from the exegetical question of whether it is to be found in Marx's mature work, Althusser's interpretation of historical materialism has given rise to an enormous amount of philosophical debate among both Marxists and non-Marxists. In the English-speaking world (and particularly in Britain) his doctrine of the abolition of the subject and the epistemology associated with it have provoked a plethora of reactions, most of them strong: it has been heralded as the Truth, dismissed as risible, condemned as scandalous and welcomed as the rejuvenation of Marxist theory. On the whole, however, it is fair to say that hostile responses have come to outweigh the friendly ones, so that it is easy to see the reception of Althusser's ideas as a flirtation, now firmly suppressed in the name of family values.

The reasons for this are far from simple – after all, the same trajectory has been followed in France. However, the tradition of Anglo-American social philosophy is peculiarly resistant to theses such as Althusser's, which challenge its deeply embedded individualism. It is therefore unsurprising that many people should have regarded his views as barely intelligible or downright dangerous, and examples of both are easy to find. On the one hand, a number of theorists accustomed to viewing society as the outcome of both actions and structural constraints had difficulty in grasping quite what Althusser was saying. They criticised him for overemphasising the role of structures and for failing to give due weight to the part played by agents in the construction of society, not fully realising that his view aimed to undercut the very dichotomy on which their objection rested.[32] The individualist assumption that, whatever the constraints under which people labour, social organisation and change is still to be explained as the outcome of individual actions which are in some sense free, proved extremely durable. On the other hand, theorists who understood the implications of Althusser's view felt at once incredulous and – for a variety of reasons – threatened. In some cases the threat was primarily a political one. The idea of the abolition of the subject conjured up a picture of impersonal and uncontrollable practices embarked upon an inevitable historical process, which was thought tantamount to Stalinism. Although this objection was voiced by critics with various political allegiances, the most clamorous and hysterical was undoubtedly the historian E. P. Thompson, whose tract *The Poverty of Theory* alleges that 'Althusserianism *is* Stalinism reduced to the paradigm of Theory. It is Stalinism at last, theorised as ideology.'[33] This charge provoked Perry Anderson to a stern, though also rather high-handed, reply, in which the supposed affinity between Althusser and Stalin is minutely investigated.[34] In many ways, as Anderson shows, Thompson's allegation is grossly unjust: for example, Althusser was far from being a supporter of bureaucratic unity within the French Communist Party; his brand of materialism contrasts starkly with that of Stalin; and there is no evidence that he felt any sympathy for the ruthless repressive policies which give Stalin's name its dark evaluative load. Despite its unfairness, however, the charge does draw attention to a series of problems in Althusser's deterministic reading of Marx which remain to be confronted. Anderson tries to sweep these aside by valiantly asserting the compatibility of determinism and free will:

> If Thompson had allowed a normal historical consciousness to inform his attention to Althusser, he would perhaps have recalled that in the history of philosophy there is no intrinsic relation between a causal determinism and a callous amoralism. If anything, the contrary is true. The most radical and implacable determinist of all, Baruch Spinoza, was known in his own lifetime as the noblest and gentlest of men, and was canonised by his successors as the 'saint of philosophers'.[35]

But Spinoza's saintliness is not the point. First, while it is perfectly true that being a determinist does not entail having a nasty character, this reply does not capture the full weight of Thompson's charge; for when he accuses Althusser of being a Stalinist he is primarily condemning not Althusser himself, but his views. Second, while Anderson is also right to imply that the determinism defended by Althusser is true now if it is true at all and is therefore compatible with our current conception of ourselves as agents, he neglects the fact that Althusser does not propose to leave this comfortable state of affairs intact. If we were to come to believe that Marx's theory, as interpreted by Althusser, is true about us, we should presumably come to see ourselves, not as agents, but as the supports of social practices. It is the implications of this – the fact that, as one commentator puts it, Althusser presents 'human individuality as the fantasy of a creature constitutionally unable to apprehend its rigidly social location'[36] – which many of his critics find threatening, and, while their nervousness may stand in the way of inquiry, they have at least seen what is at stake. For many of our current moral and political ideas are built around the assumption that individuals are agents. Why, after all, do we often regard citing somebody's action as a sufficient explanation for some state of affairs? Because, to put it roughly, we assume that their action was autonomous. We could go on to list various constraints which narrowed the range of available alternatives, but we believe, nevertheless, that within these constraints many actions are freely chosen. If we abandon this idea, as Althusser urges us to do, we obviously lose one commonplace form of explanation. But at the same time – and this is what worries many of Althusser's opponents – we lose our moral conception of individual responsibility. If there are no subjects, no autonomous agents, then there are, by the same token, no responsible agents, and we no longer have the ability to distinguish between states of affairs for which people are responsible and those for which they are not, and thus between states of affairs for which they can be blamed and those for which they can be praised. Much of our everyday morality, not to say legality, therefore disappears.

Faced with so radical a position, many of Althusser's English readers have simply retreated into their intuitively established individualist views. Such a crazy view, they think, just cannot be right, and does not require serious rebuttal and argument. I have argued elsewhere that the hegemonal position of individualism in English social theory has the consequence that it is assumed rather than argued for[37] – a fact obviously disappointing to holists in general, and particularly to those as tenacious as Althusser. However, a number of theorists have taken Althusser's views seriously, and have produced a sustained discussion of the epistemological tenets he attributes to Marx.

Of the various criticisms levelled at Althusser's argument, some of the most serious are those aiming to convict it of begging the question. Paul Hirst raised the interesting objection that, in his account of the ISAs which are supposed to constitute subjects, Althusser illicitly presupposes that subjects exist.[38] The individuals or groups who are interpellated by ISAs have to be able to perceive, listen, recognise and then internalise the discourses which these apparatuses convey; but in order to do this they must already be subjects. Something in this argument is absolutely right, but it is difficult to tell from Althusser's own discussion of interpellation whether he is really as vulnerable to it as his critics believe. To start with the kernel of truth, if people are to be constituted as subjects, they must be capable of forming beliefs about themselves as a result of being exposed to discourses. And, in order to form beliefs about themselves, it seems that they must already have some conception of 'self' as opposed to 'other'. This is what Hirst points out. Rather than being conclusive in themselves, however, his observations raise a series of further questions.

First, Althusser would presumably not deny that people acquire some sense of the difference between 'self' and 'other' early on in their lives. But, when he talks about 'the constitution of subjects', he has in mind, as we have seen, both the constitution of the occupants of particular roles, and the constitution of *agents*. The question of whether people can be *constituted* as agents (or whether, as Hirst argues, any account of this process is bound to presuppose they just *are* agents) obviously depends on what you understand by the notion of an agent. For Althusser, as I have already suggested, this seems to consist in the capacity to act autonomously: to decide, choose, change your mind, and so on. Exactly what this involves is the subject of continuing lively debate within all the traditions of European philosophy. But, for the charge brought by Hirst to stick, it would have to be shown that the idea of being constituted as a choosing, deciding subject, is incoherent. This is certainly not obvious. Babies, for example, might perhaps have a sense of themselves as the subjects of events (things that happen to them are distinguished from things that happen to others) whilst still lacking a conception of choice. Any serious attempt to grapple with this problem, however, requires a clearer conception of the 'subject' than any offered by Althusser, as well, no doubt, as a talent for developmental psychology.

Secondly, the widespread belief that many of our most fundamental ideas about ourselves as subjects are formed in early childhood gives rise to a further set of questions about interpellation. The ISAs which figure most prominently in Althusser's account are – relatively speaking – ones which enter into our lives quite late. By the time we are a position to be interpellated by religious or educational practice we already have quite a developed sense of self – five-year-olds, for example, are perfectly good at making choices, and are in many ways established agents. So we need to be able to see the constitution of the subject as a historical process, in which certain ISAs – pre-eminently the family – play an over-whelmingly important part. For they presumably do much of the work of constituting the self as agent, preparing the ground for its later constitution as an agent of a certain sort – as a member of a particular class, as having a certain gender, as having a particular nationality.

Althusser's claim that all this is done by ISAs implies, of course, that the whole story could be different; different ideological dis-courses could and would constitute subjects who would not, by our standard, be subjects at all, since they would have a radically different sense of their own identities and capacities. Besides prompting the obvious inquiry 'What on earth would that be like?' and causing Kantians to hop up and down, this picture may be incompatible with others of Althusser's claims. I have argued, against Hirst, that Althusser may conceivably be able to give an account of the constitution of the subject which does not presup-pose the existence of a *subject* in the relevant sense. But any such account must make some presuppositions and these may be more substantial than Althusser intends.

This doubt is pursued by another critic, who argues that Althusser begs the question in a different way, by assuming some fixed traits of human nature. By allotting such a major place to ideological practice, Althusser supposes that people must some-how be cajoled, duped or persuaded into roles which do not reflect their true interests.[39] In order for a capitalist mode of production to perpetuate itself, for example, a majority of capitalists and workers alike must fail to comprehend it. But why should this be so? Only because it is assumed that if people understood the system in which they were involved they would not put up with it, and it would not go on. But this is to assume that humans have a natural capacity to recognise and reflect on their interests, and that they will only stand so much injustice.

As a rebuttal of Althusser's account of the relation between individuals and structured totalities, this objection is incomplete. Ideologies *may* be needed to neutralise 'natural' human character-istics which apply to all practices. But they might also serve to overcome properties of the individual members of a society which are themselves the result of other social practices. If this were so, the existence of ideologies could be explained without resorting to an 'anthropological dimension'. Furthermore, an Althusserian who faces this criticism directly will surely reply that there is no question of individuals who have 'real interests' being 'duped' by ideology; to talk in this way to revert to the very problematic Marx was striving to transcend. The function of ideological practice is not to 'deceive' ready-made subjects, but to constitute individuals as subjects. So, although a different totality might produce subjects who were neither exploiters nor exploited, such individuals cannot be produced within capitalist societies. For they would have to have escaped the very apparatuses which constitute subjects and thus would not be subjects at all.

This is a strong answer to the question in hand, but it releases a sea of epistemological troubles. First, as we have already noticed, Althusser's account must somehow explain the enormous variety of beliefs and judgements, many of them damaging to the *status quo*, that are found in capitalist societies (and others, for that matter). For example, if the only way to be a subject is to be constituted by the existing ISAs, how are we to explain the fact that many theorists are so convinced of the necessity of intentional subjecthood, while Althusser views it as a contingency? Did the ISAs slip up in Althusser's case? He might perhaps attribute the incompleteness of his account to the fact that he is bourgeois subject, who can only glimpse an alternative view of the individual; but this defence is still a problem, for even a glimpse suggests that the ISAs of the capitalist totality may be more or less effective and this variation will have to be explained. His reply, as I have imagined it, turns away the suggestion that ISAs somehow 'persuade' people into views and roles which do not reflect their real interest, on the grounds that these apparatuses constitute subjects rather than manipulating them. But social practices only need legitimating if there is some chance that they may be rejected. So it seems that this is a further reason for Althusser to allow that the process of constitution may be more or less successful.

On the face of it, two lines of defence are seen to be open to him. One alternative is to distinguish the constitution of individuals as intentional subjects who reason, choose and decide, from their constitution as capitalists, workers or *Lumpenproletariat*, and to argue that it is the particular roles of a society which give rise to the need for legitimation. But it is unlikely that Althusser would welcome such an option, because, as we have seen, he is anxious to reject this very distinction. The other alternative is to claim that the very constitution of individuals as intentional subjects serves to legitimate capitalist modes of production, for only if individuals perceive themselves as free agents will these alienating arrangements seem tolerable. The constitution of subjects, and the simultaneous constitution of the occupants of particular roles would then both be seen as forms of legitimation. This approach to the problem looks the more promising of the two, but breeds its own epistemological difficulties, which I shall mention presently.

III

As we have seen, Althusser presents his argument at a high level of abstraction, in outline rather than in detail, and, without a more precise idea of the subject and the practices that are supposed to constitute it, it is hard to know how to go on. For some readers this sketchiness has been a source of discouragement. Others, however, have found it a challenge, and the enthusiasm of a number of social theorists has resulted in a spate of work informed or inspired by Althusser's materialism.[40] By asking a series of more specific questions about, for example, the analysis of over-determination, or the nature of political practice, writers such as Erik Olin Wright[41] and Nicos Poulantzas[42] have aimed to formulate claims and hypotheses ripe for investigation and development. At the same time, some of them have demonstrated the limits of our present ability to give Althusserian analyses of social organisation and change, thereby highlighting the extent to which Althusser's own work is programmatic. Poulantzas, for example, offers an elaborate account of the capitalist state, designed both to display the interconnections between political practice and the various other practices of the complex whole, and to show how the state responds to changing class relations. This latter ambition is dear to Althusser's heart, for he too is anxious to integrate his image of society as a whole with the role played by the class struggle. If Althusser's view is to remain true to the tenets of traditional Marxism, his belief that social change is to be explained by appealing to the practices which constitute subjects and constrain social affairs must be reconciled with the notion of social classes. On one account, these are simply to be seen as the outcome of structural constraints; their members see the world as existing ideological practices bid them see it, and act accordingly. But this thoroughgoing determinism is not easy to reconcile with the idea that the revolutionary working class may precisely be able to see through the ideological practice of capitalist society, and, taking matters into its own hands, bring about the revolution.

In trying to accommodate these two aspects of Marxist theory, both Althusser and Poulantzas encounter grave difficulties. For Althusser the problem takes an epistemological form. If we are constituted as subjects, including as class-members, how *can* we ever 'take matters into our own hands', as Marx seems to require? Furthermore, if our beliefs about society are the outcome of ideological practices, which form us in ways of which we are unaware, how can we know that Althusser's claims about the relation between individuals and structural totalities are right? How can we be sure that they are not an ideological representation like all the others? Althusser's later work offers a reply to these questions: since we cannot expect to gain untainted knowledge of ourselves and our relation to social practices, the claims of a subjectless epistemology must be assessed, like their competitors, by the standards we habitually employ.[43] But what standards are these? And has Althusser not slid into a relativism far removed from Marx's science of historical materialism?

Poulantzas' approach to the issue of class struggle suggests that he does not find Althusser's explanations by appeal to practices satisfactory. For him, it is not enough to explain social change by appealing to variations in social structures. In order to understand the history of capitalist societies one must look in addition at the balance of power between classes and the way this power is exercised. What actually happens depends to some extent on the strategies that classes pursue and on the unity with which they organise themselves and seize opportunities to strengthen their positions. How, though, is the class struggle to be analysed? In particular, can Poulantzas explain the shifting relations between classes without tacitly relying on some sort of voluntarism? Unfortunately, although he does not admit any difficulty of this kind, his appeals to class strategy are treacherous, and reintroduce the conception of the subject that both he and Althusser are so anxious to stamp out.[44]

Scattered throughout Poulantzas' studies of the phases of capitalism are appeals to the strategies adopted by classes in order to realise their interests.[45] At first glance these appear anachronistic, for our ordinary understanding of the term 'strategy' embodies the idea of intentional action. If a class is to lay plans there must be a strategist who assesses the circumstances, evaluates possible out-comes and decides what to do; and, while these properties can be attributed to groups as well as individuals, an agent (what Poulant-zas would call a subject) is needed in both cases. Strategy, in this everyday sense, is incompatible with the abolition of the subject, and it is therefore reasonable to suppose that Poulantzas is not proposing to explain the course of the class struggle in terms of the ingenuity exercised by classes and class-members in realising their goals. But to avoid this return to voluntarism he must have in mind some further conception of strategy, and it is not surprising to find him talking about it in what might be called its objective sense: the strategy of a class – the course of action which will best enable it to gain power over other classes – is estimated in the light of its objective interests and its position in the formation, and is de-tached from the beliefs and aspirations of its members. In discuss-ing the rise of fascism in Germany, for example, Poulantzas claims that, 'with the end of the First World War, a genuinely revolution-ary period opened in Germany and Italy. Revolution was on the agenda, in the sense that there were conjunctions of objectively revolutionary situations. But the working class failed to take state power . . . and to secure its objectives in critical situations.'[46] The strategy of the working class is therefore worked out in terms of the opportunities open to it in a particular situation – or rather in terms of the opportunities that Poulantzas claims would have been open to it had the class itself been different. But strategy of this sort, while it is a useful analytic tool, does not contribute much to historical explanation. For we still have to understand what makes the difference between situations where classes pursue their objec-tive interests and situations where they stray from them.

Perhaps the most obvious course is to elucidate the strategy of classes by appealing to the constraints under which they labour. Given its position in the struggle and the structures of the capitalist formation, a class may not be left with many options. And, as long as its strategy conforms to one or some of these, the task of explanation is relatively well defined. Some of the explanations given by Poulantzas fit this pattern. Others, however, do not. He argues, for instance, that German National Socialism 'handled its main enemy, the working class and the latter's relation to other popular classes, by a calculated plan to divide it'.[47] But calculation, in the ordinary sense, requires individuals to assess, judge, choose and decide. Since we are familiar with Poulantzas' rejection of voluntarism, we shall assume that this in turn is to be explained in a way that avoids treating either individuals or classes as subjects. The choices, assessments and selections which go into forming a strategy, and the ingenuity or crassness displayed in implementing it, must themselves be shown to be determined by factors other than intentions.

This, though, is where Poulantzas lets his readers down. For instead of taking the final explanatory step he leaves them with an unanalysed notion of class strategy. They know how *not* to analyse it, it is true, but are given no positive guidance which will enable them to get around the menace of voluntarism. If we now ask how we are able to get any grasp of the explanatory role of class strategy in Poulantzas' theory, the answer is that we rely on our everyday, voluntarist understanding of it. We use this to cast light on a metaphor of which we are given no other interpretation.

This inability to realise the aspirations which Althusser attributes to Marx undoubtedly constitutes a serious criticism of both theorists. It does not, however, destroy the significance of either, as the extent of Althusser's influence testifies. More than anyone else, he is responsible for the widespread current preoccupation with both materialism and ideology – preoccupations which extend far beyond the bounds of Marxism and embrace theorists of every political stamp. The problems posed by these phenomena may well elude any quick solution. But they are extremely interesting none the less.

NOTES

1. Among the signs of this are a renewed interest in up-to-date editions of Marx's texts (see, for example, the Penguin Marx); the translation of important works about Marx's intellectual development – for example, R. Rosdolsky, *The Making of Marx's 'Capital'* (German original 1968), tr. Pete Burgess (London: Pluto Press, 1977); and a wealth of exegetical works, of which some of the most detailed and interesting are G. A. Cohen, *Karl Marx's Theory of History: A Defence* (Princeton, NJ: Princeton University Press, 1978), and L. Kolakowksi, *Main Currents of Marxism: Its Rise, Growth and Dissolution*, 1 (Oxford: Clarendon Press, 1978).

2. See, for example, Perry Anderson, *Arguments within English Marxism* (London: Verso, 1980); A. Giddens, *Central Problems in Social Theory: Action, Structure and Contradiction in Social Analysis* (London: Macmillan, 1979); Charles Taylor, *Philosophical Papers*, 1: *Human Agency and Language* (Cambridge: Cambridge University Press, 1985); J. B.

Thompson, *Studies in the Theory of Ideology* (Cambridge: Polity, 1985).
3. See Louis Althusser, *Politics and History*, tr. Ben Brewster (London: New Left Books, 1972).
4. Louis Althusser, *Pour Marx* (Paris: Maspéro, 1965), tr. Ben Brewster as *For Marx* (London: Allen Lane, 1969).
5. Louis Althusser and Etienne Balibar, *Lire le Capital* (Paris: Maspéro, 1968), tr. Ben Brewster as *Reading 'Capital'* (London: New Left Books, 1970).
6. Althusser and Balibar, *Reading 'Capital'*, pp. 13–30.
7. For this view, see esp. 'On the Young Marx' and 'Marxism and Humanism' in *For Marx* and 'On the Evolution of the Young Marx' in Louis Althusser, *Essays in Self-Criticism*, tr. G. Lock (London: New Left Books, 1976).
8. Althusser, *For Marx*, pp. 166–7.
9. Althusser and Balibar, *Reading 'Capital'*, p. 178.
10. Althusser, *For Marx*, pp. 94–8.
11. See 'Philosophy as a Revolutionary Weapon' and 'Lenin and Philosophy' in Louis Althusser, *Lenin and Philosophy and Other Essays*, tr. Ben Brewster (London: New Left Books, 1971).
12. Althusser, *For Marx*, p. 99.
13. Ibid., p. 99.
14. Ibid., p. 100.
15. Ibid., p. 101.
16. Althusser and Balibar, *Reading 'Capital'*, p. 224.
17. Ibid., pp. 166–7.
18. See, in particular, G. Bachelard, *Le Nouvel esprit scientifique*, 14th edn (Paris: Presses Universitaires de France, 1978). For an excellent discussion of Bachelard's philosophy of science, see Mary Tiles, *Bachelard: Science and Objectivity* (Cambridge: Cambridge University Press, 1984).
19. This point is made by Perry Anderson in *Considerations on Western Marxism* (London: New Left Books, 1976) p. 53.
20. Althusser and Balibar, *Reading 'Capital'*, p. 36.
21. Ibid., p. 41.
22. Ibid., p. 180.
23. Althusser, 'Reply to John Lewis', in *Essays in Self-Criticism*.
24. Althusser, 'Ideology and the State', in *Lenin and Philosophy and Other Essays*, pp. 158–9.
25. Ibid., pp. 157–8.
26. Althusser and Balibar, *Reading 'Capital'*, p. 54.
27. Ibid., pp. 40–2.
28. Ibid., p. 59.
29. Althusser, 'Ideology and the State', in *Lenin and Philosophy and Other Essays*, pp. 162–3.
30. Ibid., pp. 165–7.
31. Ibid., p. 165.
32. See, for example, S. Lukes, 'Power and Structure', in *Essays in Social Theory* (London: Macmillan, 1977); S. Mennell, *Sociological Theory: Uses and Unities*, 2nd edn (Walton-on-Thames, Surrey: Nelson, 1980) pp. 90–1.

33. E. P. Thompson, *The Poverty of Theory* (London: Merlin, 1978) p. 374.
34. Perry Anderson, *Arguments within English Marxism*.
35. Ibid., p. 125.
36. John Dunn, 'Social Theory, Social Understanding and Political Action', in C. Lloyd (ed.), *Social Theory and Political Practice* (Oxford: Oxford University Press, 1983), pp. 118–9.
37. Susan James, *The Content of Social Explanation* (Cambridge: Cambridge University Press, 1984).
38. P. Q. Hirst, 'Althusser and the Theory of Ideology', *Economy and Society*, 5 (Nov 1976) 385–412.
39. William Connolly, *Appearance and Reality in Politics* (Cambridge: Cambridge University Press, 1981) p. 50.
40. For example, Michel Aglietta, *Régulation et crises du capitalisme* (Paris: Calmann-Lévy, 1976); C. Baudelot and R. Establet, *L'Ecole capitaliste en France* (Paris: Maspéro, 1971); Guy Bois, *Crise du féodalisme* (Paris: Fondation nationale des sciences politiques, 1977); R. Linhart, *Lénine, les paysans, Taylor* (Paris: Seuil, 1976); Nicos Poulantzas, *Fascisme et dictature* (Paris: Maspéro, 1970); Pierre-Philippe Rey, *Colonialisme, néo-colonialisme et transition au capitalisme* (Paris: Maspéro, 1971); E. Terray, *Le Marxisme devant les sociétés primitives* (Paris: Maspéro, 1968); G. Therborn, *Science, Class and Society* (London: Verso, 1976); Erik Olin Wright, *Class Structure and Income Determination* (New York: Institute for Research on Poverty, 1979).
41. Erik Olin Wright, *Class, Crisis and the State* (London: New Left Books, 1978).
42. Nicos Poulantzas, *Political Power and Social Classes*, tr. T. O'Hagan (London: Verso, 1975).
43. Althusser, 'Elements of Self-Criticism', in *Essays in Self-Criticism*. See esp. pp. 119–25.
44. See James, *The Content of Social Explanation*, pp. 139–45.
45. See, for example, Nicos Poulantzas, *Classes in Contemporary Capitalism*, tr. D. Fernbach (London: Verso Books, 1978).
46. Nicos Poulantzas, *Fascism and Dictatorship*, tr. J. White (London: Verso, 1974) p. 190.
47. Ibid., p. 193.

11

Home Thoughts from Abroad: Derrida, Austin and the Oxford Connection

CHRISTOPHER NORRIS

I

There is no philosophical school or tradition that doesn't carry along with it a background narrative linking up present and past concerns. Most often this selective prehistory entails not only an approving account of ideas that fit in with the current picture but also an effort to repress or marginalise anything that does not so fit. Bertrand Russell's *History of Western Philosophy* is one fairly blatant example of this strategy at work.[1] The story it tells is a Whiggish account of how thinkers managed – against all the odds of metaphysical delusion – to come out at last (with Russell and his peers) on the high plateau of logical consistency and truth. On the way to this *dénouement* Russell avails himself of various techniques for pointing up the narrative drift. His coverage takes in all the accredited 'major' thinkers, some of whose opinions Russell is hard put to summarise without remarking how nonsensical they appear from a modern (logical) point of view. Elsewhere – as with Leibniz or Kant – he takes the more accomodating line of winnowing out the structures of valid argument and consigning what remains to the history of dead metaphysical abstractions. It is this latter technique that has characterised the approach of analytical philosophers to the history of their discipline. The question is not so much, 'What did these thinkers *mean* or knowingly hope to achieve by posing the issues as they did?'; rather it is, 'What techniques exist for translating their concerns into an up-to-date idiom based upon certain (mainly linguistic) terms of analytical inquiry?' P. F. Strawson's revisionist reading of Kant is probably the best-known example of how such techniques can be used to achieve a distinctively modern understanding of otherwise recalcitrant texts.[2] What remains of Kant after this cleaning-up operation is still 'metaphysics' of a kind, but relieved of its excess conceptual baggage and couched (as Strawson would claim) in a 'descriptive' rather than a 'prescriptive' idiom. Thus philosophy comes to terms with its own errant precursors by explaining what they *would* presumably have said if equipped with the latest analytical tools.

The result of such methods is to rewrite intellectual history from a standpoint of self-assured logical grasp where present concerns decide what shall count as the relevant or useful aspects of past tradition. And the same selective process goes to construct that typecast narrative which treats the 'British' and the 'Continental' styles of philosophising as two completely separate, indeed antagonistic, lines of descent. Thus it is taken for granted that the two sides are so far apart, with so little in the way of shared methods and assumptions, that any kind of dialogue is certain to produce mere bafflement or cross-purpose talk. British philosophers with an interest in 'Continental' theory feel themselves forced into a marginal role by the highly professionalised ethos that prevails within their discipline. This feeling is only strengthened by their more or less accepting the background mythology that explains how the two 'traditions' grew up in a state of hostility often amounting to downright mutual contempt. There are several different versions of this story at present, but they all serve equally to reinforce the sense of incommensurable aims and languages. One (the 'ordinary language' version) takes its lead from the later Wittgenstein in arguing that most of the problems that have long vexed philosophers – and continue to vex these 'Continental' thinkers – result from their use of a pointless metaphysical jargon which puts them at odds with the common-sense wisdom of everyday usage. On this account, such thinkers have failed to learn the lesson bequeathed by a long tradition of misguided speculative thought. They have persisted in errors and delusions of their own creating, hooked on a kind of malign verbal magic – 'bewitchment by language', as Wittgenstein described it – which prevents them from seeing the plain sense of things. The other exemplary narrative is that which takes not 'ordinary language' but logic (or the modern refinements of logic introduced by philosophers such as Frege) as its reference point for deciding which episodes of previous or subsequent thought are to count as 'serious' philosophy. Of course there are deep disagreements between this and the 'ordinary-language' view, since linguistic philosophy in the Fregean mode holds out for a formalised logic beyond the powers of unaided self-description vested in natural language. But these two points of view come together in regarding large tracts of philosophical country as simply too obscure and treacherous to warrant further exploration. Only by avoiding the metaphysical swamps and the high terrain of speculative thought can philosophers hope to make progress through a sense of shared rational goals. And those others, such as Derrida, who question this enterprise – who think to 'deconstruct' its most basic working assumptions – can always be written off as 'literary' thinkers incapable of serious philosophical argument.

Not that this sense of being excluded from the mainstream applies only to British thinkers of a broadly 'Continental' mind. An essay by Jacques Bouveresse ('Why I am so very UnFrench') describes what amounts to the same experience from an opposite but equally embattled standpoint. Here we have a French philosopher whose interests lie mainly with the Anglo-American 'analytical' tradition; who shows small patience with Foucault, Derrida and other purveyors of intellectual 'fashion'; and who lines up squarely with those across the Channel who would identify 'philosophy' with the raising of questions capable of clear and definitive answers. Bouveresse has a list of specific complaints against the way that philosophy is carried on in present-day France. He speaks of 'the disastrous weakening of the critical sense, the progressive transformation of the knowledgeable (or presumed to be knowledgeable) public into a sort of religious community dedicated to the cult of a few consecrated stars'.[3] Hence – as Bouveresse explains – his own reaction in favour of an utterly different philosophical style, one that prizes the close twin virtues of lucidity and problem-solving power. Hence also his aversion to the habit of thought that treats philosophical questions, in Hegelian fashion, as so many stages in a grand dialectic whose progress and significance can only be grasped in historical terms. Bouveresse admits that analytical philosophy sometimes gives rise to a distorted view of past achievements which wrenches them out of their historical context in order to lend them an up-to-date appearance. But this tendency seems to him, 'all things considered, less scandalous than the tendency to make the historical understanding of authors and of doctrines . . . a philosophical aim in itself rather than an indispensable means or preliminary step'.[4] And this for the reason that *genuine* problems – as conceived by *serious* philosophers – have a lasting significance and power to perplex that transcends all mere relativities of time and place.

From his position as a kind of internal exile, Bouveresse reproduces exactly the image of 'Continental' philosophy that one finds among Anglo-American champions of the mainstream analytical tradition. In particular, he seizes on the blurring of distinctions between philosophy and contiguous disciplines, the fact that they all become 'kinds of writing' with no especial privilege attaching to the truth claims of philosophical reason. This development he associates with the tendency, among French thinkers, 'systematically to absolve errors of reasoning and method (to the extent that these are still actually perceived) in order to retain only what is essential, namely the literary qualities'.[5] It is against this levelling or relativised notion of the human sciences – with philosophy not even *primus inter pares* – that Bouveresse takes his stand. In this present situation, he writes, 'the mere fact that it continues to conceive of philosophy as an *argumentative* discipline already constitutes by itself a weighty argument in favour of analytic philosophy'.[6] What Bouveresse seeks above all is to make philosophers aware of their own distinct vocation and the fact that genuine philosophical problems cannot be reduced to the fashionable emphasis on matters of 'literary' style. The two main threats to 'serious' philosophy come about through confusing it with the *history of ideas* on the one hand and *rhetoric* (or some version of textual critique) on the other.

'Keeping philosophy pure' is how Richard Rorty describes this perennial urge to beat disciplinary bounds and fence the subject off from adjacent terrain.[7] After all, philosophy has had to give up a good many of its own territorial claims as its various sub-disciplines have either matured into self-respecting sciences or tended to split off (like psychology) with different ends in view. So it is perhaps understandable that philosophers – especially those in the analytic camp – should now take care to frame very precisely the rules that determine what shall count as philosophical argument. Despite all their differences, there exists at least a tacit consensus between those who accept the authority of 'ordinary language' and those who look beyond it to various kinds of formalised logical account. On both sides it is assumed that philosophy is a disciplined effort to elucidate the conditions of meaningful utterance – the 'conceptual grammar', as some would have it – which enable us to make sense of language. And on both sides, similarly, much of what passes for current Continental 'philosophy' can only seem a species of heady rhetorical delusion that belongs (if it really belongs anywhere) in departments of comparative literature.

Bouveresse does not mention Derrida by name, but it takes no very sagacious reader to guess that he is the main target of all these criticisms. What Bouveresse has to say about the 'literary' turn in recent French philosophy – the foregrounding of style and the lack of concern with 'serious', substantive questions – finds an echo in the many attacks on Derrida mounted by mainstream Anglo-American thinkers. Basic to these is the charge that Derrida has erased the distinction between 'philosophy' and 'literature', treating the former as a purely textual phenomenon and thus effectively subjugating *reason* to *rhetoric*. And of course – as Derrida repeatedly shows – this move has been unthinkable in philosophical terms at least since those exemplary scenes of instruction when Socrates deployed his dialectical skills against the sophists and other such mere rhetoricians. This inaugural gesture was henceforth repeated whenever philosophers came to suspect that language, through its unruly figural powers, was threatening to get the upper hand of reason and so undermine their whole enterprise. Occasionally there would spring up temperance movements – such as the famous Royal Society programme – devoted to weaning language away from its unseemly dependence on such dangerous devices. But mostly philosophers got along well enough on the standard assumption that rhetoric was anyway just an ornament to logic, so that metaphors might be a passing distraction but scarcely a threat to the business of rational argument. For Derrida, on the contrary, it is only the strength of philosophical prejudice – sustained by a persistent refusal properly to *read* its own texts – that holds this assumption in place. What philosophy declines to think through with any rigour is the salient fact of its textual constitution, its dependence on the figural resources of a language that opens up strange and unsettling possibilities of sense.[8] Bouveresse sees exactly what is at stake when he equates the current emphasis on 'literary' style with the tendency to question or suspend those rules of philosophic reason that have always ensured the predominance of logic over rhetoric. His response – as a lone voice of sanity and truth among the apostles of fashion – is to declare flatly that the rules still hold and that nothing can come of this rhetorical turn except 'errors of reasoning and method'.

Up to now I have been presenting a fairly standard picture of Anglo-French relations in philosophy and other fields of intellectual endeavour. It is a picture that is repeatedly brushed up and hung for inspection whenever some new French 'fashion' gets the treatment from mainstream British philosophers. A. J. Ayer's essays on Sartre and Camus are perfect examples of the kind, patiently explaining how these thinkers might have saved themselves a deal of metaphysical *Angst* if they had only grasped certain elementary truths such as the fact–value distinction.[9] Ayer at least had the wit – or the sense of occasion – to adopt a polemical and skirmishing style, implying that these thinkers might, after all, be concerned with real problems undreamt-of in his own logical-positivist outlook. No such reservations are allowed by John Searle when he takes Derrida to task for his flagrant 'misreading' of Austin on the topic of speech-act theory.[10] On one level this exchange can be read as just another example (albeit an extravagant case) of Anglo-American 'common-sense' logic up against the high gyrations of French post-structuralist theory. Derrida himself concludes by voicing doubts as to whether this presumed 'encounter' of traditions can really have taken place, given the extraordinary gaps of understanding that emerge along the way. But if there is – as one can hardly deny – a breakdown of communications, it is not just a case of Derrida perversely refusing to recognise Searle's plain intentions and clear-headed argument. A careful rereading of 'Limited Inc. abc . . .' – Derrida's response to Searle's critique of his (Derrida's) text on Austin – should be enough to question the idea that analytical philosophy has all the 'rigour' and deconstruction nothing more than an overdeveloped taste for elaborate verbal games.

There already exist several fairly detailed accounts of the Searle–Derrida exchange.[11] My purpose here is not so much to rehearse the arguments and differences as to reflect on what they mean – or what they have so far standardly been *taken* to mean – against the background of Anglo-French cultural debate. In Searle's view, and that of his supporters in the 'analytic' camp, the main points at issue can be summarised readily enough. Derrida has misread Austin's text in the obvious sense that he has resolved *not* to take it as a matter of faith that Austin has succeeded in saying what he means or meaning what he says. Derrida assumes, on the contrary, that the most revealing passages of Austin's argument are those where his choice of metaphors, parables or casual locutions is such as to create real problems for any close reading of his text. To Searle, these problems simply don't exist, being a product of Derrida's perverse determination to ignore the plain drift of Austin's intentions while seizing on minor points of textual detail that philosophy – 'serious' philosophy – can afford to pass over. Surely Derrida cannot be serious when he questions the idea that language is properly and essentially a means of communication? Or when he actually suggests that fictive or imaginary speech acts (excluded by Austin from 'serious' consideration) may in fact be the model and type case of performative utterance in general? Or, again, when he problematises the idea of 'context' to the point of denying that it could ever serve as the ground of appeal for deciding what speech acts properly mean in any given situation? That Derrida indeed puts his name to such arguments can only strike Searle as sufficient evidence that he is not engaged in the business of 'serious' philosophical argument. That he makes yet further elaborate play with the notion of 'putting one's name' to a text – of claiming, like Searle, some proprietory hold over future interpretations – merely goes to confirm this impression. For Searle, it is just a fact that speech acts *do* have certain conventional (but none the less real and binding) conditions attached to their proper use. To find this situation – as Derrida does – a cause of philosophical perplexity is not only to misread Austin at several crucial points but to misconceive the very nature of language.

Such – briefly summarised – is Searle's response to what he sees as a wholesale disregard for the elementary protocols of philosophical argument. Like Bouveresse, he assumes that thinking can only be led astray by attending too closely to matters of 'literary' style, or by allowing an interest in rhetoric to get in the way of straightforward logical consistency. Yet Derrida's text has a rigour of its own, a quality too easily ignored if one reads it simply with a mind to enjoying its exuberant games at Searle's expense. Admittedly there is much in 'Limited Inc.' that can hardly be interpreted as anything but a species of elaborate textual play designed to trap Searle in the typecast role of literal-minded innocent dupe. Thus Derrida quotes whole chunks of Searle's argument, but quotes them shrewdly out of context, or in such a way as to lay them open to readings totally at odds with their (presumed) intent. And this by way of reinforcing the point: that language is subject to a generalised 'iterability' – or readiness to be grafted into new and unforeseeable contexts – such that no appeal to performative intent can serve to delimit the range of possible meaning. From Searle's point of view this is just another case of Derrida wilfully grasping the wrong end of the stick. The 'iterable' character of speech acts is nothing more nor less than the precondition of their functioning at all as bearers of communicable meaning. Otherwise every form of words would be tied so completely to its unique original context that only the speaker could possibly know what it meant. So surely it is absurd of Derrida (Searle thinks) to seize upon this plainly *indispensable* feature of language and use it as a pretext for raising yet further misconceived problems about speech-act theory.

But Derrida is perfectly able to demonstrate that Searle has missed the point, here as elsewhere; that he has failed to grasp what is essentially at stake in this questioning of such ideas as 'context' and 'intention'. If Derrida were 'seriously' claiming that all communication is impossible – that we cannot, in practice, know what any piece of language *means*, because the relevant codes and conventions are radically underdetermined – then Searle's rejoinder would certainly hit the mark. But this is precisely *not* the point of Derrida's critique. What he calls into question is the right of philosophy to erect a wholesale theory of mind and language on the basis of common-sense notions that work well enough for all practical purposes but take on a different, more doctrinaire aspect when applied as a matter of philosophic principle. This is why Derrida goes to such lengths to demonstrate the ways in which Searle's text can be turned back against its own governing suppositions. He is not denying that language possesses an 'intentional' aspect that allows us – again, for all practical purposes – to interpret various kinds of performative utterance in keeping with the relevant conventions. But he *is*, most emphatically, denying the idea that philosophy can lay down the rules of this procedure by explaining how language *should or must* work if its workings are to make good sense. 'What is limited by iterability is not intentionality in general, but its character of being conscious or present to itself' ('Limited Inc.', p. 249). Searle adopts the same proprietory stance in relation to both his own and Austin's texts. That is to say, he assumes pre-emptive control over the way those texts should 'properly' be read, a power that passes by lineal descent from

Austin to Searle. And of course the central arguments of speech-act theory are closely bound up with this claim that it is possible – indeed imperative – to get Austin's meaning right. After all, it would create some awkward problems for Searle if Austin's text could be shown to elude the best efforts of so 'serious' and responsible a commentator.

But this is precisely what Derrida sets out to show, first in his reading of Austin and then – at quite extravagant length – in his follow-up 'response' to Searle. It is a question of uncovering what Derrida calls 'a type of "structural unconscious" . . . which seems alien, if not incompatible with speech-act theory given its current axiomatics' (p. 213). The theory, that is to say, seems constructed with a view to excluding the effects of that textual 'unconscious', in so far as they disrupt the kind of hermeneutic mastery envisaged by a reader like Searle. Again, Derrida is far from denying that we do require at least some *presumed* general grasp of an author's purpose in order to read any text whatsoever. Interpretation, as he puts it, 'operates *a fortiori* within the hypothesis that I fully understand what the author meant to say, providing he said what he meant' (p. 199). But this is an empirical fact about the psychology of reader-response and *not* any kind of guarantee – such as speech-act theory would claim – that understanding must indeed have taken place. Hence Derrida's insistence that the 'iterability' of speech acts is a function necessarily freed from all dependence on the truth of our intentionalist hypotheses. Any *theory* will have to get along in the end 'without in itself implying either that I *fully* understand what the other says, writes, meant to say or write, or even that he intended to say or write *in full* what remains to be read, or above all that any adequation need obtain between what he consciously intended, what he did, and what I do while "reading"' (p. 199). And such are the misunderstandings engendered in the course of this exchange between Derrida and Searle that the point is brought home with considerable force.

It might seem from all this that Searle stands squarely on the side of common-sense reason while Derrida pursues the usual 'French' line of high metaphysical abstraction. But in fact the exchange brings out an odd reversal of these stereotyped cultural roles. It is *Searle* who effectively translates the Cartesian requirement of 'clear and distinct ideas' into a speech-act theory founded on the notion of privileged access to self-present meanings and intentions. Derrida even goes so far as to claim that Searle's 'premises and method are derived from continental philosophy, and in one form or another they are very present in France' (p. 173). They derive, that is, from a tradition of hermeneutic thinking whose influence extends well beyond the movement that currently goes by that name. It is this tradition that underwrites Searle's belief in the recoverability of intentions and the power of a text such as Austin's to reveal its true meaning in the presence of an 'authorised' interpreter such as Searle.

As a self-conscious discipline, hermeneutics took rise with the nineteenth-century speculative turn in biblical commentary and language study. It was then refined and developed – often to very different ends – by thinkers such as Heidegger, Gadamer and Ricoeur. But it is not this modern, specialised discipline that Derrida has chiefly in mind when he associates speech-act theory with the 'hermeneutic' tradition. He is suggesting that philosophy has *always* been marked by this drive to appropriate meaning and truth in the name of a sovereign reason; and, furthermore, that local distinctions (as between Anglo-American 'empiricism' and French or German 'metaphysics') are of little account compared with this encompassing heritage. Austin may have believed – like Searle after him – that philosophy in its 'ordinary-language' mode was on the way to redeeming a long history of fruitless metaphysical toils. Yet he set about this task of demystification by claiming an authority – supposedly vested in common forms of speech – that infallibly rejoined that same logocentric tradition. 'Metaphysics in its most traditional form reigns over the Austinian heritage: over his legacy and over those who have taken charge of it as his heirs apparent' (p. 236). Where this covert metaphysics appears most insistently is in Searle's need to establish a series of enabling preconditions for speech-act theory. These require (1) the authority of Austin as original source of these ideas; (2) that Austin's texts make their meaning fully available to 'serious', authorised interpreters; and (3) that understanding can thus be rendered proof against Derrida's style of perverse 'misreading'. On the contrary, says Derrida: there is nothing in his own account of Austin that is not provoked by the odd turns of metaphor, the fictive examples and self-deconstructing arguments that Austin himself so frequently produces. In this sense Derrida can stake a fair claim to having *read* Austin more attentively – more 'rigorously', even – than a faithful exponent such as Searle.

For there are two kinds of 'rigour' in question here, and not (as

Searle would have it) a straight choice between argument on the one hand and mere verbal games on the other. Searle's is the kind of analytical rigour that knows *in advance of reading* precisely what protocols a text must obey if it is to count as 'serious' philosophy. Thus Derrida cites a passage from Searle where he states the conditions that are sure to obtain 'once one has a general theory of speech acts'.[12] This 'once', Derrida notes, has a curious double function, serving in effect both to map out a future programme for research and to determine its conclusions in accordance with a present ideal. 'Floating as it does between the logical and the chronological', Searle's casual phrase 'organises the suspense among all the presumptive heirs' ('Limited Inc.', p. 237). What it chiefly suggests is that the work of achieving this 'general theory' was programmed in advance by Austin (who unfortunately died too soon to carry it through), and now falls to those – such as Searle – who are fully in possession of Austin's intentions. So this is the one kind of 'rigour': an assurance of right-minded grasp that always already shares the purposes of those whose ideas are worth 'serious' attention. It is a form of pre-emptive self-authorisation that Derrida finds neatly figured in Searle's use of the word 'develop'. 'Searle might thus be considered to have "developed" the theory: to have produced it, elaborated, and formulated it, *and* at the same time to have merely extended it in detail, guided it to adulthood by unfolding its potential' (p. 236). By such means can 'theory' place itself in full command of a still 'developing' but henceforth safely institutionalised field.

The other kind of 'rigour' is that which Searle refuses to recognise in Derrida's text, touching as it does at many points upon the 'structural unconscious' of his own and Austin's writing, while also contriving to escape the closed circle of self-authorised discourse. It is a rigour invisible to those who read in the assured expectation that texts will reproduce their own tidy notions of logical consistency. But this is not to say that Derrida's text is unconcerned with 'logic' or with the kinds of counter-argument that must rise against it from the standpoint of analytic reason. What is in question here, Derrida writes, is the power of logical concepts (or preconceptions) to determine in advance what shall *count* as an adequate reading of philosophical texts. 'The law and the effects with which we have been dealing . . . govern the possibility of every logical proposition, whether considered as a speech act or not' (p. 235). And this means in turn that there cannot exist any protocol of method, reason or law that would ultimately 'provide a decision' or 'impose its norms upon these prelogical possibilities of logic'. Which suggests that Derrida is broaching something like a Kantian transcendental deduction, an argument to demonstrate ('perversely' enough) that *a priori* notions of logical truth are *a priori* ruled out of court by a rigorous reflection on the powers and limits of textual critique. To think the 'prelogical possibilities of logic' is, for Derrida, to open up a region of inquiry beyond all the certitudes of method and reason that have organised traditional philosophical discourse. Here, as in his other works, it involves a reflection on *writing* (or textuality in general) as that which everywhere precedes and articulates the 'laws' of logical thought. His response to Searle may give the impression of totally rejecting reasoned argument in favour of elaborate verbal chicanery designed to head off serious debate. In fact, as I have argued, it should rather be seen as possessing a fugitive but none the less rigorous logic of its own, a technique for drawing out those ruses of 'unconscious' signification that haunt the language of speech-act theory.

II

Derrida ranks Searle among the 'self-made, auto-authorised heirs of Austin.' His point is to expose that habitual presumption which enables philosophers to go (as they think) straight to the conceptual heart of a text without wasting time over matters of resistant or (to them) unrewarding detail. Hence Derrida's contrary insistence: that it is often in the margins or obscure minor detail of a text – in the footnotes, perhaps, or a passing parenthesis – that its strains and contradictions stand most clearly revealed. Such passages are the starting-point for many of Derrida's most powerful deconstructive readings. The very fact that they bear a problematical relation to the rest of an author's work – or, beyond that, to the ruling assumptions of philosophical discourse – may have caused them to be tucked away out of sight in a footnote or simply passed over by commentators in search of more enduring truths. It is precisely by seizing on such uncanonical texts, passages or details that deconstruction seeks to resist the homogenising pressure of received ideas.

Derrida is not alone in finding fault with analytical philosophy for its habit of reading precursor texts with an interest firmly fixed on its own pet problems. A recent essay by Michael Ayers offers some particularly striking examples of the way that past thinkers are brought up to date by application of modern criteria.[13] Thus he quotes some passages from Russell on Leibniz, explaining how a process of 'rational reconstruction' can pick out the elements that are still of genuine interest in Leibniz's thinking (mainly, for Russell, his logical doctrines) and leave all the rest to the historian of ideas. Any 'inconsistencies' that then show up can be attributed either to accidents of time and place – 'such as the desire to maintain an appearance acceptable to religious orthodoxy' – or to deeper logical contradictions within the philosopher's system of thought. For Russell, it is these latter kinds of problem that repay serious attention, since they belong to philosophy in its genuine, analytic form and not to the mere history of the subject. Still more confident in this regard are some programmatic statements from a book on Hume by H. H. Price. When Hume 'makes mistakes', according to Price,

> we must try to get him out of them, by suggesting other alterna-
> tives which he might consistently have adopted. We must try to
> go behind his language, and when he is obscure . . . we must
> try to make him clear. . . . 'What he really meant', we say, 'is
> perhaps not quite what he said.' . . . After all, if we can use
> them [our 'illustrious predecessors'] so, it is really the highest
> compliment we can pay them.[14]

Ayers points out some of the problems involved in this confident assumption that past thinkers can be lifted clean out of their historical context and engaged in a dialogue whose terms are dictated entirely by present concerns. Its effect, he argues, is to blind philosophy not only to important aspects of its own prehistory but also to differences in the intellectual currency of past ideas which decisively affect their *logical* standing. Doing without history to concentrate on 'pure' philosophy is a self-defeating exercise that issues in circular reasoning and multiplied instances of misinterpretation.

It also gives rise to those specific forms of *textual* blindness and repression that Derrida notes in Searle's attempt to appropriate the 'authorised' version of speech-act theory. Indeed, the two tendencies are closely related: on the one hand a programme that erases historical difference in the name of analytic reason, and on the other a selective way of reading that elevates concepts above the mere detail of textual signification. Ayers makes the point by remarking that 'rational reconstructions' in the analytic style ignore not only large tracts of intellectual history but also large chunks of the text under review. What thinkers such as Russell tend to imply in their dealing with intellectual history is the notion 'that there exist in some Platonic heaven a few "great types of possible philosophies" which are accessible to pure reason and to which we can refer directly when in need of an interpretative hypothesis'.[15] It is the same belief that Derrida detects behind Searle's assumption that Austin's true meaning is there to be discovered in his text by a patient application of preconceived methods. And it is *against* this deep-seated prejudice – the ruling supposition, as Derrida thinks it, of philosophy and 'Western metaphysics' in general – that deconstruction insists on the need to read closely and not be seduced by the false promise of absolute conceptual mastery.

I have suggested that it is wrong to view the Derrida–Searle 'debate' as simply a ritual exchange of hostilities between two utterly different philosophical cultures. Wrong because, first, the issues involved transcend such localised differences and take in – according to Derrida – everything at stake in the philosophical enterprise. Wrong again, because Derrida's deconstructive strategies are not just a kind of irresponsible playing with words, but a rigorous and consequent thinking-through of the problems thrown up by philosophy's forgetfulness of its own written or textual character. And the picture is misleading for a third reason, since Derrida is responding to something in Austin's text that he finds characteristic of 'English' philosophy, in so far as such national distinctions make any sense. The three-sided encounter (Austin–Derrida–Searle) takes on a strange topographical dimension where boundaries are constantly crossed and confused in the shuttling exchange of 'traditions'. Thus Derrida can ask, 'isn't Searle ultimately more continental and Parisian than I am?' (p. 173), and claim, furthermore, that what eludes Searle's grasp in the reading of Austin's text is precisely what invites – even pre-empts – a deconstructive account. This series of transactions, as Derrida describes it, 'seems to be occurring – to take geographical bearings

in an area that disrupts all cartography – mid-way between California and Europe, a bit like the Channel, mid-way between Oxford
and Paris' (p. 173).

On a simplified reading this intellectual landscape can be
mapped out clearly enough. 'California' (Searle) is one point of the
triangle, representing a certain kind of American analytical philosophy, trained up on logic and a principled mistrust of 'Continental'
thinking. Oxford stands in for J. L. Austin's style of linguistic
speculation, a style less concerned with matters of 'theory' and
happy to pursue problematic cases even where they lead – as
frequently happens – to a breakdown of speech-act classifications.
It is this ludic propensity in Austin's writing – call it his 'literary'
style – that Derrida can shrewdly play off against Searle's authoritarian discourse. As for Paris, it occupies an ambivalent place in
this complex topography, on the one hand a home-base for Derrida's excursions, on the other a seat of that 'hermeneutic' enterprise
that he finds oddly caricatured in Searle's performance. And this
whole situation is further confused by the fact that Derrida is here
writing for American readers, who will have a quite separate fix on
these issues of cultural difference. Thus he writes, 'I have read it
[Searle's text] in English but I am trying to respond in French,
although my French will be marked in advance by English and
destined in advance for a translation that will doubtless present
certain difficulties' (p. 173). In fact these 'difficulties' serve Derrida
as pretext for an intermittent running address to the translator,
raising (among other things) the question of where *he* – Sam Weber
– stands in relation to this shifting multiplicity of cultural contexts.

So Derrida by no means identifies with the 'French' as opposed
to some (equally notional) 'British' tradition of philosophy. In fact
his recent texts – especially *La Carte postale*[16] – have shown a
growing interest in the Oxford connection and the deconstructive
uses of certain ideas broached by such thinkers as Austin and Ryle.
What Derrida finds so congenial about 'Oxford' philosophy is
partly the absence of an American-style professionalised ethos;
partly its openness to seductive metaphors and fictive turns of
argument; and partly, no doubt, the interest in topics – such as the
difference between *using* and merely *citing* or *mentioning* certain
forms of words – that figure importantly in his own texts. The
place takes on a utopian appeal in so far as it represents a mode of
philosophising that shrewdly subverts all established orthodoxies
(including that of 'linguistic philosophy', as conceived by pro-

ponents such as Searle). So it is no coincidence that Oxford is the setting (or textual *mise en scène*) for the first 'chapter' of *La Carte postale*, presented as a sequence of anecdotal 'postcards' addressed by Derrida to various – real or imaginary – correspondents. The occasion was a visit to Britain during 1977, when Derrida spent several weeks in Oxford attending seminars and reading haphazardly in the Bodleian Library. To the 'serious' philosopher this might all seem irrelevant and just another instance of perverse self-indulgence on Derrida's part. But the point is precisely to challenge that traditional image of philosophy as a discourse of ultimate truth-telling power whose function is to rise above mere contingencies of time and place.

The postcard motif serves Derrida's purpose as a means of strategically reversing this age-old prejudice. It allows him to keep philosophical issues in play, but also to prevent them from settling down into a fixed agenda for debate. Above all, it suggests that communication is not (or not always) what philosophers – and speech-act theorists especially – imagine it to be: a closed circuit of exchange where intentions are never mistaken and messages always arrive on time at the appointed place. Derrida described writing (in *De la grammatologie*) as the 'wandering outcast' of Western logocentric tradition, denounced by philosophers from Plato to Husserl for its proneness to misinterpretation, its lack of that self-authorising power or presence vested in spoken language.[17] Writing exerts a 'disseminating' influence on language, such as to multiply the possibilities of meaning and prevent any assurance that 'true' communication has in fact taken place. And it is here that the postcard comes to signify, for Derrida, the existence of a writing at the utmost remove from traditional ideas of meaning and communicative truth. The postcard is indeed a 'wandering exile', a message most often casually inscribed and promiscuously open for all to read. At the same time it is a writing that can only make sense to one person (the presumed addressee), whose knowledge of the sender enables her to figure out its otherwise impossibly cryptic message. The postcard thus exemplifies the twofold sense in which language eludes the sovereignty of philosophical reason. On the one hand textuality exceeds all the limiting specifications placed upon language by the need to maintain a strictly controlled economy of concepts. On the other, the postcard may be seen to insist that meaning is indeed *irreducibly* specific, but tied down to local particulars of time and place that likewise escape the universalising drift of reason. In both respects it serves as an emblem of everything that is forgotten or repressed on the way to philosophical truth.

What Derrida is suggesting – in short – is that we read the great texts of Western tradition ('from Socrates to Freud and beyond') as so many messages that circulate without any absolutely authorised source or destination. The particular postcard that so caught Derrida's fancy was one that he found in the Bodleian Library, reproduced from the frontispiece of a thirteenth-century English fortune-telling book.[18] The remarkable thing about this engraving was that it showed Plato standing and (apparently) *dictating his thoughts* to a seated Socrates who obediently *wrote them down*. One can see why this image should have struck Derrida with the force of an uncanny belated recognition. One of his own chief arguments or strategies of reading – in *De la grammatologie* and elsewhere – has to do with precisely this mythical relationship between Socrates, Plato and the writing of philosophy.[19] The traditional ('logocentric') prejudice is that which equates Socratic wisdom with the authority of voice and self-presence, and writing with everything that disseminates and therefore threatens that authority. Thus Plato is the prototype of all those unfortunate philosophers who *must* resort to writing in order to communicate their thoughts, but who lay themselves open, in the process, to all manner of unauthorised reading and misinterpretation. To envisage a Socrates who *writes* is to open up a counter-tradition, however 'apocryphal', where the old logocentric mythology of origins no longer holds exclusive sway. It suggests that writing is in at the source of philosophy; that there is no thinking back to an authorised voice that doesn't pass by way of certain images or metaphors derived from writing.

Such had already been Derrida's contention in his deconstructive reading of the *Phaedrus* as an allegory of logocentric reason in conflict with its own self-generated textual paradoxes. There it was the key term *pharmakon* – caught up, as Derrida argues, in a constant oscillation of meaning between 'poison' and 'cure' – that attached itself to the topos of writing and thus undermined any straightforward univocal reading of Plato's text.[20] There is no better example of deconstruction as a form of rigorous close-reading or textual critique. But *La Carte postale* envisages an altogether different relation between writing, philosophy and its authorised self-image. Here it is a matter of mobilising all those hitherto repressed or marginal forms of writing that exist outside the received 'authentic' tradition. Thus Derrida muses on the long-running scholarly debate that has surrounded such possibly apocryphal texts as the Letters of Plato.[21] It is not only their authorship that is at issue here but also the question of where to draw the line when deciding what counts as genuine *philosophical* writing. Tradition finds room for philosophers' letters so long as they are authentically concerned with 'serious' questions and represent a genuine dialogue of minds in pursuit of some attainable truth. What it cannot take in is the notion of a writing that is cut off completely from authorial presence and addressed to no particular (professionalised) community of interests. Hence Derrida's fascination with the postcard, at once the most ephemeral kind of writing and the kind most open to interpretative guesswork by those who lack the privileged means to crack its otherwise impenetrable codes.

That Oxford was the place where all these thoughts came together in Derrida's mind is a fact of no interest according to the dominant idea of philosophical discourse. At most it is a matter of anecdotal background that belongs (if anywhere) in some forthcoming volume of Derrida's autobiography. But this is precisely what Derrida denies, this pitiless divorce between essence and accident, the genuine concerns of 'philosophy' on the one hand and mere circumstantial life history on the other. His point in deploying the postcard (of all things) as a tactical resource against the tyranny of concepts is to show how circumstance *always and everywhere* enters the discourse of philosophical reason. Philosophy is motivated by a natural desire to pretend otherwise, to treat its discoveries as a matter of timeless *a priori* truth, rather than a series of interesting notions thrown up by chance encounters with ideas and events. What Derrida likes about 'Oxford' philosophy is its attachment to 'ordinary language' *not* as some repository of ultimate truth but as a means of debunking such large metaphysical pretensions. Like Austin, Derrida is fond of inventing elaborate narratives or fictional 'cases' by which to draw out some fine point of semantic presupposition. With Austin the aim – the express aim at least – is to coax philosophy down from its heights of mystified specialist jargon and lead it back to a sense of the wisdom vested in commonplace idioms. This side of his project could hold little interest for Derrida, since it merely replaces the tyranny of concepts with the equally tyrannical regime of 'ordinary language'. But there is another dimension to Austin's writing, one that has lately given rise to some highly unorthodox accounts of his work. What is emphasised here is the seductive power of Austin's language, its habit of running away with the argument to the point of collapsing all those tidy terminological distinctions that make up the currency of speech-act theory.

Shoshana Felman has written brilliantly of Austin as a kind of philosophical Don Juan, exploring the varieties of linguistic bad faith under cover of a plain diagnostic intent to distinguish the true from the false.[22] In the end Austin's metaphors and fictive examples exert such a power over his thinking that crucial distinctions are allowed to fall away and philosophy is revealed as a kind of seductive discourse always in danger of yielding to its own rhetorical devices. The 'performative' dimension of language – its capacity to persuade, cajole, seduce – proves too much for the classifying efforts of speech-act theory. Like the amorous Don, Austin is as much deceived as deceiving, taken in by the mischievous power of false promises even as he holds them up for philosophical inspection. Theory is undone by its own fascination with precisely those aspects of language that most threaten its self-assured mastery and grasp. There could only be a genuine 'theory' of speech acts if performative language were a special case which could finally be explained on constative (theoretical) terms. In fact, as Felman shows, this distinction is undermined as the logic of Austin's argument gets into conflict with its suasive or rhetorical drift. Theory stands revealed as the dupe of its own most cherished aspirations, seduced by a dream of mastery over language that can only end up by ironically reversing those roles.

Again, it would be simplifying matters – falling back on the usual crude stereotypes – to treat this as simply a 'French' appropriation of common-sense British ideas. Certainly there is an orthodox reading of Austin, prevalent among his Anglo-American heirs, which Derrida and Felman are out to subvert. But they are also – both of them – using Austin's text as a means of contesting certain dominant trends in *French* linguistics and philosophy of language. Thus Felman takes Benveniste, rather than Searle, as her main target in that other tradition of 'straight' speech-act theory which tries to extract a coherent philosophical doctrine from Austin's endlessly elusive text. And for Derrida likewise it is a virtue in 'Oxford' philosophy that it holds out against the systematising drive that always subjugates language to concepts. Reading Austin as

Derrida and Felman read him has something of the same effect as Derrida experienced when he came across the Bodleian postcard. Like the apocryphal Socrates who *writes*, this Austin represents a scandal of displaced origins, a figure who subverts the authority claimed by his later, more 'serious' disciples.

So there is a good deal more than routine acknowledgement in Derrida's dealings with Oxford philosophy. In a sense he reverses that well-worn prejudice which holds that French thinkers are really just stylists or ingenious conceptual rhetoricians, while the serious work of philosophy goes on without benefit of 'literary' language. What Derrida finds in his reading of Austin is a speculative quality, a playfulness joined with analytical rigour, that strikes him as wholly admirable. There is one recurrent topic in the British tradition, from Russell to Ryle, which especially engages Derrida's interest. It is the matter of *naming*, and of proper names in particular: how to distinguish the 'mention' or token reference from the genuine act of using a name.

> C'est le problème '"*Fido*"–*Fido*' . . . la question de savoir si j'appelle mon chien ou si je mentionne le nom dont il est le porteur, si j'utilise ou si je nomme son nom. J'adore ces théorisations, souvent oxfordiennes d'ailleurs, leur extraordinaire et nécessaire subtilité autant que leur imperturbable ingénuité, psychoanalytically speaking.[23]

It is this same problematic – how to *know the difference* between 'genuine' speech acts and those merely cited, rehearsed or spoken in jest – that opens the way to Derrida's deconstructive readings of Austin and Searle. Oxford philosophy invites such treatment by its readiness to speculate on questions of language that often suggest deeper perplexities in the discourse of common-sense reason. 'Psychoanalytically speaking', these texts have much to tell about the workings of language at a level inaccessible to other, more heavily systematised forms of theory. It is the curious mixture of conscious and unconscious motives – what Derrida calls their 'imperturbable ingenuity' – that makes such writings a privileged zone for the psychoanalysis of philosophical texts.

And this is perhaps where Oxford philosophy impinges most directly on Derrida's interests in *La Carte postale*. It suggests – at whatever 'unconscious' level – some ways in which theory might continue to speculate on and in language without falling prey to the seductions of premature system and method. With its easy-going, gentleman-amateur style it carries, so to speak, a built-in resistance to the kinds of abstract conceptualisation that threaten all forms of philosophical activity. Deconstruction is by no means immune to such temptations, as Richard Rorty has pointed out in a recent essay.[24] Perhaps it is possible, as Derrida suggests, to work with terms such as *différance* whose non-self-identical play of sense prevents them from rejoining the logocentric order of Western metaphysics. Such terms will then be thought of as permanently 'under erasure', deployed on the page for tactical reasons but subject to a dislocating textual force that denies them any kind of semantic or conceptual stability.[25] But in Rorty's view these tactics must finally become self-defeating. Perhaps *différance* had no definite, assignable sense when it first came to light as an offbeat neologism in the texts of one Jacques Derrida. But now, as Rorty says, there is little hope of tenure for any bright young theorist who can't come up with a working definition of *différance*. The mere fact of its belonging to a shared language game – at no matter what rarefied level of discourse – is enough to give the word a certain conceptual currency. And the same applies to all those other deconstructive key terms ('trace', 'supplement', 'parergon', and so on) that Derrida deploys just long enough to keep himself one jump ahead of the current institutional game.

In *La Carte postale* Derrida goes various ways around to forestall this reduction of language (or writing) to the regulated economy of concepts. At one level this involves the 'psychoanalysis' of philosophy, *not* in the sense of digging up latent or 'deep' unconscious motives, but in order to demonstrate the disruptive circulation of messages ('from Socrates to Freud') that finds no place in official philosophical discourse. Authoritative language is that which predictably 'returns to the father' in a circuit of self-assured mastery and rational control. Like the postal system in good working order, it guarantees the passage of known information from authorised sender to proper addressee. It is against this logocentric scene of instruction that Derrida proposes a different communicative model, one that acknowledges those random, aleatory effects of meaning that philosophy has traditionally sought to repress. The mock-epistolary form of his text is designed as a further parabolic instance of the 'relays' or communicative detours to which messages are subject once they enter this open-ended network of exchange. The postal metaphor becomes another of Derrida's deconstructive gambits, an image of perpetually disseminated meaning where texts are taken up into the cross-talk of voices without fixed origin or destined point of arrival.

Like Thomas Pynchon's novel *The Crying of Lot 49*, Derrida's text is full of these obscurely suggestive postal images, conjuring up a whole repressed tradition of circulating letters, some of them (such as Plato's) possibly apocryphal, others (such as Freud's correspondence with Fliess) giving rise to much speculation. And, indeed, Derrida's essay on Freud in *La Carte postale* has to do with those speculative ventures of thought by which psychoanalysis both staked its major theoretical claims and constantly risked its own identity as a self-respecting discourse of reason.[26] There emerges an uncanny pattern of transference and delayed after-effects, such that Freud's most productive hypotheses (like that of the pleasure principle) are caught up in a tangled intersection of life and work, Freud's family history on the one hand and the future of the psychoanalytical movement on the other. It is the element of *risk* – the chancing of ideas that may have repercussions beyond all present foreknowledge or control – that fascinates Derrida in his reading of Freud. To theorise is always, in this sense, to *speculate*: to embark on a quest whose beginning cannot know its end, since events and ideas will only fall into place through a pattern of belated (*nachträglich*) recognition whose 'logic' is that of the unconscious and its devious effects. The speculator places himself beyond any point at which 'theory' can be confidently separated off from 'autobiography' or matters of anecdotal background. Freud's investment in the future of psychoanalysis is played out in his own hypothetical ventures, his family relations and his vexed dealing with various friends and disciples. It is a chancy undertaking – like his grandson's celebrated *'fort–da'* game – where the pleasures of mastery and self-assured knowledge must always go along with the element of risk.

This might all seem utterly remote from the interests and the ethos of Oxford philosophy. Yet there are many passages in *La Carte postale* where Derrida suggests some affinity between psychoanalysis and the kinds of linguistic 'therapy' carried on by thinkers in the Oxford tradition. In both cases there are powerful institutional pressures at work that would reduce interpretation to a matter of preserving the common-sense *status quo*. Thus psychoanalysis becomes a technique for reconciling patients to the 'normal' conditions of an alienated social existence. And linguistic philosophy is often regarded in much the same way: as a therapy designed to talk language down from its various bewilderments and 'lead it back', in Stanley Cavell's words, 'through the community, home'.[27] But there is another interpretation – of psychoanalysis and 'ordinary language' alike – which would draw precisely the opposite lesson. Henry Staten has put the case well in his recent book on Wittgenstein and Derrida:

> If Wittgenstein's arguments seem to establish a new ground of security, on the other hand remember that Wittgenstein is not primarily making arguments but teaching a linguistic skill. . . . Wittgenstein develops a style of writing which is radically errant, which unlids all the accidence concealed by 'normal' uses of words in order to show how many different routes it would be possible to take from any given point in the discourse – routes which we had simply not thought of because we were bemused by normality.[28]

Once 'ordinary language' is shorn of its residual metaphysics – the idea that ultimate truths are somehow vested in our 'normal', everyday forms of speech – linguistic philosophy takes on a very different aspect. Rather than reinforce existing conventions or naturalised 'forms of life', it works to reveal the unlooked-for possibilities latent in all communication. And this brings philosophy close to psychoanalysis in just the way that Derrida implies through the manifold intertextual tropes and devices of *La Carte postale*. The aim would no longer be that of therapeutically instructing philosophy in the ways of common-sense linguistic wisdom. It would now be a question of following up all those leads, analogies and 'random' associative hints that Derrida finds so aptly figured in the postcard 'from Socrates to Freud'.

Derrida operates with two distinct metaphors of the postal system, corresponding to two different 'epochs' of language and truth. On the one hand is the legalised channel of regular exchange where messages are sent 'under proper signature to the proper recipient'. This network is kept in good working order by the same laws that guarantee the authenticity of self-present meaning, the rules of correct interpretation and the 'restricted economy' of language in general. But there is another, liberating aspect of 'the post' where the system – as Derrida puts it – appears to 'take a leap' and suggests what possibilities might be opened up if these rules were perceived as mere normative conventions. Of course Derrida is not arguing – absurdly – that we should just do away with the postal system, or (as translated into philosophical terms) that we should scrap the rules and conventions forthwith and treat texts as open to *any* kind of wild anachronistic reading. What *La Carte postale* sets out to provide – in deliberately extravagant form – is a notion of how things might go with philosophy if it managed just *occasionally* to suspend its own constitutive laws of reason. The effect, as Gregory Ulmer writes, is 'to show how, out of the richness of detail available in the familiar model, an entire system of thought different from the accepted system may be devised on the basis of *excluded*, "accidental" or *irrelevant* features'.[29] And it is precisely this sense of alternative possibilities that Derrida glimpses in the texts of Oxford linguistic philosophy.

So it is wrong – as I have argued – to think of Derrida as the latest specimen of a 'French' tradition perfectly indifferent to everything that happens on the English side of the Channel. His writings have carried on a constant dialogue not only with British philosophy but also with the English language as a kind of reflex sounding-board for French preoccupations. The fact that many of Derrida's recent texts have been written expressly for translation into English is one – the most obvious – reason for this sense of close reciprocal exchange. But one can go back to his earliest published work, an extended introduction to Husserl's *Origin of Geometry*, and find the same pattern emerging. Husserl treats the axioms of Euclidian geometry as a species of 'primordial intuition', a knowledge available always and everywhere by process of deduction from *a priori* principles. Such knowledge would exist once and for all, unaffected by mere relativities of culture or language. This 'ideal identity' subsists in the nature of all valid reasoning on geometrical matters. It is the essential condition, as Derrida writes (summarising Husserl), 'that allows communication among generations of investigators no matter how distant and assures the exactitude of translation and the purity of tradition'.[30]

This question of the origin of geometry therefore provides Husserl with a grounding rationale for his entire project of transcendental phenomenology. And it was Derrida's early close reading of Husserl – continued in *La voix et le phénomène* (1967) – that marked the beginning and shaped the future strategies of deconstruction. Already in his commentary on the *Origin* Derrida envisages a kind of writing that would utterly confound Husserl's ideal of a pure, self-originating discourse of reason. It is in Joyce that he finds this alternative exploited to the full; in a writing that attempts, as Derrida describes it,

> to repeat and take responsibility for all equivocation itself, utilizing a language that could equalize the greatest possible synchrony with the greatest potential for buried, accumulated, and interwoven intentions within each linguistic atom, each vocable, each word, each simple proposition, in all worldly cultures and their most ingenious forms.[31]

Of course *Finnegans Wake* enjoys a cult status among French critics, who think of it as the one modern text that puts into practice all the claims advanced by post-structuralist theory. Besides, it is such a polyglot work that one could scarcely interpret the above passage as indicating much about Derrida's relation to *English* literature or language. What it does bring out is the importance he attaches to a writing that can cross *between* languages and exploit their difference as a kind of reciprocal deconstructive strategy. And it is here that we should look – to this region of complex interlingual exchanges and seductions – in assessing the significance of Derrida's encounter with English-language philosophy.

NOTES

1. Bertrand Russell, *A History of Western Philosophy* (London: Allen and Unwin, 1954).
2. See for instance P. F. Strawson, *Individuals* (London: Methuen, 1963).
3. Jacques Bouveresse, 'Why I am so very UnFrench', in Alan Montefiore (ed.), *Philosophy in France Today* (Cambridge: Cambridge University Press, 1983) pp. 9–33 (quotation from p. 24).
4. Ibid., p. 20.
5. Ibid., p. 25.
6. Ibid., p. 25.
7. See Richard Rorty, 'Keeping Philosophy Pure' and 'Professionalized Philosophy', in *Consequences of Pragmatism* (Minneapolis: University of Minnesota Press, 1982) pp. 19–36 and 60–71.
8. See esp. the essays collected in Derrida's *Margins of Philosophy*, tr. Alan Bass (Chicago: Chicago University Press, 1982).
9. See, for instance, A. J. Ayer, 'Albert Camus', *Horizon*, 13 (1946) 155–68.
10. See Jacques Derrida, 'Signature Event Context', *Glyph*, 1 (1977) 172–97; also John R. Searle, 'Reiterating the Differences', *Glyph*, 1 (1977)

198–208, and Derrida's response to Searle, 'Limited Inc abc . . .', *Glyph*, 2 (1977) 162–254. All further references to this last essay are given by page number in the text.

11. See discussions of this text in Christopher Norris, *Deconstruction: Theory and Practice* (London: Methuen, 1982); Michael Ryan, *Marxism and Deconstruction* (Baltimore: Johns Hopkins University Press, 1982); Gayatri Chakravorty Spivak, 'Revolutions That As Yet Have No Model: Derrida's "Limited Inc."', *Diacritics*, 10 (1980) 29–49.

12. Searle, 'Reiterating the Differences', *Glyph*, 1, p. 205.

13. Michael Ayers, 'Analytical Philosophy and the History of Philosophy', in Jonathan Rée, Michael Ayers and Adam Westoby (eds), *Philosophy and its Past* (Hassocks, Sussex: Harvester, 1978) pp. 41–66.

14. H. H. Price, *Hume's Theory of the External World* (London: Oxford University Press, 1940). Quoted by Ayers, in Rée *et al.*, *Philosophy and its Past*, p. 50.

15. Ayers, in Rée *et al.*, *Philosophy and its Past*, p. 44.

16. Jacques Derrida, *La Carte postale de Socrate à Freud et au-delà* (Paris: Aubier-Flammarion, 1980).

17. Jacques Derrida, *Of Grammatology*, tr. Gayatri Chakravorty Spivak (Baltimore: Johns Hopkins University Press, 1976). See esp. ch. 2, 'Linguistics and Grammatology' (pp. 27–73).

18. See Derrida, *La Carte postale*, in particular pp. 101–18.

19. See Derrida, *Of Grammatology*, pp. 3–26.

20. Jacques Derrida, 'Plato's Pharmacy', in *Dissemination*, tr. Barbara Johnson (London: Athlone Press, 1981) pp. 61–171.

21. Derrida, *La Carte postale*, p. 92ff.

22. Shoshana Felman, *Le Scandale du corps parlant: Don Juan avec Austin ou la séduction en deux langues* (Paris: Seuil, 1980).

23. Derrida, *La Carte Postale*, p. 108.

24. Richard Rorty, 'Deconstruction and Circumvention', *Critical Inquiry*, 11 (1984) 1–23.

25. On this topic of 'erasure' (in Heidegger and Derrida), see Spivak, Translator's Preface to *Of Grammatology*, pp. xiiiff.

26. Derrida, 'Spéculer – sur "Freud"', in *La Carte postale*, pp. 275–357.

27. Stanley Cavell, *Must We Mean What We Say?* (Cambridge: Cambridge University Press, 1969) p. 43.

28. Henry Staten, *Wittgenstein and Derrida* (Lincoln, Nebr., and London: University of Nebraska Press, 1984) p. 75.

29. Gregory Ulmer, *Applied Grammatology: Post-Pedagogy from Jacques Derrida to Joseph Beuys* (Baltimore: Johns Hopkins University Press, 1985) p. 147.

30. Jacques Derrida, *Edmund Husserl's 'The Origin of Geometry': An Introduction*, tr. John P. Leavey Jr (New York: Nicolas Hays, 1978) pp. 101–2.

30. Ibid., p. 10.

12

A Modern Writer's France

JOHN FOWLES

I am afraid I must disgrace the pages of a scholarly publication such as this. The notion of the novelist as intellectual and book-man, as universally well read and well informed about which is going on in the contemporary literary world, has been gaining substance all through this century, at least in academy, if some of the letters I receive are any guide. They assume knowledges in me of the modern novel, of literary theory, all of that, that I lack either totally or as nearly so as makes no difference. All novelists, at least when writing novels, are really to be classed in terms of Lévi-Strauss's *pensée sauvage*; we are not cultivated people. As the great anthropologist pointed out, that does not mean we primitives are not also in pursuit, like scientists and other sternly sane people, of a *mise en ordre*, a fitting of life into a chest of drawers. But the methods and principles of our fitting, and indeed of our chests of drawers themselves, are often remote from reason, tradition, the protocols of scientific analysis and all that venerable *galère* (in the university context) of desirable qualities.

Some novelists, such as Malcolm Bradbury and David Lodge, are of course also distinguished academics, and others become quasi-academics because they are reviewers; that is, they have to sound expert. I cannot, from my own very limited experience, imagine anyone reviewing for sheer love of it, for pleasure, indeed for anything much more than the welcome supplement of income it brings to those two Cinderella professions, writing and teaching. Even reluctant reviewers must, willy-nilly, learn quite a lot. I have reviewed very little in my life; and have equally fled (as a fly a spider's web) every kind of literary 'world', or circle, that has threatened to enmesh me. I read of such worlds, say in terms of seventeenth and eighteenth century *salons*, or of present-day campus society, with a kind of incredulity that anyone taking part in them could ever have enjoyed, or can enjoy, them.

My long-held opinion is also that lack of memory (of the indexing, encyclopaedic, good-teacher kind) is of very great benefit to a maker of fiction – indeed, one very sufficient reason why highly intelligent academics and scientists so seldom make satisfactory novelists. Knowing everything objective about a highly subjective art is a fearsome handicap; and Monsieur Jourdain's sort of innocence is a better presage for it. A novelist needs a memory of the re-creative sort, the ability to summon up scenes, events, characters and the rest for his or her readers; but this very seldom requires the accuracy and particularity of recall that so many suppose. When I hear of novelists being sunk in 'research', I grow immediately suspicious.

The required virtue is much more akin to a being at ease with the instinctive and the only half-conscious, a sort of knowing one's own junkroom. I have collected old books all my life, sufficient by now to amount to quite a small library. Remembering where everything is has escaped my powers, though not, for some mysterious reason, what everything I somewhere have. I ought to install, as my wife keeps telling me, some rational system, that would allow me to move smoothly to the right shelf in the right case; it would certainly spare frequent fruitless and cursing searches. Yet I am a novelist, and this haphazard and disorganised way I keep my books, as I indeed write them, somehow suits me best. It is, in short, very far from the sort of memory that has names, titles, dates, exact details at its finger-tips – precisely the memory that every university values so highly and tries to instill in its students.

The prospective nightmare during my own Oxford finals in French concerned a paper on sixteenth-century grammatical theory. The subject had bored me beyond belief in tutorials and reading, and I had done no work on it at all. The night before the examination I borrowed a friend's swotted-up notes, and duly regurgitated them the next morning on paper; the next day again I had forgotten the subject entirely, and have remained in the same wicked state of ignorance ever since. The only alpha mark I received in a not very distinguished second-class degree was, needless to say, awarded for sixteenth-century French grammatical theory.

I say all this by way or warning that, though I would happily claim to have been deeply formed by France and its culture, I am as ignorant of post-war contemporary French literature and all its underlying theories as I was long ago of its ancient grammatical theory. All this has had singularly little influence on me. What very skimpy reading I have done of Derrida, Lacan, Barthes and their fellow *maîtres* has more often left me baffled and frustrated than enlightened; and has led me – in a way I know must seem appallingly old-fashioned – to attribute many twentieth-century French cultural phenomena to a nefarious Germanic influence that crept over the country in the late nineteenth-century, and which has blanketed, blurred, betrayed all that lucidity, wit, elegance, etc., associated with an older tradition. I must admit this attachment to the *eau Perrier* of that old tradition is due in considerable part to sheer lack of comprehension of the muddy clouds that seem to me to spring from too much prose of the gurus mentioned above. I suspect that even if I were French I would not understand; not being French in fact envelops everything in a kind of double ambiguity. I am not quite sure what they mean, but, like the Irishman, not sure that I would understand even if I did understand.

It took me many years to realise the great abyss between the French and English traditions of language use, or rhetoric; the pervasive influence of the metaphorical on the first, and of the literal on the second; life perceived through the intellect, through forms and concepts, and life perceived (more or less) as it appears; words as pure algebra, words as practical and Euclidean; as carefully bred garden pansies, and as, in Lévi-Strauss's pun, wild heart's-ease. No doubt expert comparative linguists will cry in outrage at such a crude distinction, and I must, if I am forced, retreat behind the sub-title of this book. Such an abyss, wrong though I may be to suppose it, forms very much a part of my own imagined France.

I may read a French text and feel I have understood it perfectly in every semantic and grammatical sense; but, because I am not born French, nor bilingual, a final understanding – indeed *the* final understanding – is forever beyond me. Like every writer, I read a text in my own language against a kind of absent text, made of all the alternative words and turns of phrase that might have been used; in French, alas, I have no such instinctive thesaurus. In practical terms this does not worry me as perhaps it should. I think of it privately as 'the ghost', which haunts every contact I have with France; but all old houses have a ghost, and what we shall never quite finally know is, in my philosophy of life, an essential part of any attraction and enjoyment. I should not like France ever to become, in an emotional sense, at its heart, not foreign to me. This ghost of never completely knowing is, I believe, the quintessential part of any true and lasting love, whether between persons or nations.

I suppose the dark side of the abyss was best demonstrated in the *nouveau roman* episode, that classic case of a wine that does not travel. Its exposition, in the hands of its main theorists, such as Robbe-Grillet and Butor, was fiercely logical; with a handful of exceptions, its practice, to us backward British, bewilderingly dull. A kind of honorary French part of me by no means thought that of every *nouveau roman* he read; but his quarrelling English twin insisted that this was obsessively impractical, by the values and standards of *his* traditions. Novelists may reject the societies they live in morally and politically, but not all normal readers, into the bargain.

I was assured on all hands during a visit to Paris in 1981 that the *nouveau roman*, like the structuralist and deconstruction debates, was ancient history, long dismissed by the contemporary French mind. Story now ruled, the Balzac it had been found pointless to imitate was re-installed. ('By a small oversight they buried themselves', one literary journalist drily told me, 'instead of him.') When I remarked that the theories remained very much on some British and American minds, I was met with dismissive shrugs: typical, that the Anglo-Saxons should be so far behind.

Everyone in 1981 (including M. Mitterand) knew that the greatest living French writer was Julien Gracq. As it happens I do not disagree with that verdict – and think the general ignorance of his work in Britain a very sad thing indeed – but the point I am trying to make is the folly of our occasional academic *engouement* for movements and theories that require a native soil, their own specific language and culture, even to exist, let alone to be exercised. I might import the vinestocks, the exact methods of Burgundy or the Rhône valley, to England; I am not going to produce their wines. Intellectuals may adore the sophistication, complexity, the sheer incomprehensibility of much of the Gallic theorising; but we novelists never took it to our hearts, I am afraid. We never saw it as our duty to bore our readers; just as nowadays I think few of us accept the implications of the extremer forms of deconstruction, which so cleverly deny us any clear reason for writing in the first place.

I did once plan – and indeed started to write – a publisher's nightmare, a novel to be half in English, and half in French. My written French was in any case nowhere near adequate for the task, but what finally killed the idea for me was the impossibility of feeling truly at home in both cultures, of expressing both methods of viewing, and reacting, to experience. I have in recent years done some translating of plays for the National Theatre, and have found it there too. Superficial meaning flows easily enough from one language into the other; yet deep down they seem to me never to marry, never quite to fit. I can even see this in, so to speak, my own mirror, in having my own work translated into French. Annie Saumont, who has done all my recent books, has excellent English. She is furthermore a gifted writer of fiction herself, with several books in her own language. I know I am very lucky to have her, and was delighted when she won a prestigious translation prize a few years ago, for *Daniel Martin*. Yet her solutions to the problems my texts pose quite often set me back at first reading; not because they betray general sense, but usually because of what they leave out of the exact nuances of the English meaning, or (more rarely) the circumlocutions she is forced to to express them. Always I have a little private reaction to her work on mine, and it is a humiliating one not for Annie, but for myself: I still don't understand either French or the French.

I was lucky, when I got to Oxford in 1946, to find myself under Merlin Thomas at New College. As I soon discovered, other students envied his students their good fortune. He was young, quick, friendly, and had a sense of humour, sometimes Rabelaisian. I went up originally to read French and German, but my German tutors paled beside Merlin, and in my second year I thankfully (I sometimes regret it now) gave up German. Of course I had other French tutors, but they also tended to pale beside Merlin. One was Dr Enid Starkie, a famous figure in the faculty at that time, and in *le tout Oxford* also. I was a heretic, and never really took to her. Her French accent was bizarre. I remember smuggling a French friend into one of her lectures. When she began to recite something from Rimbaud he turned to me in profound puzzlement: 'What language is this?' Then there was old Professor Rudler, lecturing on *la passion chez Racine*, a very unpassionate performance indeed (later in France I was to hear Nadal on Corneille, the very antithesis, rather like some grand ornament of the

French bar pleading a case of *crime passionnel* before a rapt jury of students). A friend of mine and myself watched the audience rapidly diminish as the course of lectures proceeded; when it arrived at precisely two, ourselves, we decided it our moral duty to stick the course out to the end; which we did.

The time we were obliged to spend on Old French and its literature was then very generally hated, and regarded by most of us as supremely pointless, a torture we (supposedly) owed above all to the fact that Sir Alfred Ewert was head of the faculty. It took me a shameful number of years to realise that for me, at least, it had been one of the most valuable parts of the course, and certainly in the art of story-telling. If I had been told at the time I should one day be introducing a new translation of Marie de France in America (as I was, in the 1970s), I should have laughed. I hope the quotation from *La Chastelaine de Vergi* that is epigraph to my first published novel, *The Collector*, shows my symbolic debt. I still read Marie from time to time; and fall in love with her all over again.

Merlin managed to get me into the then newly instituted Maison Française in the Woodstock road, under Henri Fluchère. Our rooms all had important paintings, and I slept for a year with a Léger on the wall above my head. The food was also distinctly better than generally then in Oxford. We had lunch and dinner every day with Fluchère and his attractive French housekeeper. It was the rule that at table we must speak French, something of an ordeal for most of us, given the very low value then put in the faculty (Dr Starkie was typical of it in this) in speaking French with any fluency or with decent accent. There were quite often distinguished French guests, such as Darius Milhaud (only too happy to drop into English, outside the sacred dining-room), and then our contributions would virtually cease. On one occasion the guest was an odd little man in scoutmaster's shorts, and the rule about speaking French was waived. We knew he was some professor from 'the other place', but not why, lunch over, he was surrounded on the lawn outside by an excited gaggle of English faculty students. That was my only encounter with the famous Dr Leavis.

We were all a little bit in awe of Fluchère. Very recently I read Courteline's fictionalised memories of life in a nineteenth-century French cavalry barracks, the sarcastically titled *Les Gaîtés de l'escadron*, and felt a strange faint echo of life at the Maison Française. It was certainly nothing to do with Fluchère himself – a kind and drily humorous man behind the façade – or the comparatively civilised life of the house; much more, I suspect, the finding ourselves pitched into a foreign setting and culture, away from the 'home' of England, and embarrassed by our own ineptitudes and naïveties in it, like so many recruits to an ancient regiment.

Modern students will find it hard to believe how ignorant most of us were in those days of the actual France. The war had banned us from Europe, of course; and also, because of military service, had delayed entry into university, so we were mostly well over normal age. Of course we got to France in vacations, but I think even then most of us went with English friends. It remained a foreign place, going there was still something of an adventure. We had occasional contacts with students, but few with any other kind of French.

By pure chance one summer I got a job in a French wine factory, helping process the *vendange*, quite the hardest and most unromantic work I have ever done. We were not even allowed sleep, because lorries from the more distant vineyards would come rumbling in at all hours, often the middle of the night, and we had to be up to receive them. My knowledge of really blue *argot* leapt during those weeks; and we put things in the vats that have stopped me drinking that particular kind of *apéritif* ever since. When I left, I hitched a lift in a Citroën on the nearest road. It was driven by an unusual millionaire from Lyons, a gentle elderly man with heart trouble. He was looking for someone to help crew his yacht at Collioure nearby – a small ten-ton ketch, not millionaire-like at all. With him was his friend, a married but much younger woman from Paris. For several weeks I virtually lived alone with them, in paradise after my bout in hell. M, the friend, was also unusual: fiercely honest as well as very goodlooking. She had a very brave record in the Resistance, among other things. Of course I fell in love with her – she was only a few years older than I was myself. The only reward I received was to be allowed to become something of her confidant and her butt: what the Resistance had really been like, why she loved both her Parisian husband and the gentle millionaire (and could never love me – and how ridiculous and sentimental my transparent near calf love for her was); her feelings about life, the impossible naïvety of the English, the monstrous selfishness of her bourgeois compatriots. She was as well read as she was left-wing, and not only in the fashionable authors of the time, Camus, Sartre, Aragon. Her scorching honesty, even about her own faults, her humour, her impulsive moods, her sometimes savage teasing – all that was dazzling. She was like something one has read about in books, but here by some miracle was in the flesh. I have never been able to see countless French heroines, from Joan of Arc on, through Phèdre to Antigone, without the ghost of her face behind. 'M' did not stand for Marianne, but, so far as I was concerned, it might well have done so. She was, with Merlin, by far the best tutor I ever had on France.

I went from Oxford for a year to the University of Poitiers, where I was appointed to the faculty of English (once again thanks to Merlin Thomas) as *lecteur*; reader I may have been in title, but in all else I was like an *assistant* at a *lycée*, and a bad one. Above all else Poitiers made me realise how ignorant I was of English literature. Absurdly, most of the reading I did that year was in my own language, not French. The head of the English faculty I did not get on with; but L, the *professeur-adjoint*, was much more sympathetic, with a *normalien* mind far sharper and more learned than mine was ever to be, far more stringent and severe in its logic, far more dry. We used to go on long walks to listen to the plainchant at the neighbouring monastery of Ligugé, and I also taught spare-time in the city's Jesuit college. But the French Catholic mind has always remained closed to me. Claudel, and other impassioned icebergs, I never read with pleasure.

Years later, when I discovered Gracq, I was amazed to hear that he was, or had been, a close friend of the *adjoint* L (who indeed features as L in *Lettrines*). The brilliant L's story in later years has been sad; but the memory of him has survived.

So too has that of various French students I came to know well. A principal private interest with me all my life has been nature, and it was through these friends that I came to know French nature, in Poitou and the Vendée. My most vivid and happy memories of Poitiers lie far more in bird-watching expeditions, impromptu shooting-trips and the like, than in anything academic; the naturalists' Mecca of the Brenne; glorious meals, *raie au beurre noir*, *moules au pineau*, endless oysters beside the bay of Aiguillon; *beurre blanc* – which remains to this day my favourite sauce – beside the Loire, as also that region's wines, especially from that delectable little area round Savennières, just east of Angers (about to die,

I want a glass of Madame Joly's Coulée de Serrant in my hand; you may keep your Montrachets and the rest). I didn't really begin to know rural France until that time. But I will come to that.

I faced something of a crisis at the end of my year at Poitiers. Of all I learnt from both Merlin Thomas and L, perhaps the most useful was something negative: that I could never be a true teacher, even far below their levels. I had begun a first novel at Poitiers. I knew it failed, even by my own jejune standards, and that to become a true novelist would take me many years. Teaching *is* a convenient profession for would-be writers, in the time it allows for the other activity; but it becomes a trap, and in proportion to how seriously the teacher takes his teaching. I had applied for a job at a bizarre-sounding college in Greece, clearly a dead end in academic terms. Then Merlin wrote, to say he had heard a post as French master at Winchester was vacant, and would be happy to recommend me. It came to a day when I had a choice: go to Winchester, and a sensible and modestly promising future, or to Greece, and exile myself from all that Oxford, and England, stood for.

I chose Greece partly in a mood of deference to the *acte gratuit* and the existentialism of the time. But that is another story. When I eventually returned to England, I was badly under the Greek spell, and France seemed like a distant episode in the past. What brought me back to it was another chance: an antiquarian bookseller. Francis Norman's shop, just off Heath Street in Hampstead, must, in its flagrant untidiness, its always endless dusty piles of books, have seemed typical to a casual passer-by of any other lazy second-hand dealer's; those of us who went in very soon knew we were in a book-lover's paradise. Francis Norman was, behind his shyness, a very distinguished scholar, a delightful man, a prince of booksellers – I might almost say a Maecenas, for his prices were often ludicrously low. At the end of the many years I knew him (and lived for his catalogues, long after I had left Hampstead myself), our conversations often took a distinctly unusual form for the normal antiquarian bookshop. I would hand him some small treasure I had unearthed, say a *mazarinade* from the time of the Fronde, price anywhere else in London at least five pounds.

'Honestly, you can't let this go for just a pound.'

'Dog-eared. Not worth cataloguing.'

'But it's complete, for goodness' sake. Not a tear.'

'I really don't want more for it.'

'This is ridiculous. You know I'm not an impoverished teacher any longer. I'm jolly well going to give you more.'

'Oh well ... I suppose ... if you must ... I don't know ... would one pound fifty be too much?'

Very occasionally he had not to be beaten up in price, but satisfied that you were worthy of the book. I remember once having to argue with him for nearly half an afternoon to prove I deserved a Commenius; that I knew the great Czech was a genius, the patron saint of European education and all the rest; in short, that I could promise to respect and love the book as much as the seller himself did.

He always carried a large stock of French books, and they, or those I bought, were the road that led me back to France. What I discovered in that shop was the France that no university can teach its students: not in the least that of the famous writers, and the classics, but an endless *galimafrée* of minor poets, minor plays, forgotten memoirs, forgotten theological and political debates, Revolutionary pamphlets, trial reports, eccentricities, collections of anecdotes. Of such trivia I have gained over the years quite a collection; and of a kind any self-respecting book-collector would turn from in horror. Famous 'firsts' do not interest me in the least; countless things that no one has read again since they were first published, yes. One obscure *trouvaille* at Francis Norman's gave me the germ of *The French Lieutenant's Woman*: Claire de Durfort's *Ourika* of 1804. Only in two cases can I confess classics have influenced me. One French writer I have always deeply liked and been seduced by is Marivaux, while the one novel I have always adored, from schoolboy days, and read countless times, is Alain-Fournier's *Le Grand Meaulnes*. I know it has many faults, yet it has haunted me all my life. Fournier's own life itself has driven me again and again to the Sologne, to stand where he stood – to Yvonne's lost château, before Uncle Raimbault's shop at Nançay, in that tiny attic bedroom above the school at Epineuil. His novel lies somewhere behind all of mine. I have my own professional influence-tracers nowadays, but none seems to me to realise the effect of this one on me adequately.

I was able to go to France very little in the 1950s and early 1960s. That is when Francis Norman's shop was so important for me, its books my only French reality, and indeed much more an imagined one than anything else, and nine parts out of ten a past reality. But since those years I have been to France – or I had better say *my* France – almost every year. My France has no cities (above all, no Paris), no museums, no libraries, no famous châteaux, no auto-routes – and, with one or two exceptions such as Fournier, no literary connections. Through various circumstances I have lost touch with everyone I once knew there, so it also has no French friends, of the human kind, anyway.

What my France consists of is endless obscure countrysides, their tiny towns and lost villages, the remoter the better; some, especially all that lies south of the great curve of the Loire, from Nantes to Nevers – La Vendée, the valleys of the Creuse and the Vienne, down through Auvergne to the Causses and the Cevennes – I am usually revisiting, not seeing for the first time. I know many corners of them far better than I do many parts of England, indeed think of this France as not foreign in any meaningful sense, so strong is it in my mental landscape, in *pensée sauvage* terms. Friends can't understand why we don't live in France, at least have a holiday home there; but the pleasure lies (for me at least) in the random, drifting, returning nature of this kind of relationship with France, the way it allows me to indulge the many faces of my imagined country.

I was on just such a holiday only a few weeks ago. We revisited some favourite botanical sites on the Causse Noir and the Causse de Larzac, near Millau, which I first found several years ago. It may seem strange for a writer to let a glimpse of a few rare flowers dictate his holiday, but so it is. (As most British naturalists now know, France is a kind of miracle as regards countless species rare in this country; being there is a little like a child being given the freedom of a sweet-shop.) Then on, the rare orchids remet, to see a bridge in the Cevennes. An *abbé* was brutally murdered on it in 1702: a bleak upland bridge, a very un-Junelike evening. The lady of the drapery and gift-shop at one end of the bridge, where the *abbé* had once lived, seems taken aback that this mad Englishman should be interested in this unmarked place and remote event. We discuss Mazel's account of the murder (he was there) a minute or two; she has read that, but not Marion or Bonbonneau. I buy a pot of the delicious local honey she sells. Such days, in a heaven of flowers in the morning (*Cephalanthera damasonium* growing with *C. longifolia*, unheard-of), at the scene of an obscure historical incident (but one that has always fascinated me, it was the spark that started the Protestant Revolt) in the evening – such is my France.

Yet it is not the naturalist or the historical dilettante that primarily drives me back to it. Far more, a kind of more general aesthetic lack, if I do not souse myself in it every so often. I mentioned my liking for Gracq earlier. That is certainly based on the subtlety of his novels, such as *Le Rivage des Syrtes* and *Un Balcon en forêt* (for my money, the finest – *et le plus fin* – novel of the Second World War), but also on those descriptions of rural France that appear in *Lettrines* and elsewhere. Years before I had read him, or even heard his name, I had firmly decided on my own favourite small area of the Loire – that stretch of the south bank that runs to and past St Florent-le-Vieil, past the Ile Batailleuse and the Ile Melet (where my wife and I long ago picked for ourselves the one place in France where we would happily break our own rules, and live – once one of those *fermes épanouies sur leur terre-plein fortifié qui défie la crue.* This farm is in ruins, long uninhabited, now more heron-perch than anything else, but I dream of owning it every time I see it. The chance that this landscape is a favourite of Gracq's also, and has been memorably (*Les Eaux étroites*) described by him, like his childhood at St Florent, is perhaps a poor reason to like him as a writer. But I admire his sharp and sometimes quirky views (the *étrange manque de liant* in Flaubert, yes) of life and literature also; above all the shrewd, rich meditations in the quite recent *En lisant, en écrivant*, essential reading for both practising novelist and serious student. A *goût de terroir* runs through all I know of his work; a rootedness, a nostalgia, an almost peasant independence, despite all his sophistication and complexity in other ways.

I am trying, through Gracq, to put my finger on what I most love in France, imaginary France; why I may claim it has formed me deeply. At heart it is not the literature, ancient or modern, its wit and elegance, its delicacy and perceptiveness; its variety. It is nothing political or social; it is not its wines and foods, all its subtleties and richnesses in the *art de vivre*. If anything, it is a richness of freedoms, and even there not so much in allowing people to choose from such richness, but in making the choice available. It remains the mother of so many things besides those du Bellay listed in his famous poem, and not all desirable; yet it is for me the eternal homeland for all those whose personal *mise en ordre* partakes of *pensée sauvage*.

I sometimes imagine what I would be if I did not read French, however less than perfectly, did not know its culture, however erratically, did not know its nature and its landscapes, however partially. I know the answer. I should be half what I am; half in pleasure, half in experience, half in truth.